FRANCE AND THE LEVANT

*From the Bourbon Restoration
to the Peace of Kutiah*

BY

VERNON JOHN PURYEAR

With an introduction by
HENRI HAUSER

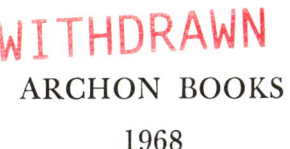
ARCHON BOOKS
1968

FIRST PUBLISHED 1941 THE UNIVERSITY OF CALIFORNIA PRESS
REPRINTED 1968 BY PERMISSION
IN AN UNALTERED AND UNABRIDGED EDITION

SBN: 208 00721 0
LIBRARY OF CONGRESS CATALOG CARD NUMBER: 68-8025
PRINTED IN THE UNITED STATES OF AMERICA

INTRODUCTION

BY

HENRI HAUSER

VERNON J. PURYEAR has made himself known in recent years by his works on the Near East, or rather, on the role of the problems of the Near East in the policies of the great European Powers. His starting point is the idea—a correct one, I believe—that from 1815 to 1856, and even up to 1871 and 1878, the conflicts that directly concerned Turkey, Egypt, Greece, Syria, and the Balkans, have been among the most serious problems of European history and have reacted directly on the alliances and the mutual oppositions of the Great Powers.

The attention given to his books and articles in France is easily understood, because these questions have always been an integral part of our foreign policy. Since its first appearance we have been keenly interested in his study of the origins of the Crimean War. It shows us how, in 1844, the Entente Cordiale had begun to disintegrate, precisely by reason of the antagonism of French and British policies in the Levant; how Tsar Nicholas and Nesselrode had attempted to utilize this antagonism to persuade Aberdeen that the Entente Cordiale, still officially in existence, should be replaced by an Anglo-Russian accord, which should be turned against France; and, finally, by what inverse evolution there had been set up, after the coup d'état of December, 1851, a new Entente Cordiale which was decidedly anti-Russian. We are not unaware of the fact that this thesis has been opposed by Professor Temperley. The controversy is not closed, and one sentence of the present volume reproaches this illustrious British historian for having unduly transformed into a docile diplomat and pacifist the man we have called the fiery Stratford Canning. *Historici certant.*

That work took 1844 as its point of departure. But M. Vernon J. Puryear realized that in history nothing begins, that nothing can be explained except by its antecedents. Making use of the regressive method, so to speak, he next discussed British commercial policy in the Near East during the period 1834–1853. He now announces a forthcoming book on Napoleon and Eastern Europe. The present volume covers the period between this coming work and the last one published, namely 1815–1833.

The author has done a prodigious amount of archival research—prodigious especially when we consider the fact that he does not live in Europe and that he is able to devote only brief visits to his researches. Whatever may be the judgment that will be given on the execution of his work and on his conclusions, we shall be grateful to him—and we Frenchmen in particular—for having put at our disposal a very considerable quantity of documentary material, in part heretofore unpublished. Archives of the Quai d'Orsay, national archives, deposits in the departments of war and of the navy, archives of the Chamber of Commerce of Marseille, all have been methodically explored, and the exactness of the references will permit us to base our discussion of the author's theses on the texts themselves. London, Vienna, and Berlin were visited with the same care. The only archives missing from the list are those of Russia, and the author is the first to admit that his information is less definite with respect to that country.

But his bibliography of printed works is extremely important, and what adds real interest to it is that it is to a great degree critical. Its division into chronological periods renders it very usable. Naturally, specialists will find certain gaps in it, but my impression is that these are unimportant.

To qualify as "imperialistic" the policy of France in the Near East between the fall of Napoleon and the appearance of the Syrian-Egyptian difficulties seems to me to exceed reality. I see simply, on the part of France, an effort that has been continuous, in spite of the changes of regime and of policies, to regain the position which she had occupied historically in the Near East and which the English thalassocracy had caused her to lose; an attempt also to take advantage of the complications of the Near East in order to resume fully her position as a Great Power.

Let us lay aside this discussion of terms, for the subject that we have just outlined is the one that M. Puryear has presented. Very wisely he has avoided everything that belongs to general diplomatic history, referring to works that have already appeared on that subject. He has kept within his own limits, never separating economic factors from factors properly political.

For, as it appears from the texts which he has so patiently col-

Introduction vii

lected, the problem of "empire" presents itself especially, except perhaps in the adventurous views of Polignac, as a commercial question. Near Eastern commerce, from Richelieu to the Revolution, had been one of the principal sources of French wealth, and French exports to the Near East had dropped from the fourth place, which they occupied in 1789, to the ninth place in 1815. Between 1767–1789 and 1819–1821 French trade in the Levant had lost from 50 to 75 per cent of its importance. Therein lies the whole problem. Note that under the old regime this trade was chiefly from Marseille. Marseille, which M. Paul Masson has so carefully studied, was truly "the gate to the Orient"—a sort of trade-republic whose free initiative was often opposed to the narrow outlook of the central authority. Neither the absolutism nor the narrow commercialism of a Colbert could agree with the independent spirit of these merchants nor with their broad conception of their business. And it was Marseille that had triumphed in the struggle.

Hence it is especially Marseille that, during the Restoration and the July Regime, urges France to regain her position in the Levant, in Egypt, and in the Black Sea. These considerations play their role in all the political manifestations of France. It is interesting to note, for example, in M. Puryear's book, the commercial repercussions of the Hellenic revolt. The whole matter cannot be explained merely by the struggle of the Cross against the Crescent, by the classic love for Hellas, witnessed to by the *Messéniennes* of Casimir Delavigne or by the *Orientales* of Victor Hugo. Following again in part the Egyptian plans of Bonaparte, France first aided Mehemet Ali to build a fleet, which brought her again into conflict with England; for the latter, as M. Hoskins has shown in *British Routes to India* wished to revive the caravan traffic which, between the western Red Sea and Alexandria, would connect the steamship lines to Bombay with those of the Mediterranean.

This evolution of the French policy is suspended when the Greek revolt becomes a war for independence. We see, in M. Puryear's book, how much the European imbroglio of that period is reminiscent, in more than one aspect, of the one we witnessed in the Spanish civil war: the doctrines of neutrality and of nonintervention, the efforts, more or less sincere, to limit and to localize the conflict, the suppression of piracy, and the question of volunteers. All these questions are mingled with those of the partition of the Ottoman

Empire; for example, those that are imputed to Metternich, which M. Puryear discusses from the point of view of Schiemann's theories.

He brings to us an analysis of the commercial conditions of the Peace of Adrianople. He shows France returning, before and after the revolution of 1830, to her Egyptian policy. When the Algerian affair complicates still further the problem of routes in the Mediterranean, she has the idea of making the pasha the master of all of northern Africa, from Sinai to distant Melilla. It is interesting to notice the Catholic policy, which has affirmed itself as a policy of crusade during the Greek insurrection, end, despite the expedition to the Morea, in a sort of reëstablishment of the Caliphate, of an Arabic empire, with Cairo as the capital, which would have embraced the whole of the southern shores of the Mediterranean, as it did in the eighth century—a Charlemagne, as Henri Pirenne puts it, sharing with Mohammed.

Although the negotiations did not succeed, the Franco-Egyptian friendship continued, as did Franco-Egyptian trade. To the question of trade routes to India there is now added a problem that Bonaparte could not have envisaged at the time of the blockade, namely, the problem of cotton. Marseille absorbs 40 per cent of the Egyptian export of the precious fiber, thus threatening Liverpool's monopoly. "King Cotton" becomes one of the elements of the Near Eastern question.

It is because of these considerations that France supports Mehemet Ali in his efforts to found a dynasty in Egypt and to reëstablish the policy of the Pharaohs and the Ptolemies of expansion toward Syria. It is in this territory that she comes into conflict with England. By 1833 (the Peace of Kutiah), the date at which M. Puryear stops, the respective positions are taken, and already the conflict which is to enter its acute phase in 1840 is announced. It was therefore in accordance with good method, in a book which is an introduction to the history of this crisis, to go back to 1815.

I am of course incompetent to judge what interest the American public will have in these accounts of the Near East, which farmers of the Middle West and of California may think of as "Tales of the Arabian Nights." Mehemet Ali and his adversaries are far removed from their present preoccupations; 1815 and 1833 may seem for them dates lost in the mists of the Middle Ages.

Introduction

And yet I hope the readers, or at least the scholars in the United States, will realize that the problems of competition here studied lie at the foundation of contemporary questions. The world is daily becoming smaller. The Suez Canal, Palestine, and Iraq are today nearer to New York and Washington than were Liverpool or Lisbon a hundred years ago. The Mediterranean has again become what it was before the travels of Columbus and of Vasco de Gama, one of the great arteries of world trade and one of the great centers of international politics, if indeed it is not about to become the scene of a great conflict.

In spite of the policies of nonintervention and of "splendid isolation," no one can escape participation in such a conflict, if it should occur. At an earlier date Americans were obliged to participate in the struggle against the corsairs of the Barbary Coast. To understand the meaning of the present-day problems, extending from Gibraltar to the Euphrates and from the Adriatic to the valley of the Nile, one must study the origin of those problems. At any rate, for us Frenchmen, and for our neighbors the British—for whom the Mediterranean is an imperial highway—a study like M. Puryear's is of great value.

UNIVERSITY OF PARIS (SORBONNE)
February 24, 1938

PREFACE

THIS IS a documented study of the integrated diplomatic and economic policy of France in the Near East in the period between the first Bourbon restoration and the peace that France mediated to end the first Turco-Egyptian war over Syria. With French activity as the theme, the account has been topically organized to accommodate the problems and periods that best depict the fluctuations of French policy in the Levant, though certain policies of the other Powers have been outlined as well. The third in the writer's studies of the policies applied by the major Powers in Balkan Europe, southwestern Asia, and Egypt, this book chronologically and topically precedes its companion volume, *International Economics and Diplomacy in the Near East* (1935), an account of British commercial policy from 1834 to 1853. For unbroken continuity the work should probably continue with a chapter on the Treaty of Unkiar-Iskelessi; but this phase we have treated recently in the *Revue historique*.

Since the research is limited to little-known or inadequately integrated aspects of foreign policy, the book features new findings from the archives and is not a new survey of problems and foreign policies already discussed in textbooks and other works. Only rarely have some of these better-known factors been summarized here, for the sake of continuity. The arbitrary limitations will appear most obvious for the period of the Greek War, in which we are concerned with analyzing such economic problems as the monopoly of Marseille, simulation to defeat Turkish preëmption, tariffs, and reactions to blockades rather than with recapitulating such important but well-known political factors as the Tripartite Treaty of 1827, the battle of Navarino, the military phases of the Russo-Turkish War, and the territorial delimitations of Greece. Beginning with the negotiation of the Peace of Adrianople, however, our details of diplomacy are necessarily multiplied to support the new conclusions and to fill in neglected gaps.

The research was well advanced while the writer was a fellow of the Social Science Research Council, a subsequent grant from which enabled him to complete the project. Thanks are extended to the Council and to officials of the various archives who have cheerfully accorded their aid. The rich repositories utilized, some of them for three or four different study periods, are as follows: in Paris, the Archives du ministère des affaires étrangères, the Archives nationales, the Archives du ministère de la guerre, the Archives du ministère de la marine, and the Bibliothèque nationale; in Marseille, the Archives modernes de la chambre de commerce; in London, the British Museum, together with the archives of the British Foreign Office, at the Public Record Office; in Vienna, the Haus- Hof- und Staatsarchiv; and in Berlin, the Geheimes Staatsarchiv. Especial thanks are extended to M. Stanislas de Jankovitz of the archives service of the French ministry of foreign affairs; to M. Jean Reynaud, director of the library and museum of the Chamber of Commerce of Marseille; to M. de La Roncière, director of the Bibliothèque nationale; and to the distinguished *préfacier*, M. Henri Hauser of Paris. As heretofore, Professor Robert J. Kerner of the University of California has generously aided and encouraged me with his expert advice on the problem in general and on Russian policy in particular. His timely article in the *Cambridge Historical Journal*, presenting a new and fundamental contribution to the history of Russian policy in the Levant, filled an important place in the study. My wife has cheerfully assumed the typist's tasks. The errors remaining, inevitable despite the aid I have had, are my own.

V.J.P.

DAVIS, CALIFORNIA

CONTENTS

I. Eclipse

In Quest of Levant Markets 1
  1. Economic Penetration 1
  2. The Marseille Monopoly 10
  3. Unfinished Business 14
  4. Spotlight on Greece 16
  5. Simulation 17
  6. Russia Faces the Issues 20
  7. France Considers Possibilities 21
  8. Handicaps to Trade 25
  9. Commercial Eclipse 29

II. The Tempo Changes

Internationalization of the Greek War 37
  1. England Dissolves the Levant Company 37
  2. Xantippe 40
  3. France and Egypt 42
  4. Battle of Navarino 49
  5. After Navarino 51
  6. Russia and Turkey at War 53
  7. French Expedition to the Morea 54
  8. Blockades 58
  9. Return of the Ambassadors 62
  10. Russia Advances 63

III. Focus on Adrianople

International Relations and the Peace of Adrianople 69
  1. Polignac at the Helm 70
  2. Turkey Faces Collapse 71
  3. Speculation and Policies 73
  4. The Polignac Plan 76
  5. An Alleged Austrian Plan 79
  6. Negotiations and a Plea 83
  7. The Fleets Summoned 86
  8. Peace of Adrianople 89
  9. New Bases of Russia's Policy 89
  10. The Commercial Article 93
  11. After the Treaty 95
  12. Gordon and the Frigate "Blonde" 96
  13. Partial Evacuation by France 98
  14. France Approves 99

	PAGE
15. Aberdeen Thinks Turkey Will Crumble	100
16. Polignac Foresees Turkey's Collapse	104
17. Polignac Is Pro-Russian	104

IV. Shift to Egypt

The Drovetti Plan 112

1. Egypt and French Policy 112
2. The Project 113
3. The Council Considers 114
4. Orders Are Issued 117
5. First Negotiations 121
6. The Counterproposal 123
7. Notifications to the Great Powers 126
8. Reactions 127
9. An Abrupt Shift 130
10. Huder Fails 132
11. Experiment in Algeria 135
12. French Commerce in Egypt 135
13. Specter on the Horizon 139

V. The War for Syria

French Policy and the First Syrian War 147

1. Conversations at Choubra 148
2. The Peace Disrupted 151
3. Does France Encourage the Pasha? 154
4. Objectives of the "Rebels" 155
5. French Policy Modified 158
6. Results of the Capture of Acre 162
7. The "Sphinx" Scouts for Egypt 167
8. Sebastiani Presses for Peace 168
9. Broglie and French Policy 170
10. Overtures 172
11. Instructions to Roussin 173
12. Turkey Requests Aid 174

VI. France Mediates

The Peace of Kutiah 181

1. Varenne the Intermediary 181
2. Muraviev and Halil at Alexandria 184
3. Russian Army Summoned 186
4. Ibrahim Halts at Kutiah 187
5. Egyptian Policy of France Opposed 188
6. Roussin Guarantees Peace 190

	PAGE
7. Broglie Disapproves	192
8. The Egyptian Ultimatum	194
9. The Peace Signed	197
10. Boislecomte's Negotiations	199
11. Failure of the Western Fleet Objective	203
12. Status Quo	208

VII. INFERENCE

France and the Levant	214
APPENDIX: Note on the British Fleet Episodes of 1849 and 1853	219
BIBLIOGRAPHY	223
INDEX	237

ABBREVIATIONS

AA:	Akten des auswärtigen Amtes (Berlin-Dahlem)
AE:	Archives du ministère des affaires étrangères (Paris)
AEMD:	Archives du ministère des affaires étrangères, mémoires et documents
AN:	Archives nationales (Paris)
CCM:	Archives modernes de la chambre de commerce de Marseille (Marseille)
FO:	Archives of the British Foreign Office (Public Record Office, London)
HHSA:	Haus-, Hof-, und Staatsarchiv (Vienna)
MG:	Archives du ministère de la guerre (Paris)
MM:	Archives du ministère de la marine (Archives nationales, Paris)
PRO:	Public Record Office (London)

These abbreviations are used in the notes and bibliography. The series for a given reference is indicated by the name of the nation to which the collection appertains except in references from the British archives in which the initial letter of the nation is used. For the French archives Arabic figures following the name of the nation refer to volumes; for the British archives the figures refer to series and volumes respectively. References to Archives du ministère des affaires étrangères (Paris) include two sections: political and commercial reports and instructions (AE) and memoirs and documents (AEMD).

I. ECLIPSE

IN QUEST OF LEVANT MARKETS

THE LEVANT not only allured Restoration France to trade revival, with Marseille leading the way, but it also eventually afforded the steppingstone to empire. Almost all the international relations affecting the Near East from 1814 to 1833 pass in review as the archive record discloses France in commercial and diplomatic activity to regain her prestige and influence among European states and later to prepare for her advance into Algeria.

The first decade, formative for the policy of the Restoration, witnessed the partial recovery of the Levantine trade which, before the Revolution, had brought prosperity to Marseille and to all of southern France. Recovery of the Levantine markets was well under way by 1821 when the Greek revolt and disunited home policies interposed themselves. Then Spain commanded attention. In the reign of Charles X several factors internationalized the Greek War and altered French policy to political penetration. The Bourbon monarchy acted against both Egypt and Turkey, joining Great Britain and Russia in 1827 to terminate the Egyptian intervention and, with the consent of her allies in 1828, sending an expedition to the Morea to protect the Greeks against Turkey. Equality of prestige with the other Great Powers had by that time been reëstablished; but the Levant became more than ever the key to French foreign policy as French influence in Egypt increased by rapid strides. The Peace of Adrianople having cut short the grandiose scheme for connecting the affairs of the Near East with French territorial expansion in western Europe, the conquest of Algeria in 1830 fell just short of having been made by Egypt under French auspices. Three years later the policy of France and Egypt achieved another triumph: Syria was added to the administrative responsibilities of Mehemet Ali perhaps as much by French diplomacy as by the armies of Ibrahim Pasha. This book recounts and integrates several less-known phases of these and related problems.

1. ECONOMIC PENETRATION

From the moment of the Restoration France turned again to the Levant, remembering how well it had served her commerce during the twenty-six years from the loss of her colonial empire to the coming of the Revolution. She had already learned, however, through Napoleon and his predecessors, that too much aggressiveness in the Levant would awaken enough international jealousies to cause failure of her policies. For a decade, therefore, she followed haltingly and meekly, as befitted her weakened status in 1814 and 1815, behind the other Powers in the Near East. Through commerce as well as diplomacy might she set the stage for recovery; hence her new advance was not direct, like the Bonapartean expedition to Egypt in 1798, but devious. This chapter will sketch the development of Near Eastern policies by France and the Powers in the decade beginning with the first Bourbon Restoration.

The commercial recapture of the Near East by western Europe in the nineteenth century came about from both old and new factors and was well under way long before the Suez Canal could make the recapture permanent. As cause, the attraction of trade based on liberal prerogatives of long standing was complemented by the new evidences of nationalism in the Balkans and of insubordination by Ottoman pashas. The revolt of the Serbians, the rising power of Egypt, the detached practices of the pashas of Acre and Scutari, and the preparations for a Greek revolt all presaged, as we now know, the ultimate dissolution of the Turkish Empire. Indeed, the weakness of Turkey only advertised the ease with which economic penetration through more liberal trading prerogatives was possible for Europeans. Obviously the old economic prerogatives in Turkey would be guarded by the Great Powers—the more so since the Near East afforded a striking contrast to the restrictive trade of western Europe after Napoleon. Commerce in the Levant was both held and extended as the European merchants and governmental agents worked throughout the Ottoman Empire by negotiation, intrigue, intimidation, flattery, and bribery.

Whatever direct French commerce and shipping with the Levant continued after Napoleon was carried on chiefly by foreigners. The city of Marseille was, in 1815, in its greatest decline for a century. In 1798 there had been eighty-one important French commercial houses in the Levant and Barbary, collectively claiming, with their annual 70,000,000 francs of trade exchanges, the preponderant part of the entire foreign commerce there.[1] In 1816 there remained

[1] For notes to section i, see pp. 32–36.

only twenty-three such houses; though statistics for their trade volumes are unreliable, all reports agree that the trade of each remaining French firm was relatively smaller than before.

Hopes were expressed for a speedy revival of the trade immediately after the Restoration. France had almost to begin anew, but she did have the previously established legal bases for the Levant trade as her point of departure. These were (1) the series of capitulatory grants by Turkey, initiated in the original grants to France (1535) and expanded during almost three centuries; (2) the Franco-Turkish treaty of 1802, which carried the trading prerogatives of French merchants into the Black Sea; and (3) the tariff of 1802, which had complemented the treaty—altogether, a liberal legal system for trade in the Ottoman Empire. This system, shared by the principal Powers, now gave France no exceptional advantages. Except that Turkey reserved the right to prohibit certain items of trade and to preëmpt others, all authorized Europeans might trade with comparative freedom upon paying the usual duty of 3 per cent at all Turkish ports; and, contrary to general opinion, France did not, from the standpoint of political actualities, find herself particularly intimate with the Turkish government in 1815.[2]

The Marquis de Riviera was named new ambassador to Turkey and head of the French consular administration in the Levant, replacing Andeassy, Napoleon's last ambassador at Constantinople. Appointed in August, 1814, Riviera was instructed not only to advance commerce with the Ottoman Empire but also to make it the medium for a more direct and consistent French political policy.[3] The detailed instructions stated that France must labor all the harder through diplomacy to reëstablish her position in the Levant, with Malta now under England and Venice under Austria. The legal bases for trade, disrupted during the last years of the empire, were to be restored and protected; no new concessions were sought, the Turkish rates being considered moderate and the safety of French commerce and subjects already established. To clarify the seeming confusion among French merchants themselves respecting the rules under the much-debated economic monopoly of Marseille (which will be treated later) Talleyrand restored most of the regulations that had been effective in 1785.[4] Already the former French naval station in the Levant, which had been forced from its position by the maritime supremacy of England, had resumed its normal duties,[5] especially its function of protecting commerce against the prevalent piracy of the region.[6]

Riviera made slow preparations to assume his new duties, the "Hundred Days" intervening. When, in December, 1815, he finally departed, he had supplementary instructions to enforce the restored regulations, especially the restrictions on French and foreign traders for the quite limited benefit of Marseille. He was also to aid in developing French trade with the southern provinces of Russia, since Russia here possessed exceptional resources for the supply of grain and timber. To attract more French shipping to the Black Sea, Riviera might encourage the dispatching through the Euxine of even such exchange products as were destined for St. Petersburg and Riga. Times had changed, he was told, since the days of Colbert; now the markets of the Baltic were dominated by Great Britain. "It can only be hoped," continued the new instruction, "that French commerce, weak and timid as it will be in entering this new field, can overcome all obstacles." It was argued that commodity price ranges and the absence of important competition should favor the development of French trade with southern Russia, for which French industry was already organizing.[7]

Such trade, however, soon proved difficult and unprofitable. The removal of Turkish restrictions against Black Sea trading had been hailed with enthusiasm in France; but during only one year of the Napoleonic period—1808, the reaction to the alliance of Tilsit— had even temporary realization of the expected trade profits been permitted. The new plans, also based on the freedom of navigation stipulated in the treaty, recognized that the ultimate development depended upon Turkey's control of the Straits. This control, however, permitted Turkey to interpose important restrictions—for example, her capitulatory right to preëmpt grain or any other commodity which passed the Straits if it were needed by the Turkish inhabitants. She denied firmans (formal authorizations) for passage to the first two French grain ships, which had loaded at Odessa for Livorno and Genoa. When asked the reason, the Turkish authorities informed both France and Austria that the transshipment of grains from one ship to another within the Straits was forbidden under Turkish rules. Thereupon, to secure the necessary firmans, Deval, French chargé d'affaires, duplicated the device introduced by the British under similar circumstances in 1813—a false declaration of the cargoes and their origins. This admitted simulation was approved by the French foreign office, with an injunction that French agents should "oppose with energy all innovations by the Porte which might compromise French commercial relations with the Russian ports of the Black Sea."[8] So great was the interest of Frenchmen in the possibilities of the Black Sea trade that an imposing joint-stock *Compagnie de la Mer Noire* was projected in July, 1816. Its prospectus indicated that its activities would be for the most part in exchange trade, without precise territorial limits. Its headquarters would be established at Marseille, with divisional headquarters at Odessa and Constantinople and branches at Kherson, Moscow, Kiev, Taganrog, Galatz, and Sinope.[9] The project proved ephemeral, as had several similar plans in 1803.

The end of the Napoleonic wars presaged a new economic era for Great Britain. The factories sought new markets; further improvements in transportation were under way; and the strong navy protected trade overseas. Restrictive factors were protectionist policies such as the grain law of 1815, upheld by the eighteenth-century type of aristocracy that still governed England, and the rapid expansion of protective tariffs throughout Europe, as illustrated by the French tariffs which kept France almost closed to English manufacturers. British policy was directed toward keeping open the existing markets wherever possible and toward finding new markets in the less developed regions of the world. Thus India acquired a new importance, South America loomed large, and the trading possibilities of the Levant were at last coming into fuller appreciation. Malta and the Ionian protectorate gave new bases for economic penetration into the Levant, while the liberal trading privileges of Turkey encouraged the utilization of that area. English legal rights for trade were extensive. The Black Sea had been opened to England in 1799 and again, more specifically, in 1802, while the Anglo-Turkish Treaty of the Dardanelles (1809) gave treaty formality to the unilateral capitulatory grants.

The direct economic activities of British traders in the Levant and the control of the British consular system in Turkey were consolidated by the politically influential English Levant Company, whose trading privileges were open to all British subjects upon payment of the usual fees.[10] The actual and potential trade importance of Turkey soon led to an extension of the British consular representation there. A man destined to influence British commerce in the Levant considerably for the next quarter of a century, John Cartwright, the company's consul at Patras, became consul general at Constantinople in 1817.[11] Under the British system the consuls were also traders. Only in rare appointments, like Cartwright's, were the consular duties and salaries adequate to encourage the officials not to use their trading privilege; consequently a company consul usually found his official duty in opposition to his personal financial interest.[12] The Black Sea had a new appeal for the British also, as illustrated by the consular changes there.[13]

A vexing problem was that of the bilateral tariffs. Normally operative for fourteen-year periods, they all expired between 1816 and 1820. Turkey, under the disadvantage of low specific duties after commodity prices had risen, wanted new tariffs negotiated promptly.[14] It was even difficult to secure Turkey's enforcement of the tariffs as the period neared for their renewal.[15] The Franco-Turkish tariff of 1802 expiring first, Riviera's first important negotiation with Turkey was to arrange the new tariff (November, 1816). This replaced specific duties previously scheduled for some three hundred and fifty articles of trade by a proportional duty listing the thirty-nine principal articles, the listing including an application of the principle of "current prices at given places." Restrictions prohibited imports of tobacco and gunpowder into Turkey, and exports of grain, oil, soap, Mocha coffee, and copper from Turkey.[16] The French merchants did not like the new tariff because under it some slight advantages in rates were enjoyed by their competitors; hence the French government would not permit its immediate application, advancing the claim that it infringed the most-favored-nation clause of the capitulations, although admitting that the prescribed duties were considerably below the stipulated general rate of 3 per cent. The Chamber of Commerce of Marseille made detailed comparisons of the new tariff with that of 1802, and with the applicable Austrian, Russian, and British tariffs, pointing out that under the new schedule the French would have to pay triple what was paid by the British and Austrians on cotton goods. Thus placed on the defensive, Riviera worked out his own comparative table, showing that, although the items specified in his tariff were not uniform with the others, the variations worked both ways, some benefiting French commerce.[17]

Riviera's prompt negotiation suggested to the French the desirability, in the future, of waiting until the other Powers had signed their tariffs before agreeing to one which would be applicable to themselves, and this became French policy on the problem. Under the usual system, an old tariff was automatically continued, despite its expiration, until a new one should have been negotiated. In March, 1818, a new tariff was signed between Austria and Turkey, and Prussia soon accepted the Austrian schedule. Russia offered to sign a new tariff, but Turkey refused, pending the solution of the political matters then under discussion. Turkey insisted on a new tariff with Great Britain in 1819 and overcame the arguments of the Levant Company by threatening to take 3 per cent in kind. This produced the new Anglo-Turkish tariff of 1820. At one step in the negotiation Liston, the British ambassador, overruled an attempt by Turkey to exclude the produce of the ports of the Black Sea.[18]

The application of Riviera's tariff was deferred four years. Now that three of the other Powers had signed their new tariffs with Turkey, France felt free to permit the operation of her tariff; but she applied to her benefit all newer and lower specific duties found in the other schedules.[19]

The government at Paris had meanwhile accorded its encouragement to the reviving Levant commerce. Protection against piracy was a constant and necessary aid; sometimes the government made inquiries, or offered suggestions. The minister of the interior, Vaublanc, observed in a letter to the Marseille Chamber of Commerce in 1816 that there was no active French commercial firm at Acre, and directed attention to the fact that French ships at Smyrna were in the service of foreign commercial houses.[20]

One of the newest problems of the Levant was the increasing importance and power of Mehemet Ali in Egypt, whose reported monopolies of commerce, as well as those by certain other Turkish pashas, were subjects of governmental inquiry. Under the Ottoman system, as we have seen, certain items were excluded from the tariffs because of Turkish prohibitions against unrestricted trade in them. The monopolies of Egypt grew out of the initiative taken by Mehemet Ali himself to determine the exceptions to the Turkish tariffs which would apply in Egypt. Eventually he excepted almost every important item of trade, both of import and of export. Even so, a wide field for foreign speculation was still possible, the compensating factor for foreign loss being the strong government of the energetic pasha. Mehemet Ali gave the foreign merchant protection in Egypt at a time when most other Turkish provinces were suffering from the weakness or misconduct of their governors.[21] Protests at Constantinople against Egypt were ineffective, the Porte not having the requisite power for the coercion of the pasha, especially at a time of actual and threatened rebellions in the Balkan provinces.

Barbary piracy in the Mediterranean was a common problem. France joined in a concerted but unsuccessful effort through diplomacy to get rid of it. The most efficient protection against piratical raids was perhaps that offered by the British Mediterranean squadron to British commerce, especially after the fleet established its position through the bombardment of Algiers in 1816. The Barbary regencies nevertheless made quite a lucrative business of their piracy against all those who could not defend themselves. Russia at first sought to check it by negotiating directly with Turkey; then Tsar Alexander I in 1816 proposed a maritime league against the regencies if Turkey found herself unable to give proper guarantees for the security of commerce. Fearing that Alexander would find it desirable to appropriate a Mediterranean naval station to help him carry out his part of the projected undertaking, the British would not agree. The French government also declined to participate at that time, assigning as its reason the temporary weakness of the nation. Meanwhile the Porte did little or nothing to repress piracy; Riviera suggested it was purely the religious reason which prevented Turkey's offering interference.

Barbary piracy was inevitably among the problems which confronted the Congress of Aachen in 1818, where different plans for its eradication were discussed by Metternich, Richelieu, Castlereagh, Wellington, Hardenberg, Bernstorff, Nesselrode, and Capodistrias. The result was the protocol of November 20, which recognized the importance of opposing piracy and stipulated that direct negotiations with the regencies would be in order. Castlereagh and Richelieu offered the services of England and France as agents for such negotiation, and the offer was accepted.[22] The plan devised was to make impressive notification of the decisions of the congress to Algeria, Tunisia, and Tripoli. Anglo-French action under the plan was deferred until the autumn of 1819. The methods used, and the negative results recorded, are illustrated by the French documents on the notification made to Hussein, dey of Algeria. Rear-Admiral Jurien de La Gravière acted with Rear-Admiral Freemantle of England. The consuls of the two Powers at Algiers gave Hussein advance notification of the approaching appearance of the joint mission. The admirals, in an audience with the dey on September 5, told him that all the major Powers of Europe were "irrevocably determined" to put a stop to the system of piracy which was contrary to the general interest of all the states and that, if the regencies persisted in their piracy, they might expect a league to form against them which would place their existence in jeopardy.[23] The dey listened with indifference to the reading of the protocol of 1818 and declared he could not renounce his right to visit ships "to determine whether they were friends or enemies"; but he refused to put his reply into writing.[24] At the same time the Powers advised Turkey that the regencies were exposing themselves to danger by their continuance of piracy. The Porte, Riviera reported, seemed irritated by the whole proceeding.

French trade in the Levant made substantial, but not spectacular, recovery in the five years from 1815 to 1820. The recapitulation in 1820 showed that several French firms were doing a profitable business in Turkey, others had retired, and many were quite new. All agreed that constant political protection was still necessary.[25] Beaujour, inspector general of French commerce in the Levant, reported the imports and exports for 1816 and 1817 as totaling 23,000,000 francs.[26] The best available concise summary of the comparative trade is provided by Cesar Moreau.[27] From this it would appear that in 1787–1789 the Levant had ranked fourth in imports by France and ninth in exports from France; in 1819–1821 the Levant ranked seventh in imports by France and thirteenth in exports from France. Moreau's figures in terms of francs probably are exaggerated, but they show that the relative total trade value of Levant commerce from France in 1819–1821 was from one-half to three-fifths of its average for the immediate prerevolutionary era.

The greatest handicap to the recovery by the French of trade in the Levant was their failure to provide an adequate basis for reciprocal trade. The Restoration monarchy, in fact, established a generally prohibitive tariff system for agricultural products.[28]

2. THE MARSEILLE MONOPOLY

The interest of the government of King Louis XVIII in the revival of French trade in the Levant was of especial importance to its French center. The population of Marseille had been 120,000 in 1789, when the city yet enjoyed its privileged position based on traditional mercantilism. Its privileges were suppressed in 1791. A feebly protective consular duty of 2 per cent was authorized from 1793; but the population declined steadily even from 1802 to 1806, called "the years of hope" by M. Masson, and also from 1807 to 1814, "the years of deception." It had dropped to 80,000 by 1814. Trade revival was reflected in the new prosperity of the city; the population climbed to 110,000 by 1821, surpassed the 1789 figure about 1825, and reached 132,000 in 1831.[29]

Clarification may now be made of the references to Marseille in the foregoing analysis of Riviera's instructions. Soon after the first Bourbon Restoration the Chamber of Commerce of Marseille had sought the reëstablishment of all the regulations which had given the city its former monopoly of French trade in the Levant and its privileged position in the economic life of southern France. The system had been one of the numerous bulwarks of the old regime, so the government of the Restoration acted with some favoritism to Marseille. On February 20, 1815, the ministry of the interior notified the Chamber of Commerce of the confirmation of the regulations of 1785, qualified by the statement that the regulation concerning foreigners "could not be revived by this confirmation."[30] This excluded the mainstay of the preferential system, a protective duty of 20 per cent payable to Marseille on merchandise from the Levant if borne by foreign vessels or for foreign account. However, the confirmation did restore the other safeguards, including the control by Marseille of the licensing and bonding of French merchants who traded in the Levant,[31] the inspection by Marseille of French goods destined for the Levant to assure their uniform qualities (which before 1789 had implied a direction in the methods of production), and the stationing of an inspector general in the Levant to serve as overseer of French commerce. Under the former system operations in the Levant had been further unified by the periodic meeting of the French merchants of the various Levantine ports in assemblies called *nationales* to deliberate on their common problems and to regulate prices. The entire consular personnel had been always alert to advance trade, but the directing agency for this unified and monopolistic control for the most part had been the Chamber of Commerce of Marseille, although the trade was carried on by individual merchants. Despite the limitation which centered the profits from the Levant trade chiefly in southern France, the Marseille system had proved more successful than that of the less aggressive English Levant Company.

The new regulations included the 2-per cent duty, as in 1793, which did not satisfy Marseille. The issue of the nominal and easily evaded consular duty as against the reëstablishment of the high protective rate continued to be debated for over a decade. Soon after the second Restoration detailed studies began. Talleyrand inquired of Riviera, on August 21, what fees might be properly made collectible for consular services and whether the former duty of 20 per cent should be restored.[32] The prohibitory surtax on foreign shipping was favored by both Marseille and Toulon because, they pointed out, the freight rates for Greek, Genoese, and Russian merchant vessels being lower than those of French vessels, foreign ships were employed almost exclusively for the import of Levantine produce into France. Talleyrand and his ministry had been forced out in September, and his successor, the Duc de Richelieu, opposed that aspect of the monopoly, perhaps because of the positions assumed by the rival chambers of commerce in central and northern France.[33]

Soon reports from the Levant indicated that the new regulations restricted French trade even without the 20 per cent, whereas the French bonding system did not conform to the requirements for traders of other nations;[34] other objections opposed the inspection of drapes by Marseille alone.[35] Notwithstanding, the Chamber of Commerce of Marseille in June, 1818, renewed its request for the reëstablishment of the 20 per cent.[36] Three years under the 2-per cent duty had demonstrated both its failure as an object of protection and the weakness of its application. Although the regulation stipulated 2-per cent duty on all merchandise entering French ports directly from the Levant in foreign boats, payment was evaded by the simple device of having foreign boats in the service of French merchants touch at an Italian port before proceeding to Marseille.[37]

The discussions of the request from Marseille centered on

whether or not the regional advantages for Marseille were superior to the national claims advanced by other sections of France. The Chamber of Commerce of Carcassonne, for example, opposed Marseille's request, which was denied after reference to the general council of commerce at Paris. Marseille then sought a higher and effectively administered duty to replace the 2-per cent and finally, as a minimum concession, the effective application of the 2-per cent duty. The Marseille Chamber of Commerce utilized the occasion of the new Levant problems and a change of French ambassadors to Turkey in 1820 to advance its arguments anew. The revolt of the pasha of Scutari against the sultan and the threatened revolt of the Greeks had led the French foreign ministry to send an expert in Near Eastern affairs to Constantinople; Latour-Maubourg, who had distinguished himself at Constantinople during the Napoleonic period, had been named to succeed Riviera. The chamber requested the new ambassador on January 26, 1821, to try at least to enforce the 2-per cent consular fee against foreign ships. Latour-Maubourg, friendly to the chamber's views, wrote that he was supporting it in his discussions with the minister of foreign affairs and the minister of the interior and ventured the opinion that the government was about to grant this request of Marseille.[38] The documents show that directions soon required the strict enforcement of the 2-per cent duty.[39]

The coming of the Greek War gave a different perspective to the economic problem, of interest alike to the government and to Marseille. The new problem was how much the war, whose duration could not be foretold, might interfere with French trade. First reports disclosed that Austria, at least, found profit from the war trade. The governmental reaction appears in the commercial instructions to Latour-Maubourg, dated October 8, 1821.[40] Another interesting factor appearing was the beginnings of French favoritism for Egypt. Pasquier directed that efforts be made to clear up the uncertainties which beset French commerce in the Levant, requesting the ambassador's opinion on the desirability of restoring the former Marseille monopoly or a similar system. The activities of the Turkish pashas restricted French commerce, especially in Egypt, where, however, Pasquier admitted that the preponderance of Mehemet Ali would make useless any corrections the Porte might order. Drovetti, now returned to Egypt as consul general, might secure some ameliorations from that pasha; but as for the monopolies by the pasha of Acre, Latour-Maubourg was directed to ask the Porte "to put an end to them." The idea of turning French commerce over to the Greeks as carriers was sharply opposed by Pasquier, who thought the non-Muslim subjects of the Porte already had so many privileges as to be a detriment to European traders and probably in part responsible for the decline in French shipping. The ambassador was granted discretion concerning the method deemed best for correcting the problem presented by non-Muslim Turkish subjects, except in one respect: the unauthorized use of the French flag to cover shipping in the Levant was to be halted. It was presumed that the new determination to enforce the 2-per cent duty against foreign traders would help to rehabilitate the languishing French commerce and make unnecessary any governmental subsidies for it.[41] Latour-Maubourg, quite occupied with the protection of French commerce when the war got well under way,[42] assigned collection of the 2 per cent to a special collector.[43]

The Marseille chamber now sought to advance still another step, claiming that 2 per cent was not adequate for the protection of French shipping against foreign competition. It sought either an additional levy of 5 per cent on Levant shipping which arrived by way of Italian ports or a flat 10-per cent rate on all Levant produce which arrived in foreign boats. Objections were at once raised at Paris: it would be inconvenient to change the items of Levant trade which had been included in the Franco-Turkish tariff; the 2-per cent rate seemed adequate for the purposes of the chamber; and the raw materials from Turkey, needed by French industry, would be unduly raised in price by a higher levy. Regretting that the general council of commerce at Paris did not share the same view, Latour-Maubourg wrote the chamber that he was not concerned so much with details as with the principle; and he believed that France should "approach the former system as soon as possible." He invited the chamber to prove its own case to the Paris authorities, finding himself unable to meet the arguments from Constantinople.[44]

Latour-Maubourg did not remain long at Constantinople, leaving the embassy under the direction of Count Beaurepaire, chargé, shortly after penning this letter. Beaurepaire opposed the Marseille monopoly as detrimental to French trade. Already a new method of evading the 2-per cent levy had been found, the simulation of ownership of cargoes destined for France. If owned by foreigners, they were shipped in the name of a French subject,[45] for which there was no punishment provided.[46]

Occasionally there were further attempts at strict enforcement of the limited duty;[47] but gradually the question of the Marseille monopoly was permanently adjourned, the merchants of Marseille losing. The discussions proved that the Levantine commerce of France had come to be regarded as national instead of regional in scope.

3. UNFINISHED BUSINESS

The Russo-Turkish political negotiations, which Riviera watched so closely, were of interest to all Europe, the crux of the Near Eastern question in 1815 being the ability of the inherently weak Ottoman Empire to survive. The hostility of Russia in addition made the continuance of Turkey in her role within the European balance of power still more problematical.

The end of the Napoleonic period permitted Russia to return to her unfinished business with the Porte, the two alternatives before Tsar Alexander being pointed negotiation or war. The principal conflict concerned divergent interpretations and nonfulfillment by Turkey of certain provisions of the Treaty of Bucharest (1812) relating to the Danubian provinces and to the freedom of commercial navigation within the Straits. On the other hand, the treaty had not been fulfilled by Russia in the evacuation of Georgia and other provinces on the eastern shores of the Black Sea, held by Russia because the Treaty of Gulistan with Persia (1813) had supported her claims to them.

The negotiations, broken off abruptly with the Napoleonic invasion of Russia in 1812, were resumed in November, 1816, by the new Russian minister, Baron Stroganov, a somewhat bellicose individual. Sent to Constantinople to attempt through negotiation "to reconstruct the Russian system in the east on solid bases," Stroganov had been instructed to try to win the following concessions as interpretations of the Treaty of Bucharest: (1) Turkey was to assure the full enjoyment of Moldavian and Wallachian liberties under Russian protection, these liberties now to include, specifically, the regulation of their imposts according to the methods established by the hospodars (Princes Ypsilanti and Murousi), tenure of the hospodars for seven-year terms and their eligibility for reëlection, and the establishment of quarantines for their Danubian frontiers; (2) Turkey might place Serbia under Russian protection, or, if impossible, every advantage feasible tending toward the admission of Serbia's autonomy—including economic freedom—might be solicited; (3) Turkey was to surrender her claims, terminate her traffic in slaves, and permit the unhindered development of Russian commerce, in the contested Asiatic provinces; (4) Turkey was to demolish her fortresses on the islands of the Danube delta, specifically required by the treaty; (5) Turkey was to execute all of Russia's economic prerogatives.[48]

Stroganov found the negotiations slow and difficult. Turkey insisted upon the restitution of the Asiatic littoral of the Black Sea and at first did not admit any "explanations" of the Treaty of Bucharest; Stroganov in turn declined to discuss the Asiatic frontier until the principles sought by Russia were accepted. Fearing an Austro-Russian coalition, Turkey early in 1817 agreed to negotiate all the disputed points except the Asiatic littoral. New instructions directed Stroganov to employ conciliatory methods, the first successful result being an agreement on one of the Danubian problems, the territorial delimitation along the Danube. For three years the other problems were debated, and, after a semblance of agreement was recorded upon the interpretations of the commercial prerogatives claimed by Russia, Turkey refused to give any guarantees for the future validity of her "explanations." The following confirmatory commercial agreements were specifically claimed by Stroganov: (1) a new act to clarify and guarantee the Peace of Jassy (1792) against the depredations of the Barbary pirates; (2) another act, registered in all the Ottoman tribunals, to assure Russia the enjoyment of the many advantages of her treaty of commerce with Turkey (1783), especially the exemption of her commerce from all nonstipulated levies; (3) a declaration which would permit Russia to share all the honors and privileges enjoyed by France, England, and the other Powers; and (4) the confirmation of the right to station Russian consuls anywhere in Turkey.[49] Meanwhile, Russia held the Asiatic littoral.

Such was the status of Russo-Turkish relations when the Greek War for Independence caused Tsar Alexander to shape new policies and face new difficulties, especially wartime commercial problems, in Turkey.

4. SPOTLIGHT ON GREECE

A striking comparison in the commercial activities of the Ottomans and the Greeks may be noted. While the official classes of Turks had done little to increase their own meager inclinations for trading pursuits, the Greeks had made commerce one of the principal avenues of their preparation for national independence. Their intensified commercial activity began in 1798, at the time of the rupture between France and Turkey over Bonaparte's expedition to Egypt. Later, the renewed war between France and Great Britain, especially its Peninsular aspect, had had the incidental effect of providing the Greeks, as well as the Egyptians, with large economic profits from a considerable clientele. Because of the naval preponderance of England in the Mediterranean the Continental system had been ineffective in the Levant from its inception, the Greeks expanding their carrying trade especially because of the ease with which they secured Russian and British flags for their vessels. Indeed, during the Napoleonic wars Turkey had found it expedient to adopt a rather liberal policy toward the Greek merchants. Their trading activities had been continued after 1815, and they had supplemented their profits by engaging in piracy. A combination of circumstances thus had made the Greeks in fact the most active merchants in Levantine waters. Their numerous vessels plied between Odessa and Malta, Marseille, and the other principal ports of the Mediterranean, in most of which the Greeks maintained prosperous commercial houses.

The principal reasons for the Greek rebellion against Turkey were the development of nationalism and commerce and the weakness of Turkey; the model for it was the open insubordination of Ali Pasha of Scutari (March, 1820). Doubtless many Greek leaders believed that they might count on the moral and material support of Russia, the indecisive character of the Russo-Turkish negotiations arguing that Tsar Alexander might combine aid for his coreligionists with the liquidation of his own claims against Turkey. Without the promise of such support, however, Alexander Ypsilanti and others opened an unsuccessful revolt in the Danubian Principalities from March to June, 1821; in April the important and long-continued Greek nationalist revolt was under way in the Morea.[50]

Russian sympathy, like that throughout Christian Europe, was with the Greeks in the internecine war; perhaps Alexander was between two fires—his liberal personal views, which favored the Greeks, and his desire as a conservative ruler to maintain with Metternich the principle of legitimacy and the bulwarks of peace. The decision placed Russia as officially neutral, duplicating the policies of the four other Great Powers. A second common policy sought the protection of commerce in the Levant. Four of the Powers, acting independently, attempted to localize the war, thus seemingly aligning themselves against the potentially alternate war policy of Russia.

5. SIMULATION

The insistence of Russia upon the protection of her commerce through the Straits was important from the outset, Turkey herself raising the question anew by an order of May 14, 1821. It was natural that Turkey should supplement her military and naval action against the Greeks with whatever commercial restrictions were in her power. Seeking to diminish the Greek profits from commerce and to prevent the anticipated flow of Russian grains and other produce through the Straits, she issued an order for the preëmption of foreign produce found within the Straits. Killing two birds with one stone, she would thus also assure the Turkish military and civilians an adequate supply of grain and oil. The new order supplemented the standing restriction on oil, which for years had been successfully evaded by means of fictitious manifests. That the extension of preëmption applied specifically to Russian produce cannot be doubted; the order announced Turkey's intention "to enforce the purchase, at the current price, for the use of the Turkish government, of the cargoes which might arrive from the Black Sea." The preëmption order encountered the diplomatic opposition of all the Great Powers; the ambassadors of England and France only complained that the Turkish price for grain might not be equitable, whereas Stroganov protested the measure altogether, declaring that its execution by Turkey "would be regarded as amounting to a cessation of friendly intercourse" with Russia.[51] The more tolerant English and French attitude may be attributed in part to their anti-grain laws, under which they could hardly wish their traders not to utilize the most convenient market. That the Turkish order for them meant only a selective market, to be utilized as they preferred, may be deduced from the initiative taken by the British merchants in asking their embassy to issue fictitious manifests whenever they wished to prevent the preëmption of their cargoes of grain. The first preëmpted cargoes netted their British owners handsome profits. Thereafter, the differences between Turkish and Mediterranean grain prices served as the merchants' barometer: if the Turkish price were higher at a given time, they permitted their cargoes to be preëmpted and collected the bonus; if the market price were higher elsewhere, they sent their prohibited cargoes through the Straits by declaring them to be something else. Although there were obvious political barriers at the moment, they well understood that if necessary they might at any time invoke their treaty rights to cover the produce of Russia which they carried. "There is in point of right," they reasoned, "a difference between the prohibition of export of Turkey's own produce from its own territory, and the stopping of foreign vessels laden with foreign produce and passing through the Bosporus under the positive stipulations of treaties."[52] Later it was discovered that the necessary bribes for Ottoman officials cut into the otherwise satisfactory profits and that other difficulties were encountered.[53]

The contrasting Russian attitude is readily explained, although she too might employ simulation. The Turkish restriction represented an arbitrary use of the Straits, and there was no guarantee that simulation would be permitted indefinitely; the market prices fixed by Turkey depressed the wheat prices at Odessa; the threat of preëmption tended to make the grain trade uncertain.[54] Probably because of the opposition of Russia, Turkey on August 9, 1821, suddenly lifted the embargo on wheat, continuing that on oil.[55] Thereupon Russia insisted upon the freedom of passage for all her commerce, as guaranteed under her treaties with Turkey, and summoned Turkey to accord the free passage of the Bosporus to the commercial vessels of all the Powers which did not yet enjoy that privilege.[56] In May, 1822, after newer and greater differences with Russia, the Porte again placed restrictions against Russian commerce in the Straits.

We have already noted the earlier French approval of simulation as a method of evasion of Turkish preëmption. As for the British, Cartwright gives us the method, and Strangford, the new ambassador at Constantinople, the approval. Cartwright's directions to the acting chief secretary of the British embassy on May 23 were as follows:

It would appear that the Porte continues to object to granting firmans for vessels coming from the Russian ports in the Black Sea and bound for England with certain articles, and it may therefore be necessary, in making applications for firmans, to present fictitious manifests, as had been for some time practiced. You will therefore be pleased, when cargoes arrive, the passage of which is objected to, to combine with the dragoman charged with obtaining the firmans a fictitious manifest to be presented to the Porte, a copy of which as well as the true manifest will be sent to me. The same will be observed in regard to cargoes proceeding from England to Russia, the passage of which may be objected to by the Porte.

This was approved by Strangford, who wrote Cartwright as follows: "I must, therefore, on the ground of immediate expediency, approve entirely of the directions [regarding fictitious manifests] which you have issued to the acting chancelier of this embassy."[57]

An analogous problem arose from the renewal of the practice under the capitulatory system, almost forgotten since 1813, of the Turkish inspection of all foreign vessels which passed the Straits. Also designed to handicap the rebels, the renewed visiting of all foreign commercial vessels was intended to prevent Greek passengers and sailors from shipping as members of the crews of friendly vessels; but again the order struck primarily at Russia. As early as March 29, 1821, Turkey resumed the former practice, Stroganov at once protesting that such action was "in opposition to treaties between the two governments, derogatory to prerogatives, producive of delays, and prejudicial to commerce."[58] Turkey retained her order but changed her method to one of simple questioning of the ships' captains. Quite obviously another form of simulation might be employed here; as we shall see, Turkey later changed her order.

A unique case coming from the Turkish inspection of foreign vessels related to a Russian war vessel in June, 1821, when Turkey announced that she would not permit its departure from Constantinople until after the required search. Stroganov insisted that the vessels of the government were not subject to inspection and he was joined by the Austrian internuncio in the new protest. Russia won her point, although Turkey in rejoinder insisted that she was within her rights because such a vessel, under Turkish rules, should not have been at Constantinople in the first place.[59]

6. RUSSIA FACES THE ISSUES

The relations of Russia and Turkey had entered a new phase. In addition to the old problems which arose from the conflicting interpretations of the Treaty of Bucharest and the new commercial handicaps to her trade, Russia soon had a sizable set of other demands, respecting the Greeks, to be made upon Turkey. These she made, although seemingly she did not plan to utilize the then favorable occasion to go to war in defense of them. She sought the reconstruction of the destroyed Greek churches, guarantees for the free exercise of the Greek religion, distinctions to be drawn by Turkey between the Greek rebels and the submissive Greek populations, and one military measure, the withdrawal of the Turkish forces from Moldavia and Wallachia.

Turkey answered these demands evasively. Declaring the Greek War a religious conflict, she charged Russia with being an accomplice of the Greeks. Counterclaims included a demand for the expulsion of the refugees who had fled to Russia and denial of any Russian right to interfere in the affairs of Greece. Russia's firmness made the new negotiations difficult. Every capital in Europe followed carefully the successive changes in the political tempo at Constantinople; as early as the end of July, 1821, interpretations pointed to a new crisis in Russo-Turkish relations. Turkey, flushed with her success in the Principalities, at that time again declined or evaded the Russian demands. A respite was won in August, as we have seen, when she made the concession of withdrawing her order for preëmpting foreign grain. After much discussion Stroganov at the end of the year broke off relations.Thereupon Turkey announced that she would not insist upon the return of the refugees, would remove a part of her troops from Moldavia and Wallachia, and would make some proposals to try to satisfy the other demands of Russia. These half measures were not well received at St. Petersburg, and Russian troops eventually entered the Principalities.[60]

Quite problematical was the reaction now to be expected from the other Great Powers. Disliking the prospect of a change in her relations with them, Russia submitted, for their objective examination, a concise statement of her claims, and proposed to arrange in concert an agreement with them on the best methods for assuring to the Turkish provinces "the benefits of a happy and inoffensive political existence." Prussia, without direct interests in the Levant other than her small trade there, accepted the Russian point of view at once. Austria and Great Britain, however, considered the possibility of an immediate fall of Turkey, especially if Russia pressed her claims vigorously. Staunch believer in established order, Metternich had opposed the Greek revolt from the outset; but he was unwilling to go so far as to advocate intervention in favor of Turkey. Castlereagh likewise had followed a "hands-off" policy. Now, through a memorandum of October, 1821, both Metternich and Castlereagh in a guarded way extended their "hands-off" policy almost to that of nonintervention, perhaps to be especially applicable against Russia. What either would have done if Tsar Alexander had made the attack on Turkey which they feared is not known, Castlereagh not having recorded an answer to that hypothetical question before his sudden death a year later. Publicly, however, England let it be known that she sympathized with Turkey in the Russian phase of her problem.[61] Castlereagh did not contest the issues of the specific Russian grievances against Turkey but regarded the continued existence of Turkey as the paramount issue. Metternich apparently was soon convinced that Alexander would remain true to the conservative principles of the Holy Alliance.

7. France Considers Possibilities

France seemed more favorable to the views of Russia, according to the shrewd Pozzo di Borgo at Paris. Indeed, under the impression that France wanted to see a localized Russo-Turkish war and convinced that France would remain strictly neutral in such a conflict, Pozzo in October, 1821, suggested that Russia might take definite action against Turkey. His opinion was that, if such a war came and expanded and if Austria occupied one province of Turkey, France would be content to occupy an island. Pozzo felt confident that neither Prussia nor Austria would enter a coalition hostile to Russia, but that Great Britain would be the principal opponent.[62]

Under guise of a hesitant policy, France under the new and changing conditions had already decided to take again a more active part in European politics. From the outbreak of the Greek revolt, France sought to pacify the two Near Eastern factions, trying to calm the irritations of the Greeks and to have Turkey confine her punishments to the Greek rebels alone. The strained relations of Russia and Turkey led France to take common diplomatic steps with England, Austria, and Prussia to prevent the expansion of the Greek War into a Russo-Turkish war, since the common efforts of the Powers through 1821 had not yet won Russia's promise to refrain from pushing her demands to war.

By October, 1821, Premier Richelieu regarded a prolonged Turco-Greek war as inevitable; according to a memorandum of his observations, the longer it lasted, the better would be France's position to profit by circumstances. Almost confirming Pozzo he thought that, instead of following the pattern of the previous centuries of French friendship with Turkey, the better policy now would be for France to concert with Russia, for Turkey and Sweden had been largely replaced by Russia and Prussia in the European system. The alternative to unity with Russia was a close coöperation among all five of the Powers, to prevent such gains "in power and intensity" by the revolutionary principle that it could later become dangerous. Richelieu was convinced that Great Britain would not take an active part in the war, but that the negotiations might possibly align France and Russia diplomatically against Austria and England. Because France had a considerable part of her naval force in the Mediterranean, he believed that armed neutrality was the best policy for France at the moment.[63]

On the same day that Pozzo di Borgo reported his interesting and analytical observations on French policy (October 8), Pasquier wrote the political phase of his instructions to Latour-Maubourg, the new French ambassador who, we already know, was soon to depart for Constantinople. Tracing the events which had led to the Levantine crisis, he emphasized especially the relations of Russia and Turkey. Latour-Maubourg was to act as a conciliator and at the same time as the representative of a Power which desired to preserve Turkey. This attitude was "based on several centuries of friendship [with Turkey], in which there were not now any barriers in rivalry or conflicting interests." In one respect a pro-Russian type of policy was authorized, Latour-Maubourg advising the Turks, in the interest of peace, to renounce their demand for the extradition of the refugees and to evacuate the Danubian Principalities. Hypothetically envisaging the appearance of the Russians at the Bosporus, Pasquier directed the ambassador in that event to take all necessary precautions to guarantee the persons and property of French subjects. The fleet was ordered to move nearer to the scenes of conflict, and Commander Halgan was authorized to follow the instructions of the new ambassador, at whose service a war vessel was placed. If it were found advisable for the vessel to pass the Dardanelles, necessary precautions must be arranged in concert between the ambassador and the commander.[64]

A more active French participation in European affairs might have taken either a Turkish or a Spanish direction, considering the disturbances of the time. The theses of a memorandum drawn up by Latour-Maubourg in December suggested that France might well prepare for events that probably would occur, presumably a war between Russia and Turkey. France, he said, could not ignore a struggle "in which the existence of French subjects and the prosperity of French commerce were continually menaced and compromised in the ports of the Levant," a point of view also supported by Richelieu. Certainly France should make some sort of demonstrations in the waters of the Levant as a counterpoise to British naval movements and to the probability of British commercial expansion at the expense of the French. Richelieu had indicated that France might take an attitude which, without menacing the neighboring Powers, would nevertheless provide protection for French commerce and subjects. Latour-Maubourg therefore recommended that a *corps d'observation* be stationed at the mouths of the Rhone. An appended note by the war ministry suggested that such a corps would have the double object of readiness for service in Spain if necessary and for embarkation from Toulon to other regions if events made such a movement advisable.[65] The French actually stationed a large corps on the Spanish frontier, as is well known.

Count Villèle replaced Richelieu on November 28, 1821. (A succession of foreign ministers served under him during the six years he led the ministry: Montmorency to December 28, 1822, Chateaubriand to June 6, 1824, and Damas to January 4, 1828. The principal agents of France at Constantinople during the period were Latour-Maubourg, who served less than two years, and Guilleminot.) Richelieu continued neutrality as the basic French policy in the Greek War, shown by the instructions of the ministry of marine to Halgan on January 15, 1822. France did not follow Russia in lending her flag to the Greeks; as an effective way of enforcing neutrality the commander of the Levant squadron was directed "not to tolerate the use of the French flag to cover any foreign ship."[66]

Montmorency by March, 1822, shared the general opinion that a rupture between Russia and Turkey was likely, the policy of France in that event being already formulated. Denying the existence of any private understanding with Russia, France announced to England that in such an event she would remain neutral, her situation and the nature of her interests in the Levant not permitting hesitation on that point. Of greater concern were the further problems of the possible ruin of Turkey because of a Russian attack and the potential expansion of such a war into a general conflict. Opinion at Paris held that, if a general war eventuated, "the ruin of the social order in the old world must be regarded as certain." More significantly, France considered the question of a possible partition of the dominions of the sultan. No advance arrangements having been made for such a contingency, France desired to preserve the unity of the five Great Powers in such an event, "claiming the right to participate equally with the others in territorial advantages" which might accrue. She argued that French territory now showed a relative decline from what it had been in 1792 because of the accretions won by the other Powers in 1815. A new ambassador, the famous Chateaubriand, was dispatched to London. He was instructed to ascertain, if possible, the attitude of the British government on the Turkish territorial questions, being careful, however, to avoid saying anything on that subject which the British might use against the French at Constantinople.[67]

With respect to the Near Eastern antagonists, French policy by June, 1822, was interpreted as favoring both Turkey and Greece in different particulars. On the one hand, the fall of the Ottoman Empire was to be prevented; on the other, the Greeks were to be assured the preservation, within the empire, of their religion, property, and civil and political rights.[68]

Methods of giving effect to the favoritism for the Greeks were indicated by the instructions to Rigny, on May 27, 1823, authorizing him, "for motives of policy or of humanity," to use his own discretion in sometimes providing convoys for nonneutral vessels. The Turkish paper blockade of the Levant against the Greeks was opposed; to be respected, the instruction stated, blockades must be effective. The commander was to discourage attempts to run through real blockades, and he was not to submit to any new duties on shipping in the Levant.[69] Another illustration of the point was the suggestion of a less vigorous opposition to piracy. The minister of marine on October 25, 1823, wrote Rigny that he had no positive opinion as to what to do about piracy; he had told the foreign minister that, although the laws against piracy were quite positive, it was necessary to distinguish the real pirates from others. If French naval vessels made attacks on doubtful vessels, the official French policy of neutrality would be infringed; hence Rigny was to proceed against pirates "only when their illegality and their brigandage were adequately proved."[70]

8. HANDICAPS TO TRADE

By the time of the Congress of Verona the Powers had before them the clearly marked international-trade effects of the war in the Levant, Russia being the most outspoken in opposition to the handicaps by Turkey. The French merchants likewise complained, while the Levant Company kept the issues before the British government.

At the time of the renewal of preëmption of grain (May, 1822), Cartwright summed up the restrictions to foreign trade in the Black Sea, listing four difficulties: Turkey (1) refused to authorize the passage of oil through the Straits, necessitating fictitious manifests; (2) asserted her right to seize any part of a cargo of Russian, English, or other produce in transit through the Straits if Constantinople should be in need; (3) restricted the transport of Turkish produce, such as Egyptian, into the Black Sea; and (4) often delayed the issuance of the firmans for passage. All of these handicaps were regarded as contrary to the wording of the Russo-Turkish commercial convention of 1783, which applied to Great Britain under the most-favored-nation clause of the treaty of 1809.[71]

The British in certain circumstances held Turkey to the letter of the Russian treaty, because they feared the imposition of a transit duty, which would have affected their competition with Austria and Russia.[72] In August the company informed the British foreign office that its "commercial relations with Turkey were becoming more critical, and perhaps less intelligible than ever."[73] In addition to rigid quarantines generally applied throughout the

Levant,[74] three other grievances had now been recorded by the company against the Turkish government; the sequestration of the property of certain Greek merchants at Smyrna, some of whom were indebted to British firms,[75] the forced registration of all foreign vessels chartered by Turkish subjects, and the prohibition of trading by all Powers that did not possess proper treaty grants.[76]

For Russia the Greek War contributed to a temporary diminution of the new export importance of her southern ports.[77] Moreover, her commercial problems expanded in proportion as she showed eagerness to accord aid to Greek shipping. In 1822, for example, Turkey began to show new zeal in her searches of Russian vessels which passed the Straits, at that time restoring the order for the searching of all foreign vessels: a Turkish officer was actually to board each vessel and to inquire pointedly of its master respecting the ship's nationality and cargo.[78]

Thus Turkey attempted to lessen the practice of simulation, to which all the Powers had taken recourse. She announced also that changes of flags for commercial vessels would not be recognized, and that transshipment of produce within the Straits would not be permitted; even the order of preëmption of grain and oil at her discretion was reaffirmed.[79] Private assurances that the new rule concerning searches would not apply to British, French, and Austrian vessels led the representatives of these Powers to admit the abstract right of Turkey to make the regulation.[80]

It was expected that Russia would bring her issues with Turkey before the Congress of Verona. In doing so, Tatischev clarified the Russian position, and added the welcome information that Russia did not intend to press her demands to the point of war. George Canning evinced sympathy for Russia, admitting that Turkey, as Russia's natural enemy, was doing all that she could to interfere with the commerce of the fertile southern provinces of the tsar. Yet he considered that Great Britain, herself the ruler of millions of Mohammedans, was hardly in position to make war on Turkey because she was the overlord of non-Muslim peoples. The British representatives at the congress, Stewart and Wellington, were instructed to avoid pledging Great Britain to take part in any projected intervention in the Greek War.[81] France, Austria, and Prussia also supported Russia in her commercial claims against Turkey, at the same time discouraging intervention in the Greek

War. Spanish intervention was the more important problem at the congress, however, Wellington perforce assuming an attitude of detachment when a French invasion of Spain was authorized. Great Britain tendered the good offices of Strangford at Constantinople, and through him Russia soon undertook new negotiations for a settlement with Turkey.

Tsar Alexander, in opposing the Turkish regulations of 1822, insisted that all ships bearing the Russian flag be accorded the passage of the Straits in conformity with the precise stipulations of the convention of 1783. Turkey in rejoinder introduced an interpretation which might exclude Russian commerce with Greece from the benefits of the treaty by stating that the convention clearly provided for exceptions in times of war.[82] Just when Strangford began working for a resumption of Russo-Turkish diplomatic relations, early in 1823, Turkey preëmpted a quantity of Russian grain found in transit through the Straits; Alexander nevertheless invited Strangford to press for a solution of all the unsettled issues with Turkey.

The first lessening of the handicaps to the shipping of foreign produce through the Straits during this period occurred on May 23, 1823, when Turkey promulgated some new regulations for the benfit of her own subjects that permitted them to embark Russian produce in the Black Sea and either sell it to Turkey or send it to other markets, under free transit of the Straits. However, all ships were to make the customary stops for firmans of passage, frequently causing a delay of eight, and sometimes as many as twenty, days. Strangford got Turkey to agree to expedite the issuance of firmans for British ships.[83]

The navigation of the Straits presented some problems for the British, a minor cause of friction between Turkey and the Levant Company at the end of 1823 being the exclusion of an armed merchant vessel from the Bosporus. This proved to be an interesting case in the almost continuous exclusion of foreign vessels of war from the Dardanelles and the Bosporus during modern times.[84] Difficulties confronting trade were continuous. The principal British merchants at Constantinople[85] held a special meeting on March 6, 1824, at the residence of the British consul general in Pera, at which a petition was drawn up to ask for the correction of trade grievances. Several corrections were suggested: an inquiry was asked to see whether or not the British ambassador in 1813[86] had relinquished the British right to free trade to and from the ports of the Black Sea, and if possible to arrange to terminate the necessity for fictitious manifests; security was desired for the British right to export from Turkey all tariffed products upon payment of the duties and to transship them without further payments; request was made that Turkey be prevailed upon to issue promptly all firmans for passage, the regulations announced in 1823 having failed of enforcement; demand was made for the suppression of all abuses attendant on the "visiting of ships." Other requests were for an effective protection of brokers, for prompt payment of an indemnity for delays experienced in the tardy loadings of vessels chartered by the Turkish government to carry grain from its provinces, and for the settlement of all bona fide claims for sequestered Greek property, especially that in Smyrna.[87] Despite the insistent concern of the members of the Levant Company over these handicaps to British trade, the British government throughout the period seemed to regard them as quite minor matters. By analysis, they represent problems of trade profits for the British merchants, not unreasonable and extensive Turkish interference.

French grievances were of similar type, although less insistent because of the smallness of the French trade in the Ottoman Empire. According to a letter by Guilleminot (October 10, 1824), so many questions or reclamations sought by French companies and individuals appeared that the embassy was kept busy, "usually without success," attempting to get damages.[88] In August of the same year protests were sent to Paris from Consul General David of Smyrna and from the Marseille Chamber of Commerce against the Turkish internal duties.[89] In the various démarches for correcting the Turkish abuses, the French agents went unassumingly along with the other Powers.[90]

Meanwhile, interest had shifted to the Russo-Turkish negotiations. In these Strangford was the intermediary, serving with a sort of mixed commission. Of the four sets of Russian claims, relating respectively to Greece, the Principalities, the Asiatic littoral, and commerce, those involving Greece were sharply separated from the others, owing to the insistence of Austria. In their own interest, as well as in the interests of peace, the British energetically supported the Russian views in most of the issues. In July George

Canning instructed Strangford to warn Turkey against the continuance of her "unreasonable" attitude toward Russia and to advise that the only way to preserve peace was through methods of conciliation. He pointedly supported the Russian claims in reference to commerce and to the frontier forts. A British protest was delivered to Turkey against the seizure of Russian grain transported in foreign ships. Canning, fearing that the absence of any quarrels between Russia and the other Powers at that moment would aid in the development of a bellicose policy toward Turkey, suggested that the Porte maintain internal peace "as the best method of guarding the empire from attack from without."[91]

The negotiations proved successful for the most immediate points of difference. Russia's commercial claims were granted in substance, although they were not established with great clarity until the Peace of Adrianople. Turkey announced her willingness to conclude the desired commercial conventions for the passage of the Straits by all Powers not already having the privilege and to end the other vexations to commerce of which Russia had complained.[92]

Thereupon Tsar Alexander sent Minciakii, his consul at Patras, to Constantinople to make definitive arrangements. Minciakii negotiated for the complete withdrawal of the Turkish forces from Moldavia and Wallachia. Again Strangford aided in the discussions; but he advised Turkey to ask Russia for a reduction of her own forces in the Principalities, which he said were there in violation of treaties.[93] Minciakii eventually succeeded in winning Turkey's consent to withdraw her forces.[94]

The Turkish evacuation of the Principalities permitted the resumption of normal Russo-Turkish diplomatic relations. Russia named Ribeaupierre as minister to the Porte. His departure for his post being, for various reasons, unduly delayed, Minciakii meanwhile acted as chargé d'affaires.

9. Commercial Eclipse

Whatever the handicaps to trade offered by Turkey or the irregular methods necessary for British or Austrian trading activity, merchants of both of these Powers at least did a good deal of business in the Levant. In contrast, the trade outlook for France seemed quite gloomy. The statistics speak for themselves: in 1823 the French commercial flag was represented at Constantinople by only sixteen vessels; that of Austria by over 600; even Naples, Sicily, Spain, and Sweden all surpassed France.[95] In 1824 Austria sent 530 vessels to Constantinople, Russia sent 438, and England sent 358.[96] French trade had so far declined that the government on December 15 reduced its consular representation in the Levant. It closed the consulate general at Bagdad, the consulates at Basra, Trebizond, and Syrian Tripoli, and six scattered Levantine vice-consulates.[97]

The method that should be used to restore French commerce in the Levant was again the subject of inquiry. When he was in Marseille in February, 1824, Guilleminot asked for suggestions from the Chamber of Commerce. The chamber renewed the stock argument and sought restoration of the Marseille monopoly, the plan which already had been repudiated by the French general council of commerce and several important city chambers. A collection of data in one volume of the consular archives evidences that studies were made in 1824 on various aspects of the problem. All of the conclusions emphasized that French laws, not the Turkish restrictions, accounted for the unfavorable light in which French commerce appeared. An analytical memorandum by Louis Castagne surveyed the available statistics on trade. Castagne made seven pointed recommendations, favoring: (1) the issuance of captains' authorizations with more facility; (2) the use of foreign sailors on French boats; (3) the suppression of the obstacles interposed by the French administration to the transfers of ownership of vessels; (4) the lessening of the burdens for registration; (5) the prompt and facile issuance of clearance papers for ships; (6) the abolition of the quarantine for ships returning from the Levant; and (7) the arming of some French merchant ships. Guilleminot was away on vacation for several months, and Beaurepaire, in supporting the recommendations of Castagne, made the additional suggestions that the foreign sailors in French service might be naturalized and that they might be utilized to lessen the cost of operation of French vessels; that the restoration of the Marseille monopoly would aggravate the malady instead of curing it; and that French marine laws imposed handicaps on French shipping which did not touch the foreigner who operated in French ports. Beaurepaire concluded that the whole system was such that it was then to the advantage of Frenchmen to use a foreign flag, such as the Russian, even in the port of Marseille. These papers having been referred to Marseille, responses were made by Rostand for the chamber. In his reply to specific questions are the following points: In general, France had enough ships for the requirements of the Levant trade—although in 1822 there were not enough vessels, there were too many available in 1823; as for the arming of vessels, it would be necessary in the first place to determine whether there were adequate reasons for considering that phase at all; foreign ships navigated at less expense for the simple reason that they used smaller crews and paid smaller salaries; the French right to navigate the Black Sea should be especially protected and the French flag not lent to vessels not having such a right under the capitulations. In the same series appears a copy of a letter written on August 9, 1822, by Latour-Maubourg which emphasized many of the points made by Castagne.[98]

King Charles X ascended the throne shortly after the reports mentioned above were prepared (September 15, 1824). Meanwhile Baron Damas had replaced the aggressive Chateaubriand at the foreign office. The first contribution of Damas to the problem has already been indicated. It was he who suppressed the various consular establishments on December 15.

Thus far we have treated many of the basic economic problems which accelerated the interest of France and the Powers in the Levant during a difficult decade. France attempted to restore her lost markets in the Near East, while Marseille unsuccessfully sought to regain her ancient monopoly; French commerce, however, had suffered an eclipse. Feeble international efforts had been made to halt Barbary piracy; Egypt was developing into an autonomous province; the negotiations between Russia and Turkey had only partially settled their outstanding differences when the Greek revolt shook the foundations of the Turkish Empire. Political and commercial policies, whether French or general European, were so interrelated as to develop simultaneously. Turkey, holding aloof from commercial pursuits, struggled to keep her empire intact while the Great Powers held her to the letter of her former commercial grants to them.

NOTES TO SECTION I

[1] See P. Masson, *Histoire du commerce français dans le Levant au XVIIIe siècle* (Paris, 1911), *passim*.

[2] This is shown by the diplomatic and consular dispatches for the early years of the Restoration.

[3] AE Constantinople 77; AEMD Turquie 31. The table of abbreviations employed for the archives is given on p. xvi.

[4] Talleyrand to Riviera, August 12, 1814, AE Constantinople 78.

[5] AE Constantinople 77.

[6] Cf. E. Jurien de La Gravière, *La station du Levant* (Paris, 1876), I, 1.

[7] AE Constantinople 78.

[8] *Ibid.*

[9] AEMD Turquie 14. Sinope would have been the port for exchanges with Tokat and the regions beyond.

[10] The consul general at Constantinople represented the government as well as the company, however. He was appointed and paid by the company, but had a regular commission under the crown (FO 78 T 96).

[11] FO 78 T 89.

[12] It was not until 1825 that the British government began gradually to restrict the trading activities of the consuls.

[13] Southern Russia was outside the jurisdiction of both the Levant Company and the Russia Company. After the Peace of Amiens, British consular representation at Odessa had been assigned to a merchant, Henry S. Yeames. Upon his death in 1819 his son, James Yeames, was appointed "consul general for the Russian ports of the Black Sea." Soon thereafter the consul general was assigned a regular salary. His principal duties were to tabulate trade statistics, which he did very well, to keep abreast of the political developments, and to extend British protection to Ionian and Maltese traders in addition to the British. (Planta to Yeames, April 2, 1819, FO 65 R 118.) Taganrog was given a British consular agent in 1818. The uncertainties of the grain requirements in England, however, postponed the extensive participation of English traders in the Black Sea trade until the eighteen-forties.

[14] Foreign tariff agreements with Turkey listed the specific duties payable on listed commodities, thus obviating the necessity of discussion of values each time the customs payment was made. The western negotiators always attempted to have low unit payments stipulated, somewhat below the normal 3-per cent levy by Turkey. An added advantage of the tariffs was that they gave the European merchants the benefits of any interim price increases in the values of their produce or of any advantages accruing from the cheapening of Turkish money in international exchange.

[15] For example, the Prussian minister protested on September 25, 1817 (AA, Rep. 6 Türkei No. 2, vol. 1).

[16] These were the usual restrictions applicable at the time. The prohibitions against grain and oil led to the extensive use of simulation, as will be shown in the next section. In the early 'thirties the most important restricted export item was raw silk from Brusa.

[17] AE Constantinople 80.

[18] Liston to Castlereagh, May 25, 1820, FO 78 T 94; Cartwright to the Levant Company, May 25, 1822, FO 78 T 136.

[19] Except for commercial problems, the activity of Riviera during his first years at Constantinople was not very great. In 1817, for example, his official reports consisted for the most part of his month-to-month impressions of political developments, especially the Russo-Turkish negotiations to be treated later (AEMD Turquie 31). There were intermittent complaints about abuses to trade, one example having come from French merchants in Smyrna in April, 1820 (AE Constantinople 80).

[20] CCM, dossier, Commerce du Levant.

[21] As an illustration of the quite general European complaints against Mehemet Ali's economic system, we may utilize the grievances against the export monopoly which Henry Salt, British consul, listed in 1820. The pasha's monopoly of exports extended to all the principal agricultural products of Egypt; he permitted the mixing of inferior with good qualities of produce; he sold largely to the officers of administration at his ports, giving them the extra profits of brokerage speculations; and he arbitrarily regulated prices. (Salt to Planta, June 30, 1820, and to Londonderry, November 6, 1821, FO 78 T 96 and 103.)

[22] AEMD Turquie 31.

[23] *Ibid.*

[24] E. Plantet, *Correspondance des deys d'Alger avec la cour de France* (Paris, 1889), II, 542–545.

[25] AEMD Turquie 19.

[26] AEMD Turquie 9.

[27] Cesar Moreau, *Examen comparatif du commerce de la France avec tous les pays du monde* (London, 1828).

[28] Illustrated by the new laws affecting grain, the most important item available from southern Russia and the Levant, the transition from protection to virtual prohibition occurred from 1814 to 1821. Napoleon's decree of 1810 had permitted the free import of grain although prohibiting its export; by the law of November 20, 1814, the Bourbon monarchy established a sort of sliding scale for both imports and exports. A temporary exception was allowed for ten months beginning in November, 1816, because of crop shortages in France. At the expiration of that period a more stringent restriction against grain imports was decreed, in imitation of the laws which favored the agrarian producer in England. The law was further modified in 1821 to raise the minimum prices below which no imports would be allowed. This caused the prohibition of grain imports in fact between 1821 and 1830, except during February, 1828. As in England, one consequence of this policy in France was the appearance of a free-trade party. Thus French merchants contented themselves of necessity with only the brokerage for foreign account and the transport phases of the important grain trade of the Levant. This was one of the reasons why French merchants turned with alacrity to the cotton trade of Egypt in the late eighteen-twenties and early 'thirties and in part also explains why French policy was eventually oriented toward almost independent Egypt instead of being more comprehensively revitalized in Turkey.

[29] P. Masson, *Les bouches du Rhône* (Paris, 1922), IX, 39.

[30] CCM, dossier, Commerce du Levant, 1802–1815.

[31] The required bond for individual traders was from 40,000 to 60,000 francs (AEMD Turquie 9).

[32] AE Constantinople 78.

[33] A memorandum by Deval at Constantinople in February, 1816, supported the new claims for virtual free trade, at least on a trial basis. He had noted in 1814 and 1815 that French drapes in the Levant lacked uniformity and were surpassed in quality by those from Belgium. For other grades of textiles, such as muslins, French manufactures were in demand but faced the competition of Saxony, Switzerland, and England. He found the French merchants content to carry on routine commerce, but seeking little expansion. Hence Deval suggested that it might be well to institute a trial period in which foreign carriers would be free to sell French goods. "I believe that the Greeks can carry on French commerce at less expense than the French merchants," he wrote, "for several years they have enjoyed the same customs rates as those of the European Powers." Among the advantages of this plan, Deval said, were these: France would save the expense of maintaining retailing establishments in the Levant, the Greeks might coöperate with the French houses already in the Levant, and, content with less profit than the French, they would encourage the consumer's use of more French manufac-

tures. Deval proposed also that Belgian and Swiss drapes be embarked at Marseille on French ships; in short, that the Marseille monopoly be abandoned. The direct reply to this communication was noncommittal. Richelieu acknowledged it with thanks as one of some seventeen dispatches by Deval (*ibid.*).

[34] AEMD Turquie 9.
[35] CCM, dossier, Commerce du Levant.
[36] J. Julliany, *Essai sur le commerce de Marseille* (Marseille, 1842), II, 221.
[37] CCM, dossier, Commerce du Levant, 1802–1855.
[38] *Ibid.*
[39] Latour-Maubourg to Pasquier, minister of foreign affairs, June 21, 1821, AE Constantinople 81.
[40] See pp. 22–23 for the political aspects of the instructions.
[41] AEMD Turquie 19; AE Constantinople 81.
[42] The Turks seized a quantity of Greek merchandise at Smyrna, for example, part of which had been held on consignment from France, against which the chamber at Marseille complained (AE Constantinople 81).
[43] CCM, dossier, Commerce du Levant.
[44] Latour-Maubourg to Marseille Chamber of Commerce, June 20, 1822 (*ibid.*, and AE Constantinople 81).
[45] AE Alexandrie 23.
[46] AE Constantinople 83.
[47] In May, 1825, for example, Drovetti was ordered to see that the French merchants stopped providing their facilities for the evasion of the duty (AE Alexandrie 22).
[48] G. Yakshich, "La Russie et la porte ottomane de 1812 à 1826," *Revue Historique*, XCI (1906), 281–306.
[49] *Ibid.*
[50] The Ypsilantis had known in advance that Austria was hostile to Greek ambitions and that Russia probably would not support the Greeks in military measures against Turkey (Ypsilanti, *Mémoires* [Paris, n.d.], p. 86).
[51] Cartwright to Liddell, May 25, 1821, FO 78 T 136.
[52] Cartwright to Strangford, May 20, 1821, *ibid.*
[53] Sometimes a vessel would be detained thirty or forty days and then released after Turkey found she had no immediate need for the cargo. Other cargoes were taken at reduced rates; the payment for some was deferred by Turkey (Cartwright to Liddell, August 25, 1821, *ibid.*; cf. G. Canning to Strangford, February 24, 1823, FO 195 T 40).
[54] Yeames to Planta, January 21, 1822, FO 65 R 130.
[55] Fictitious manifests thereafter were employed for oil. When the embargo was lifted, several British ships with cargoes of grain were at Constantinople awaiting appropriation of their cargoes. Strangford at once summoned Turkey to see that their owners did not suffer financial loss (Strangford to Cartwright, August 9, 1821, FO 78 T 136).
[56] Yakshich, *op. cit.*, (1907), pp. 74–89.
[57] Cartwright to George Wood, May 23, 1822, and Strangford to Cartwright, May 24, 1822, FO 78 T 136.
[58] I. de Testa, *Recueil des traités de la porte ottomane*, I, 233–241.
[59] Cartwright to Liddell, June 12, 1821, FO 78 T 136. By Turkish rule, the Straits were closed to foreign warships. In the Treaty of the Dardanelles (1809) England agreed to have her ships conform to the Turkish rule. The first European Convention of the Straits was signed in 1840 (Puryear, *International Economics* [Stanford University, 1935], pp. 146–179).
[60] Cf. Yakshich, *loc. cit.*
[61] This was shown when Strangford, in his first audience with the sultan, termed Great Britain "the friend and ally" of Turkey and spoke of the interest of the British crown in the integrity of Turkey (T. Schiemann, *Geschichte Russlands unter Kaiser Nikolaus I* [Berlin, 1904–1911], I, 307–308).

⁶² Pozzo di Borgo to Nesselrode, October 8, 1821, *ibid.*, pp. 565–572.
⁶³ AEMD Turquie 19. These reflections of Richelieu follow a note by Codrika on the status of Turkey. The note depicted the Turks as a weak agrarian people who were unable to extend their commerce with Europe but who nevertheless would be able to defeat the Greeks.
⁶⁴ Pasquier to Latour-Maubourg, October 8, 1821, *ibid.*
⁶⁵ MG, D² carton 1.
⁶⁶ MM, BB⁴, carton 426.
⁶⁷ These instructions of March 27, 1822, are published *in extensa* by G. Teissier, *Canning et Chateaubriand* (Paris, 1934), pp. 77–97, quoting AE Angleterre 615.
⁶⁸ AEMD Turquie 19.
⁶⁹ MM, BB⁴, carton 445.
⁷⁰ *Ibid.*
⁷¹ Cartwright to the Levant Company, May 25, 1822, FO 78 T 136.
⁷² Cartwright to Liddell, August 26, 1822, *ibid.*
⁷³ Liddell to Planta, August 19, 1822, FO 78 T 112.
⁷⁴ AA, Rep. 6 Türkei, No. 2, vol. 1.
⁷⁵ Bosanquet to George Canning, October 10, 1822, FO 78 T 112. The French complained of the same thing, as we have seen.
⁷⁶ Parliamentary Papers, Turkey, No. 16 (1878), No. 28. The first instance in which Turkey actually enforced her commercial restrictions against England occurred in January, 1823. The "Thames" was stopped at Constantinople because it attempted to transport Egyptian produce into the Black Sea. To prevent the establishing of a precedent, the Board of Trade requested the foreign office to intervene for the release of the "Thames" and to get Turkey to permit unrestricted shipping to and from the Black Sea. Almost immediately another ship, the "Aurea," was stopped for the same reason. In both cases Turkey rightly claimed the payment of duties on Egyptian produce in transit to Odessa, which would have been due if Danubian produce had been transported through the Straits to the Mediterranean. After three months of discussion the British paid the duties and the ships were released. Thereafter bribery was used to contravene the restrictions. (FO 78 T 136, 191.)
⁷⁷ See Vernon J. Puryear, "Odessa: Its Rise and International Importance, 1815–1850," *Pacific Historical Review*, III (1934), 198–199.
⁷⁸ Testa, *op. cit.*, I, 233 ff.
⁷⁹ Latour-Maubourg to Montmorency, September 18, 1822, AE Constantinople 81.
⁸⁰ Cartwright to Liddell, July 10, 1822, FO 78 T 136.
⁸¹ E. J. Stapleton, ed., *Some Official Correspondence of George Canning* (London, 1887), I, 200–213, II, 375.
⁸² Professor Schiemann states that both the Russian and Turkish positions seem well founded, from the wording of the convention itself (Schiemann, *op. cit.*, I, 330, note).
⁸³ FO 78 T 136; cf. Parliamentary Papers, Turkey, No. 16 (1878), Nos. 29 and 30.
⁸⁴ The "Thalia," carrying nine guns and bound from Marseille to Odessa, was detained at the entrance of the Dardanelles from September 30 until December 3 on the Turkish interpretation that the vessel was a warship and hence excluded from the Straits by the Anglo-Turkish treaty of 1809. Representations by Cartwright, submitted through Strangford, satisfied the Turkish authorities that the vessel was not a ship of war, but during the discussions another point was raised. Because it was a ship of 672 tons, slightly larger than the limit of 600 tons stipulated by the Russo-Turkish commercial convention of 1783, Turkey wished to impose a similar restriction on British commercial navigation. Cartwright thus concluded his reports of the affair: "It is to be apprehended, I think, that the Porte wishes to impose upon our

[British] navigation the restriction on the amount of tonnage which has been admitted by Russia in her treaty with the Porte, for the navigation of the Black Sea. The regulations being also obligatory upon us would authorize, no doubt, the Porte to refuse the passage to the Black Sea of an English vessel of the size of the 'Thalia,' though they could not, I presume, justify such a pretention in regard to English vessels bound for Constantinople from the Mediterranean." (FO 78 T 136.) For a discussion of British contraventions of the rule of closure of the Straits to foreign warships, see Appendix, pp. 219–222.

[85] These were: Messrs. Cartwright, T. N. Black, Barbaud, Sarelli, Wright, Graves, Sandison, Hardy, Simmons, and Wood.
[86] Documents on the problem are in FO 78 T 136.
[87] Cartwright to Liddell, May 10, 1824, *ibid.*
[88] CCM, dossier, Commerce du Levant.
[89] AE Constantinople 82.
[90] On January 24, 1824, for example, the ministry of foreign affairs thanked Beaurepaire for his efforts to remove the handicaps to transit commerce (*ibid.*).
[91] George Canning to Strangford, July 12, 1823, FO 195 T 40.
[92] Sardinia (on October 25, 1823) was the first state to profit by this concession (G. E. Noradounghian, *Recueil d'actes internationaux de l'empire ottoman*, I, 102). Spain, Sweden, Denmark, and Naples were accorded commercial access to the Black Sea in 1827.
[93] *Ibid.*, II, 104.
[94] The agreement was reported on July 29, 1824 (Stapleton, *op. cit.*, I, 150).
[95] AE Constantinople 82.
[96] AA, Rep. 6 Türkei, No. 2, vol. 1.
[97] AE Constantinople 82.
[98] *Ibid.*

II. THE TEMPO CHANGES

INTERNATIONALIZATION OF THE GREEK WAR

FOREIGN INTERVENTION in the Greek War of Independence was the result of the developments after Turkey summoned her powerful Egyptian vassal, Mehemet Ali, to aid her in putting down the Greek rebellion. This, with its inevitable political sequels and the continuance of the Russo-Turkish antagonism, internationalized the Greek War. Many new policies emerged between 1825 and 1829. French policy was significantly advanced in the Levant, although its application was contradictory in alternately favoring and opposing Egypt. The British government strengthened its position in Turkey by taking over the consular organization of the Levant Company and sought to escape isolation in the Greek question.

1. England Dissolves the Levant Company

The large place in Turkish affairs which was held by "the Right Honorable, The Governor, and the Right Worshipful, The Company of Merchants of England Trading to the Levant Seas," under whose direction the British consuls served in Turkey, was no longer tenable with the new political problems of such magnitude and delicacy as those of the Greek War and the strained Russo-Turkish relations. The government of Great Britain more than once found itself in the inconsistent position of upholding policies which were not always approved by the English Levant Company. To end the competition, the company was dissolved.

There were several general and specific reasons for the dissolution. (1) The increased civil and criminal jurisdiction of the company burdened its organization, the increase coming from two causes. First, changes in the rules made it comparatively easy for any British subject to engage in the trade of the Levant under all the privileges of the company. Traders being no longer limited numerically, exclusiveness in the opportunities of membership was lost, and monopolies became unprofitable. Second, there was an increased demand for consular protection owing to the Ionian and Maltese problems after 1815. Although no changes were authorized by Parliament in their behalf, these new subjects having no independent commercial jurisdiction, it was found necessary to provide consular protection under the company's organization for their traders in Turkey. (2) Constant complaints charged inefficiency against the officers of the company.[1] Practice tended toward noninterference by the government in company management. In exchange for the fees, charged and administered exclusively by the company,[2] the British merchants expected efficient service. (3) The ultimate management of the consular establishment was a factor. Sometimes conflicts of jurisdiction occurred between the ambassador and the consul general. Under the company laws, the connection between the ambassador and the consular organization was through the consul general of the company, who, although head of the consular system, was himself amenable to the ambassador on important matters. Differences of opinion led the ambassador and the consul general each to appeal to his respective superior. One referred questions to the British foreign office; the other asked for instructions from the company, also in London, which objected to occasional interferences by the ambassador. It claimed that the arrangement of 1804, whereby the government had assumed control only of the embassy, should be observed on both sides.[3] (4) Conflicts in policy were the essence of the problem. The Levant Company complained of the Turkish abuses to trade; but it complained more against the Greeks. The government did not interpose objections to the export of arms and ammunition to Greece,[4] whereas the company was more active in selling war supplies to Turkey. Greek ships, profiting from governmental encouragement, in turn interfered with the trade of the company. Illustrating the difficulty of operating two agencies of British administration in the Levant, company merchants at Smyrna protested that they were not given proper protection by the home government. A suggestion was made by the company that the British fleet give the desired protection;[5] in pursuance of its policy of neutrality between Turkey and Greece the government refused, since interference would have been regarded as intervention in favor of Turkey.[6] Several months later the government advised the company, in reply to a complaint that Greek cruisers searched English vessels, that this inconvenience was "unavoidably incident to a state of neutrality" and that, although the fleet would suppress piracy against British commerce,

---

[1] For notes to section ii, see pp. 65–68.

piracy was not to be confused with the belligerent right of search.[7] This virtually duplicated the policy already adopted by the French government. Investigations disclosed that "the Company favored and aided Turkey through the expedient of covering Turkish property with fictitious papers, and gave passes to Turkish and other foreign vessels not entitled in any way to carry English colors."[8] Like the French, the British government by interpretation had begun to direct its policy of neutrality toward favoritism of the Greeks. Indeed, it has been said that some British imperialists entertained ambitions to see Greece fall under an exclusive British protectorate, possibly assuring British supremacy in the Mediterranean and mastery of the Dardanelles, but that George Canning feared the formation of a great coalition against England if such a plan were attempted.[9] Once the British fleet aided the company but inadvertently opposed neutrality in forcing the Greeks to restore a cargo captured in a blockaded port. The government at once dispatched positive orders that strict neutrality must be maintained in the future. This blanket order was not liked by the company. Objections interposed at London charged that the Greeks were more disposed to piracy than were the Turks, that Turkey had established a paper blockade of practically every port which could be used in dealing with the Greeks, that the blockade was broken daily because Turkish vessels were not on hand to enforce it, and that there was no precise definition of a blockade anyway. In reply, Canning changed the order to make it apply only "to places really or actually blockaded,"[10] the same policy as had been adopted by France.

The steps in the dissolution of the Levant Company may be noted. George Canning notified the company at the end of January, 1825, that a bill was soon to be submitted to Parliament to transfer jurisdiction over the consuls in the Levant from the company to the crown, the government proposing to take over the personnel intact and treating each individual as if he had been in government service from the beginning. The notification was accompanied by the "hope" that the company would acquiesce "in a measure which had no other object than the advancement of the public interests, without prejudice to those of individuals." A later pointed request for the surrender of the company's charter[11] was acceded to at a general meeting of the company, called a "court," on February 23. Parliament on June 10 passed the act which repealed the concessions to the company and transferred the direction of its consuls to the crown.[12]

2. XANTIPPE

Although relatively insignificant for the affairs of the Levant at the time, another British activity early in 1825 which might have related directly to Greece was the special mission of Stratford Canning to St. Petersburg.

Tsar Alexander had invited the Great Powers to a conference with Russia on the question of Greece; France, Austria, and Prussia had accepted. Great Britain, on the other hand, had only permitted her ambassador at St. Petersburg to take matters *ad referendum*. George Canning saw no reason to rush matters, an opinion based on presumably authentic advices that Russia would not make a separate understanding with Greece.[13] Arrangements proceeded to hold the conference without the British. Such procedure did not please the British foreign secretary, especially since he could not be sure that the still unsettled Russian issues with Turkey, independently of Greece, might not themselves lead to war.

This perhaps accounts for George Canning's decision to have his cousin Stratford appear at the Russian capital while the conference was in session. The approaching conclusion of the agreement between Russia and England on a North American territorial question provided the opportunity for the special envoy to be commissioned ostensibly to conclude the negotiation on that matter. The appointment of Stratford Canning marked him for the first time as the outstanding Englishman who dealt with Near Eastern affairs, a role which he played until after the Crimean War. Indeed, Clarendon called him "Redcliffe Pasha" and "Sultan Stratford" during the days of the conflict in the Crimea. By his instruction dated December 8, 1824, he was to proceed to Russia by way of Vienna with authority not only to sign the convention regarding commerce, navigation, and territory on the northwestern coast of North America, but also to enter into detailed discussions of the Turco-Greek question. The principal point in the latter was to endeavor to persuade Alexander to return his minister to Constantinople.[14] Ribeaupierre, although appointed, had not yet assumed his duties.

In conference with Metternich and the kaiser at Vienna, Canning sought to divert Austria from her policy of opposition to the Greek revolt. Although it later appeared clear that Metternich wished to avoid a conflict with England, this is what he recorded after the departure of the British envoy:

> Canning's mission has failed entirely, and we have expressed ourselves to Russia in a way which will leave no doubt as to the firmness of our intentions. We will use the proper means to strengthen our squadron in the archipelago and in the Ionian Sea; the Emperor has authorized measures which as far as possible will guarantee our commerce and navigation in these seas from the additional dangers to which attempts of Greek cruisers, tolerated and protected up to a certain point by British authorities, may expose them.[15]

Arriving in St. Petersburg on January 29, 1825, Canning found the other diplomats already in conference on the problem of Greece. The convention on northwestern America was signed promptly, following which Canning threw out the suggestion to Nesselrode that he was also instructed to enter into conversations on Greece. Nesselrode considered the statement, asking what proposals Canning brought. Canning declined to open the discussion, rather placing himself in the position of wishing to answer questions raised by Nesselrode. Unwilling thus to open the back door of the conference to the British, Nesselrode in turn did not venture any questions or discussions of importance, reserving his comments for the conference proper. In several subsequent meetings with Nesselrode, Canning made persistent efforts to draw him into full discussions of the problem. These attempts always met the same abrupt result. At the conclusion of each such session during several weeks of that type of "negotiation," Canning assumed an attitude of resignation, repeatedly saying to Nesselrode that, if the Russians would not discuss the question of Greece frankly with him, there was nothing left for him to do but to ask for his audience to take leave of the tsar. Nesselrode always very considerately offered to arrange promptly such a meeting for him. Two indecisive discussions were recorded; the audience of leave was eventually held, and Canning left Russia on April 15. The manuscript volume of Canning's reports on the mission may be summarized in a sentence. Declining to tender opinions themselves, the Russians had expressed a willingness to hear Canning's proposals, but these he had declined to give until after he had heard those of Russia.[16]

A significant sidelight appears in one report: Nesselrode on one occasion frankly told Canning that he had acted in a receptive mood only in order that Canning might have no reason to report to his government that Russia had refused to hear him. Nesselrode later termed Canning's attitude "overbearing."[17] The mutual personal dislike formed at the time rankled for years afterward, affecting many of the affairs of the Near East and contributing mightily to the coming of the Crimean War. The failure in the attempted negotiation was followed shortly by the appointment of Canning to the post of British ambassador to Turkey (June, 1825). Meanwhile the conference at St. Petersburg likewise had all but failed. Owing to the attitude of England and the divergent opinions of Russia and Austria, about all it did was to give additional clarification to the various issues.

3. France and Egypt

Beginning about 1824 the policy of France was to strengthen Egypt within well-defined limits. Some pro-Egyptians like Drovetti already had envisaged the possibility of such close connections between France and Egypt that the Egyptian navy might be used by France in the future to balance more nearly her naval inferiority to Great Britain in the Near East. A new phase of the Greek War provided the first opportunity for a French advance. Here we shall see that a comprehensive French military mission was sent to serve Egypt, naval vessels were constructed in France for Mehemet Ali, French engineers directed similar construction at Alexandria, and French commerce with Egypt was extended. The close relationship for which Drovetti so long had labored began to be realized.

The revolt of southern Greece had been localized for three years. Because most of the Powers regarded Turkey as indispensable to the equilibrium of Europe, the Greeks had not been able to muster the direct support of foreign governments. The sympathies of Christian Europe were with the Greeks, however, as proved by the volunteers for service in their ranks. As for Turkey, although the direct aid of the Christian Powers was precluded in the nature of things, their nonintervention was in fact a valuable support for her. This was true also of the commercial aid given her by foreign firms, notably the English Levant Company, which had usually favored Turkey against Greece. Although the Ottomans had been confident of their ability to check the uprisings, the war had dragged on and had favored the insurgents in 1823.

A new and complicating factor was brought into the picture when Sultan Mahmud, in 1824, summoned Mehemet Ali to aid him in subjugating the Greeks. Crete was placed under the administration of the pasha, serving as a base for the ensuing naval and military operations. The seriousness of the Egyptian move was not fully recognized by the statesmen of Europe until October, 1825, when the armies of Ibrahim, son of the pasha, operating from conquered Navarino, had ravaged a great part of the Morea.

One of the first results of Mehemet Ali's aid to the sultan was the pasha's decision to organize some new infantry regiments to replace those detailed for service in Greece. For the expanded instructional service he called upon France, one of the nations which already had sent him a few instructors. He employed a merchant, Tourneau, to go to France in the summer of 1824 for the initial negotiations. Tourneau established connections with General Belliard, famous in the French expedition to Egypt from 1798 to 1801, who consented to recruit the requested military mission. Belliard selected General Pierre Boyer, who had been with Bonaparte in Egypt and Syria and had been a leading figure in the armies of the First Empire, to head the mission and Marshal Livron, who had been a merchant in Egypt at the time of Bonaparte's expedition, to second the command. Eight other officers were chosen, including Colonel Gaudin, later to prove Boyer's rival. The duties of the military mission, which arrived in Alexandria on November 24, 1824, included the formation, organization, and instruction of the troops of Mehemet Ali, assistance in naval construction, and assistance in the organization of factories for military purposes. The foreign instructors already there, described by Boyer as principally Italian and Spanish adventurers, soon departed for other regions. The field was cleared for the introduction of French army methods, desired by the pasha, who at once requested four additional instructors,[18] bringing the total to fourteen.

The objectives of the French government in this enterprise do not appear clear from the records. The correspondence is not complete; the most illuminating letters are those preserved by the war department from the exchanges between Boyer and Belliard. There we find Belliard writing on September 5 that Boyer's establishment in Egypt was "of great interest for France" and that it "should be very important for the two countries." Six weeks later Belliard touched the question of Egyptian independence, as follows:

> The great question of emancipation [of Egypt] can only be treated verbally and with the greatest circumspection. The enterprise can and must not take place without the certainty of success, and without the patent or secret support of a strong Power, France. I repeat, this is a question of highest interest and cannot be too fully matured.

On the other hand, in the written comments of November 8 addressed to Drovetti by Damas, it was plainly stated that, although Boyer and Livron had asked for instructions from the French government, the government had declined to "take any part, even verbal," in their project; it was "content not to offer opposition, leaving them free in their conduct." Nevertheless, Douin suggests that it is practically certain that Boyer received some instructions from Premier Villèle on the attitude to be adopted. Additional credence for this suggestion was lent by the letter of Belliard to Boyer on March 1, 1825. "Certainly," he said, "with an army of 60,000 men, organized, instructed, and disciplined as it can be with the means Mehemet Ali wants to employ, with the support of France, his natural ally, his independence will be fully assured." Belliard argued that the pasha would find the support of either England or France indispensable and concluded that "sincerely friendly relations can be established more easily and more naturally with France than with England."[19]

The policy of the French government in reference to Egypt is best found in the related and contemporary problem of naval construction for Mehemet Ali. Not many weeks after the arrival of the French officers, the pasha transferred to France his request for the purchase of war vessels which had previously been declined by England.[20] Livron, who was given the responsibility of aiding in naval construction, was instructed by Boghos, acting for Mehemet Ali, on December 28, 1824, to return to France to ask the government to provide facilities for the purchase, or the construction and fitting out, of two frigates and a corvette. If the vessels were ceded by France, Livron was to solicit for Egyptian service some officers of the French marine to form a theoretical and practical naval school in Egypt. The agent was also directed to assemble information on various inventions which might be utilized by Egypt.[21]

Back in Paris, Livron undertook secret negotiations for the execution of the orders placed by Mehemet Ali for the three war vessels. Apparently there was little discussion of a transfer of French ships, but the ministers showed themselves willing to sponsor the construction of the vessels. Political and technical factors were studied fully before decisions were made. Count Chabrol, minister of marine, at once recognized that the armament of such ships in France would be regarded as an aid to Turkey against Greece, "even if only considered as an object of commercial speculation."[22]

Chabrol concluded that it would be impossible to construct the vessels of the sizes required by Egypt, especially the frigates, in the commercial shipyards of France without governmental facilities and technical assistance and without the sales of reserved governmental supplies of timber and armaments. Indeed, the production problem was so great that it was a question whether Toulon rather than Marseille should not be the construction point. The whole problem was submitted to the French council, with an explanation that the king had expressed "a desire to cultivate the good dispositions of Mehemet Ali in favor of the French and their commerce, without halting the system of neutrality theretofore observed by France between the Greeks and Turks." Chabrol specifically asked whether the government would authorize the construction of the two frigates and one corvette as a commercial enterprise, and if so, whether the construction should be at Toulon or Marseille, and to what extent the government would aid the construction by cessions of the necessary supplies. The decision of the council, on April 27, 1825, was that the ships might be constructed at Marseille as a commercial enterprise. They were not in any event to be constructed at Toulon. The government would facilitate the construction "without any official intervention," and would sanction the use of government materials. The firm of Bruat, Daniel et Cie. of Marseille then accepted the order. A marine engineer, Cerisy, was sent from Toulon to direct the company's construction of the vessels. The building of the ships soon began, secrecy having been observed as to their ultimate destination. Livron returned to Cairo on August 4. Encouraged, Mehemet Ali ordered an extra corvette, which was also authorized by the French government. The destination of the vessels becoming known in advance of their completion, the gov-

ernment found itself criticized by opposition journals for aiding the
Turks, the *Courrier français* publishing details of the whole proceeding; other French firms sought equal governmental aid if they
should wish to handle orders from Mehemet Ali. Thus placed on
the defensive, directions were sent to Toulon to suspend the deliveries
of supplies from naval warehouses. The construction nevertheless
went forward, the company finding adequate private supplies. Yet
in February, 1826, the government supplied the anchors for the
frigates, a direct aid.[23]

Meanwhile, commercial interests sought to use the new friendship for an expansion of French commerce with Egypt. Simultaneously with the appearance of Boyer in Egypt, Damas inquired of
Drovetti whether the Franco-Turkish tariff was then being enforced
in Egypt, nothing to the contrary having been reported. Damas
also advised that France was following with interest the introduction of a new type of cotton into Egypt.[24] In February, 1825, the
government asked for positive information on the Egyptian methods of cotton culture and the possibility of extending its type to the
French colony of Senegal. Drovetti seized the opportunity offered
by the new friendship to attempt to win a preponderant economic
position for France in Egypt. At the same time he reported that
Boghos, now minister of commerce and usually pro-English, was
showing favor to the French.[25] Belliard's letter of March 1 to Boyer
spoke of the "almost reciprocal" economic positions of France and
Egypt and contrasted that situation with the conflicts and competition in commerce between England and Egypt because of the
British dominance of India. He noted that French and Egyptian
interests were more solidified than ever, the Egyptian expedition
to the Morea being the principal handicap. "A good treaty of commerce, advantageous for the two states," he wrote, "might cement
the union."[26]

In July Damas notified Drovetti that a new French company
was forming for the exploitation of Egypt. With a capitalization of
fifty million francs, it was being established through the joint
efforts of several older firms in Paris. Its operation would not prejudice the interests of other French firms already operating in Egypt.
The government had approved of the new company.[27] There were,
however, two handicaps to its success—piracy and the Egyptian
monopolies. More extensive piracy in the eastern Mediterranean

had increased the European commercial dangers and further contributed to the discomfort of Europe at the Egyptian turn of Levantine affairs.[28] French interests were especially displeased at the time, for two reasons: several new depredations by Greek pirates against their vessels had been reported, and the Greeks were reportedly placing themselves under the protection of the British.[29] When Livron returned to Cairo in August, he found that Mehemet Ali appeared quite anxious to increase his commercial relations with France. The reason for the failure of the projected company was not the lack of French governmental encouragement but the unwillingness of Mehemet Ali to alter his monopolistic control of the commerce of Egypt. Despite the rhetoric of Livron, he would not agree to give the French company any special privileges.[30]

Again in Paris in October, 1825, with Egyptian funds, Livron conveyed the pleasure of Mehemet Ali that the government of France would facilitate the naval construction. He also brought a request of Mehemet Ali for ten additional infantry instructors, requiring that they serve wherever Mehemet Ali might need them, in Egypt, Greece, Ethiopia, or Asia.[31]

From 1826 to 1828, when French commerce with the Levant in general continued weak, it showed marked increases in Egypt,[32] owing principally to cotton.[33] During the same period commerce with Turkey declined, about the only thing done to benefit French commerce with Turkey in 1826 being the formation of a council of commerce, primarily concerned with the collection of information.[34] Since the analyses of 1824 were not given official cognizance at Paris until 1827, apparently Marseille, for economic reasons, favored the Egyptians against the Greeks.[35] The year 1826 in France was anti-Greek from many standpoints.

Boyer wrote to Belliard on January 25, 1826, that it was important for the new officers to be sent promptly, because of the current fear that the new tsar of Russia, Nicholas I, would attack Turkey. In that event, Mehemet Ali was planning to move into Syria and to extend his power from Acre to the Persian Gulf, fearing only the English as opponents of this plan. In secret conferences with Boyer, Mehemet Ali made known that he was checking up on Persia, to prevent that country being set in motion against him by the English. Agents were sent everywhere to prepare the way for his new démarche. He thought that the people of the Liban, for example, would raise troops for him, and he inquired what attitude France would take if England blockaded Alexandria. Freely speaking of the sultan's empire as a "phantom" one, he hoped that Russia would end it, and even spoke "of founding an empire on the ruins of that of his master." On March 4 the foreign office notified Boyer of the selection of seven additional officers for service in Egypt;[36] in July the two brigs and one corvette originally ordered arrived at Alexandria.[37]

International developments soon suspended the new Franco-Egyptian friendship; by the time the war vessels were delivered the reported accord of the Powers respecting Greece had provoked in Mehemet Ali distrust of France, reflected in the decreased authority of the French military mission. Dissensions within the mission were also apparent, owing to rivalry between Boyer and Gaudin. In September, 1826, Boyer returned to Paris, several of the officers with him, but Gaudin remained, hoping to assume Boyer's place. At the same time Consul Malivoire of Cairo hoped to replace Drovetti as consul general.[38]

The distrust of France was also shown by the renewed tendency of Mehemet Ali to effect a working arrangement with England, against which Drovetti, Boyer, and Livron had so strongly advised. Mehemet Ali now attempted to convince the British agents that it would be politically and economically justifiable for Great Britain to avoid any participation with Russia in the Greek War. The defection of Austria from the other three Powers in the question of Greece was evident; Mehemet Ali anticipated a rupture between the Great Powers. He therefore suggested an alliance between Egypt and Great Britain, threatening to turn either to France or to Austria if England refused. In subsequent discussions, only a few weeks before the battle of Navarino, Mehemet Ali offered to withdraw his forces from the Morea if England would come to an understanding with him and, being at that time in distressed finances, sought protection if he should defect from Turkey. This attitude convinced Consul Salt that Mehemet Ali would withdraw from Greece anyway. As in his discussions with France, Mehemet Ali wished not only a "league of commerce and friendship" but also British support for his acquisition of Syria, including Damascus, and for his continued hold over Arabia. But this would have given him the mastery of both the overland routes to India. The naval battle at Navarino ended these discussions, to which the British had evaded a direct answer.

Another contemporary French problem in northern Africa, destined to an unusual development after the Greek War, was the conflict with Algeria. A chain of French grievances had accumulated against Hussein, the dey of Algeria, relating to piracy, commerce, and the enslavement of Christians, the same grievances being to a certain extent common to all the Powers. The first debates on the problem in the French Parliament went back to 1820, the French periodically thereafter pressing their claims. On one occasion, in the conference granted by the dey to Deval, then French consul at Algiers, on April 30, 1827, the dey insulted the consul by slapping his face.[39] The French government at once took steps through negotiation to get amends for this and the other complaints; but, failing to win satisfaction, war was declared (June 16, 1827). The parliamentary sessions of 1827 closed without explanations by the government respecting the affair; in 1828 there was little discussion of it in the Chambers; only in 1829 was it given full parliamentary discussion. French hostility to Algeria, meanwhile, was confined to a blockade of Algiers.[40]

4. Battle of Navarino

The international negotiations which served as the background for the battle of Navarino (October 20, 1827)—a battle which made impossible the continued intervention of Egypt in the Greek War—have been recounted many times, and the broad outlines are well known. The death of Alexander (December 24, 1825) and the accession of Tsar Nicholas I provided Great Britain with a good excuse to send the Duke of Wellington to the Russian capital. There he signed with Nesselrode the protocol which established the coöperation of Great Britain and Russia for negotiations with Turkey looking to a self-governing Greek state (April 4, 1826). Greece would have "complete liberty of conscience and of commerce." England and Russia agreed to seek neither aggrandizement of territory nor exclusive influence nor commercial advantages for their subjects which would not also be equally available to the other Powers. The ultimatum of Russia to Turkey (March 17, 1826) led to negotiations and the Convention of Ackerman (October 7, 1826) which presumably adjusted all the outstanding territorial, commer-

cial, and Danubian differences between Russia and Turkey. The
Ottoman Empire had been temporarily weakened by the intervening revolt (June, 1826) of its now hereditary army corps, the
janissaries. Now it seemed to take on new life and, despite the repeated warnings of both Russia and England in the interest of the
Greeks, continued obdurate. Finally France[41] joined with Great
Britain and Russia in the Treaty of London (July 6, 1827) which
provided for coercion against Turkey to guarantee the independence of Greece. As in the protocol of 1826, the contracting Powers
disclaimed any exclusive advantages for themselves in the new
undertaking. Austria and Prussia refrained from support or even
encouragement of the move. The details of the tri-Power treaty
were submitted to the Porte, and a joint declaration (August 16,
1827) demanded an armistice between Turkey and Greece. This
the Porte refused. The allies then took steps to prevent the sending
of further Turkish munitions to Greece and the Greek islands, while
Guilleminot recommended "prudence and circumspection" to all
French traders in the Levant (September 4, 1827).[42]

Almost identical instructions to the allied naval commanders and
to the three ambassadors at Constantinople provided, always on a
contingent basis, for the application of coercion in order to win an
armistice or at least to end the Egyptian intervention. The British
and French admirals in the Levant late in August recorded the
Greek consent to an armistice; but the Turks rejected the whole
plan. Extension of hostilities was presaged by renewed Greek military measures and the arrival of large Egyptian reënforcements at
Navarino. Admiral Codrington appeared there on September 12,
notifying Ibrahim that the entire Egyptian fleet now stood under
blockade in that bay; Rigny of France later joined Codrington and
the British, as did Heyden of Russia. Ibrahim agreed not to move
his fleet without asking for instructions from Constantinople. There
matters halted for several days. Then Ibrahim was sent an ultimatum demanding his agreement forthwith to an armistice and to
the evacuation of the Morea; his evasive reply led the allied commanders to precipitate matters by the movement of their squadrons,
on October 20, into the bay to anchor alongside the Turco-Egyptian armada. The Muslim forces refused to move some
anchored fire ships when summoned to do so; soon nervous firing
upon patrol boats occurred, and a general naval battle ensued. By

nightfall the combined Muslim squadron had ceased to exist, and Ibrahim had been cut off from Egyptian supplies.

5. AFTER NAVARINO

Turkey's anger after Navarino precluded her acceptance of the allied attempts at mediation. Deprived of any new support from Egypt, she redoubled her own efforts against the Greeks, proclaiming the conflict a Holy War. As a further measure of coercion, therefore, the French and British ambassadors and the Russian minister left Constantinople in December.[43] In reprisal for Navarino, Turkey virtually closed the Straits to neutral shipping on February 28, 1828.[44]

Not alone did Turkey give vexations to neutral shipping. Indeed, in concert with Russia and Great Britain, the French naval commander in the Levant on November 29, 1827, was ordered to capture and send to Toulon the pirate vessels which operated under the Greek flag.[45] The reason for this action was shown clearly by a letter from the Marseille Chamber of Commerce to the ministry of the interior. Here it was pointed out that the Greeks had not yet reciprocated the support given by their generous friends, and that they, "brigands who used legal forms," continued to interfere with French shipping "with more audacity than before." Since the future of Greek relations with the other Powers seemed to be the question, it was suggested that the Greeks might enjoy their liberty without interfering with the remainder of Europe. They should develop their internal resources, including the industrial, but they should not "leave their country, either to continue piracy or to encroach upon commerce and navigation of other peoples." The chamber made definite recommendation that all maritime construction for Greece be refused as a means of aiding the French merchant marine.[46] The British fleet was likewise ordered to protect British and Ionian commerce against the Greeks. The allies determined not to recognize blockades by Greece in any territories other than the Morea and the Cyclades, previously approved as blockaded regions.[47] Mehemet Ali was soon chagrined to learn of the occupation by Greek forces of a part of Crete, which he considered his own territory.[48]

Despite the temporary setback of the friendly relations between France and Egypt, which resulted from the Treaty of London, the

battle of Navarino paradoxically cleared the way for a renewal of
the French coöperation with Egypt. Until after the reactions of
Mehemet Ali to the battle were known, France suspended the return of Drovetti, who was then in France, to Alexandria. News of
the friendly dispositions of the pasha for France led Damas to order
the consul general to return to Egypt near the end of the year (on
December 21). Drovetti was instructed to convey the exchanged
expressions of friendly feelings and to advise Mehemet Ali to remain neutral in the event of hostilities between the three allies and
Turkey, meanwhile recalling the Egyptian troops from the Morea.
The French government would continue to favor the construction
of naval vessels for the pasha, and French schools would continue
to be open to young Egyptians.[49]

Martignac became the premier of France on January 4, 1828, a
position which he held until August 9, 1829. His first foreign minister was La Ferronays, the friend of Russia, of Greece, and of Egypt.
Arrangements were completed on February 20, 1828, for sending
three or four French military instructors to Greece. Meanwhile,
the French ministry of war considered two possibilities: one, the
extension of the Near Eastern war to western Europe, which would
require large forces; the other, the French participation in a joint
expedition to Greece to require the evacuation of Egyptian forces,
which would require only 12,000 to 14,000 men. Entrenched as he
was in the Morea, Ibrahim Pasha still defied the allies. Isolation
from the home base stopped his reënforcements and faced him with
the alternative of withdrawing, upon arrangement with the allies,
or of carrying the war by land into the north. The latter possibility,
as well as the obvious conclusion that, if Ibrahim withdrew, the
Turks would replace him in the Morea, led France at once to adopt
the plan for an expedition to confirm by land occupation the gains
already won by the allies on the sea.

The chief of the recruiting office suggested that a "partial" war
would offer several advantages: it would occupy everybody, revive
the martial spirit in France, and excite rivalry in the army.[50] The
French government by order of March 6, 1828, organized a corps
of 6,000 men for the projected expedition. Mehemet Ali acted upon
the restored friendship with France to solicit two French engineers
through his agent, General Livron, to direct the remaking of the
port of Alexandria, constituting it one of the best in the Mediter-

ranean, and to superintend the new Egyptian naval construction now necessary. On April 15, 1828, the French government announced that permission had been granted for Cerisy, the French marine engineer who had directed the naval constructions for the pasha in France, to go to Egypt, where he became the real creator of the Egyptian navy.[51]

Egypt again expanded her export of cereal grains.[52] All of the French foreign ministers for the period of the Greek War, when they got around to it, studied the problem of French commerce in the Levant. La Ferronays was no exception. He reflected that French commerce with the Ottoman Empire had approximated seventy million francs annually before 1791; that it had been almost totally interrupted in the course of the Revolution; that it made only a feeble recovery after 1815 (twenty-three million francs being the average about 1817). His latest figures showed that some improvement had been made; in 1827 the total trade had amounted to thirty-seven million francs. But La Ferronays was struck with another fact: that the increase had been principally owing to trade with Egypt, not with the Ottoman Empire as a whole, where French trade was still weak. The trade with Egypt had grown from two millions in 1816 to twelve millions in 1827. One reason was that French manufacturers more and more had come to prefer Egyptian to Turkish cotton.[53]

6. Russia and Turkey at War

The precise policy of Russia toward Turkey at the beginning of 1828, if different in any way from that accepted by the Treaty of London, is perhaps not known.[54] It is quite obvious, however, that Russia had two bases for action against Turkey, the Convention of Ackerman and the Treaty of London, whereas France and Great Britain had only one, the treaty. The Turkish closure of the Straits to commerce was a serious infraction of the Convention of Ackerman.[55] Other infractions were reported also. For example, French reports from Jassy indicated that Turkey had fortified the two large Danube delta islands in defiance of the convention and of the Peace of Bucharest. Guilleminot on April 5, 1828, sent word from Corfu that Russia had suddenly declared war on Turkey.[56]

The Russo-Turkish war added a new and significant development in the Levant, the solution of the Greek question now becoming rather more Russian than general European in character. On April 26 Tsar Nicholas by formal declaration stated his terms for the restoration of peace. These were: (1) the reëstablishment and enforcement of all Russo-Turkish agreements, especially the Convention of Ackerman; (2) the payment of an indemnity by Turkey; (3) the granting of access through the Straits and the Black Sea for all Powers to trade with Russia; and (4) the acceptance by Turkey of the Treaty of London, giving Greece her virtual independence. Most observers thought these terms quite moderate, especially since they excluded from the war aims any territorial cessions in European Turkey. La Ferronays, and later Portalis, expressed satisfaction at the moderation of the tsar.[57] Aberdeen sought to keep the Greek question separate from the Russo-Turkish quarrel, Metternich afterwards saying that where England and France had made their mistake was in allowing Russia to make war in the first place; that he had proposed strong action to prevent it, but that these two Powers had declined to interfere.[58] In point of fact, Russia was in an exceptionally strong diplomatic position at that juncture, not the least of the factors contributing to her position being her more aggressive alignment with the humanitarian and popular Greek cause.

Nesselrode expressed appreciation for the attitude of France. He wrote Pozzo di Borgo, who always favored a Franco-Russian alliance, that, if Austria detached herself, "at least a defensive treaty with France might become quite necessary."[59]

7. French Expedition to the Morea

The French and British policies diverged rather sharply in the weeks which immediately followed the Russian declaration of war against Turkey. Wellington never approved of the war, whereas the French ministers were inclined to utilize the occasion for a more aggressive stand in favor of the Greeks, their plan being to provide the logical sequel to Navarino. The result was that France alone dispatched an expeditionary force to the Morea in August, 1828, the background of which reveals the interplay of the international affairs of the eastern Mediterranean.

France found that serving as the friend of both Egypt and Greece had its difficulties. Inevitable conflicts of policies gave Greece the better support. This was strikingly illustrated when France proceeded, at first without the support of her allies, to devise a scheme for the expulsion of the Egyptian forces from the Morea. On April 20 the French attitude was clearly shown, the government declining to comply with new requests of Mehemet Ali for money, arms, and officers. France, moreover, was displeased with Mehemet Ali's conduct in another particular, the enslavement of a large number of Greeks taken to Egypt on the boats which escaped the disaster of Navarino. Drovetti, instructed to urge the pasha to give up this "odious traffic" and again to insist upon the recall of his troops, was told that, in spite of French friendship for the pasha, Mehemet Ali alone would be held responsible for what happened if the evacuation did not take place. A strict blockade of Alexandria was threatened.[60]

Russia's attack on Turkey complicated factors for French policy. Polignac, then ambassador to London, was instructed to redouble his efforts to win over the British cabinet to support a joint expedition to the Morea. The idea was not liked at London, especially since Wellington did not agree with the Russian policy which advocated the employment of force against Turkey.[61]

The British refusal to coöperate in a joint expedition was notified by Polignac at the end of May. Two reasons were assigned: the fear of a hostile reaction in Parliament if the British government were charged with making war on Turkey—an action deemed indispensable to the equilibrium of Europe—and the reported statement of Capodistrias to the British naval commander that the appearance of foreign soldiers in Greece would cause his fall from power. France meanwhile declined Dudley's overture for an isolated Anglo-French entente excluding Russia. La Ferronays asked Guilleminot to check up, to see whether Capodistrias actually looked with disfavor on the project of an expedition.[62]

Aberdeen succeeding Dudley as British foreign secretary in June, a somewhat different course was followed with respect to Russia. Wellington had not participated in any conferences on Greece from March to June, because the new status of Russia in reference to England had not yet been clarified: allied with England and acting as neutral in the Turco-Greek war, Russia had ceased to be neutral since her war with Turkey began. The problem was given an unusual settlement on June 15 when by protocol Russia agreed to relinquish her belligerent character in the Mediterranean, there

acting as a neutral along with England and France and continuing
her hostility toward Turkey at all other points. Aberdeen agreed to
continue the relations under the Treaty of London on this new
basis. At the same time Aberdeen sent Heytesbury as ambassador
to St. Petersburg. La Ferronays at once perceived that the solution
was a fiction and that the problem of the ultimate independence of
Greece was to be left in doubt, on the assumption that Russia would
be asked to sign a treaty with Turkey as soon as her own differences
over Ackerman were smoothed over. Polignac was instructed again
to insist upon the common action of the three allies in the Near East
and to consider the measures which might be necessary to force
Ibrahim to leave Greece.[63] Almost at the same time Drovetti reported that Mehemet Ali had finally agreed to evacuate the Morea
and to free the Greek slaves when so ordered by the sultan.[64]

The inquiry whether Capodistrias wanted foreign support was
answered on June 24, when Capodistrias not only requested munitions and the continued financial support of France but added that
"the arrival of some allied troops was an imperious urgency."[65]
Capodistrias was probably favorable to the French plan of an expedition because he recognized that naval action alone, despite Navarino, would be inadequate to force the retreat of Ibrahim.[66] For
that matter, Ibrahim might have gone north by land (into Bulgaria), creating other problems. La Ferronays requested opinions
from both Guilleminot and Rigny on the number of troops to send
to the Morea, the best place for their debarkation, the means of
their provisioning, and other useful information. Guilleminot replied that, for complete success, not only must Ibrahim evacuate
his army of from ten to fourteen thousand but that the Turkish
forces still in Greece, numbering about six thousand, should also
leave.[67]

After the receipt of the request from Capodistrias, French preparations for the expedition were speeded, although its departure
was delayed to await British approval. Polignac, now instructed to
propose again a joint expedition or, if England would not join, to
let the French make the expedition alone, found Aberdeen and
Wellington at first fearful that such a move would injure the
principle of neutrality under which they proceeded or would lead to
real war with Turkey. The strong support given Polignac, however,
by the ambassadors of Russia and Austria won the British over to

the French proposal. The protocol, of July 19, authorized the armed intervention of France and defined the objects of the expedition, Russia and England accepting the principle of the expedition providing that France retired her forces as soon as the Egyptian army was out of Greece (unless Ibrahim went north into Rumelia, in which event France might station a corps on the isthmus of Corinth to prevent his return). A joint note informed Turkey of the move.[68]

The French government immediately (on July 20) ordered measures to carry out the now-approved expedition to the Morea. Lieutenant-General Maison was given the command of the expedition, which would consist of at least 12,000 men, and perhaps of 500 or 1,000 more, and would depart on August 15.[69] At the same time the decision of Mehemet Ali to evacuate the Morea was received in Paris.[70] In the notification to Drovetti (sent on July 22) it was explained that England had offered the use of warships as transports, if needed,[71] but that England would not participate in the expedition. The French object was stated to be the establishment of a blockade by land to complement the naval blockade against Egypt which the three Powers already had in effect. A few days later, in another dispatch to Drovetti, La Ferronays stated that France was going ahead with the expedition, despite the disposition of Mehemet Ali to recall Ibrahim. The expedition would serve "to chase the Turks out of the places they would hold in Greece after the departure of the Arabs."[72]

Meanwhile, Admiral Codrington had appeared before Alexandria with seven large warships.[73] In addition to restricting further campaigns against Greece, this blockade had the practical effect of preventing the possible sea transport of troops to aid Turkey against Russia; it also gave physical backing to the allied demand for the evacuation of the Morea by Egypt. On August 9 Codrington and Mehemet Ali concluded a convention whereby the Egyptian army would evacuate Greece, the Greek slaves[74] would be freed, and English and French ships would escort and convoy the Egyptian troops back to Alexandria.[75]

The convention with Egypt caused England to raise the question of the necessity for the French expedition, although Wellington, in reporting the expedition, made it clear to Turkey that England did not intend to separate from her allies.[76] The supplementary instructions for General Maison authorized the commander to act in a hostile manner only after having exhausted every resource for the voluntary evacuation of the Morea or after new recommendations had been sent to him by Guilleminot. "The object of the expedition," stated Rayneval, "is the reëstablishment of peace in Europe." The evacuation by Egypt should induce the sultan to accept the Treaty of London.[77]

The French expedition reached Peraldi on August 28, 1828. Evacuation by the forces of Egypt having begun already,[78] the principal tasks of the French soldiers were to keep order and to build roads, pending the final disposition of the Morea by the allied Powers.[79] The instructions of the French foreign office to Consul Rouen (in Greece) on May 21, 1829, indicate that France was quite willing to capitalize on the expedition. The government held that the Turkish capitulations might be duplicated in the new commercial relations between Greece and France. In any event France desired a continuance of the advantages possessed by French subjects while the Greek territory was under Turkish administration; especially so after "having so powerfully contributed to [Greek] emancipation." On the other hand, France did not want to deprive Greece of its opportunity of raising revenues by customs. Such a "benevolent and generous attitude" should not be abused by the Greek government. Instead of 3-per cent duty, France was willing to agree to 10-per cent, or not more than 12-per cent, and, in contrast to actual practice in reference to Turkey, Greece might have the additional advantage of an accurate tariff.[80]

8. BLOCKADES

There were four sets of problems resulting from blockades in the Levant at the beginning of 1829. These were: (1) the raising of the allied blockade of Crete against Egypt; (2) the blockade of Alexandria by England; (3) the Russian blockade of Turkey and its contraction to a blockade of Constantinople; and (4) the Greek blockades, one by the allies against Turkey and another, larger in scope, proclaimed by the Greek government against Turkey.

England and France simultaneously (on October 15, 1828) ordered the raising of their blockades of Crete, their original objective being no longer present. However, acting on contrary orders from Stratford Canning (who was, like Guilleminot, awaiting his opportunity to return to Constantinople), Malcolm at first refused to execute the order. The British foreign office was notified of this refusal on November 17. On December 20 Aberdeen opposed the ambassador and issued special instructions that the blockade be raised without further delay.[81] The result of the conflicting orders respecting the Cretan blockade was Aberdeen's acceptance of Canning's resignation without the ambassador's having formally tendered it. Before the dismissal the foreign secretary gave the ambassador a severe reprimand (on January 30, 1829). In this, Aberdeen presented his opinion that Canning's ideas about Greece were mostly wrong and charged that Canning had shown himself opposed to the Treaty of London and had refused to work harmoniously with Ribeaupierre, the Russian minister. Aberdeen and Canning debated the question of the Cretan orders for several weeks. On April 9 the foreign secretary named his own brother, Robert Gordon, as Canning's successor.[82]

The implications of the blockade of Crete were shown in the instructions by Portalis, new French foreign minister,[83] for the new French consul general to Egypt, Jean-François Mimaut.[84] It appears that Mehemet Ali had been worried about the attitude of the Porte following his retreat from the Morea; he was also perhaps disturbed that the convention for evacuation had been arrived at only after the pasha had agreed to provide an equal number of troops for Turkish use against Russia. Mehemet Ali felt disposed to send 15,000 troops to Constantinople by land route, but in the hope that they would arrive too late to be of service to the sultan. After the raising of the blockade of Crete, Heyden, the Russian naval commander in the Mediterranean, feared that the island would be the point from which troops would be sent to aid the Porte. Hence he stopped some ships there. France and England requested explanations. Heyden stated that he had acted on false information and that he did not intend a new blockade of Crete. Because the consul of Russia had left Egypt, Mimaut was directed to act as the intermediary between Heyden and Mehemet Ali.[85]

Mehemet Ali reacted quite favorably for French policy, as shown by the first conferences held with Mimaut. On July 7, 1829, he formally promised Mimaut that he would conform his foreign policy to the views of France. The pasha was especially pleased that France and England had kept the communications open between Egypt and Crete, in contrast to the attitude of Russia. On

August 17 Mehemet Ali countermanded the orders to send an expedition to relieve the Turks.[86]

Many documents for this period concern the Turkish handicaps to trade, upon which a great part of the responsibility for the Russo-Turkish war was based. In point of fact, the handicaps were not shared to any great extent by neutrals, there being, for example, only one fixed Turkish charge for a French boat seeking to pass into the Black Sea—the fee for the necessary firman. In addition, however, several donations had to be made to various Turkish agents before the ship was actually cleared for passage; but these were rather definitely prescribed, the total amounting to only about $10 a vessel. All the foreign Powers felt a sort of grievance against Turkey because of the principle involved, for she still seemed to regard it as a privilege for ships to be permitted to go into the Black Sea. By the time of the Treaty of Adrianople all the Powers accredited to Turkey shared the privilege, but not all on the same conditions. Strictly speaking, Russian and Austrian vessels in peacetimes were permitted to go into the Black Sea even when they carried Ottoman produce. Sardinians had the right to enter the Euxine, but the Porte reserved the right to preëmpt the produce they carried. Although this apparently was never applied against Sardinia, it theoretically might be. In short, there were various usages and classifications for foreign vessels;[87] hence Louis Castagne could well report at the end of 1828 that neutrals suffered little because of the Russo-Turkish war and that Austrian commerce was especially active. While Turkey levied extraordinary duties on goods admittedly en route to Russia, Russia prohibited the shipment of grains from her southern provinces if destined for Turkey.[88]

Now neutral shipping was given a real handicap—the Russian blockade of the Dardanelles and the Gulf of Saros, directed against the European supply by sea of staple foods and munitions of war destined for Constantinople. The French conformed, notification having been made on October 6, 1828.[89] England did not admit the validity of the measure until after Russia exempted all neutral shipping. Aberdeen had threatened to break off relations with Russia under the Treaty of London in order to secure the desired exception, basing his conclusion on the agreement by which Russia acted as a neutral in the Mediterranean.[90]

Turkey effectively evaded the blockade through overland transports of war supplies from Enos, Contessa, and Adamitti. Hence, in the spring of 1829, Ricord, commanding the Russian war fleet in the Aegean, was ordered to extend the blockade westward to include these gulfs. Turkey now at once began to seize camels and other beasts of burden, the only remaining means of commercial communication with the interior, to convey supplies by land from Smyrna, and to exclude Turkish produce from the shipping ports.[91] The extension of the blockade was opposed vigorously by the new British ambassador to Turkey, because, he said, "the injury inflicted upon the Turks by no means is commensurate with that sustained by Russia's allies." The effects were felt severely by British traders in the Levant during the three months of its operation. General stagnation resulted at Smyrna. The Turks having seized the means of transport with the interior to facilitate their transport of war materials, the interchange of produce stopped. Gordon was of the opinion that Christian lives and property would be sacrificed before Turkey would suffer in consequence of the blockade, so it was reasoned that Russia would have defeated her own purpose in that respect.[92] Following the raising of the extended blockade, Aberdeen instructed the British consul at Smyrna to conform to the blockade of the Dardanelles, that is, not to issue clearance papers for British ships without a declaration from their masters that war materials were not being transported to Constantinople.[93]

Aberdeen feared that Russia would extend the blockade to Salonica and Smyrna. Lieven assured him that the tsar had not intended to include Contessa and that the blockade there would be raised.[94] Aberdeen desired a disavowal written into the protocols at London but accepted instead an official note from Lieven in June announcing the raising of the blockade of the regions beyond the Dardanelles and Gulf of Saros.[95]

At about the same time the Greek government, already enforcing with European consent a blockade of the Morea and Cyclades, published a blockade of the coasts of Attica, the Negropont, and the Gulf of Volo, and extended it to the western coasts of Greece and to the island of Crete. Gordon at once announced that the British fleet would prevent the slightest interference with the free commerce of British subjects. The blockade of Crete was regarded as totally illegal, since the allies were not to permit Crete to be incorporated with Greece.[96] This attitude was approved by Aberdeen, who said it was the duty of the British government "to protect the lawful commerce" of British subjects. Portalis censured Aberdeen for opposing the Greek blockade, but Aberdeen held to his policy.[97]

9. RETURN OF THE AMBASSADORS

In the early months of 1829, Russia seemed to desire a closer connection with Great Britain, rather than with Austria.[98] There were indications that a powerful opposition party in France was resisting the pro-British policy of King Charles X and his government.[99] The three allies continued to work together harmoniously in reference to Greece.

It had for a long while been apparent that a part of the weakness of the system of the allies was their inadequate representation at Constantinople, where the negotiations on Greece must eventually center. Russia, England, and France had agreed by the spring of 1829 on the more important questions respecting Greece. To win Turkey's acceptance was now the principal order of business. In April the allied nations evidenced a new solidarity when the French and British ambassadors were ordered to return to their posts at Constantinople. Russia, still at war with Turkey, was to be represented by the Austrian internuncio. Both western ambassadors were directed to negotiate a solution of the Greek question if possible;[100] but they were not to treat any problems arising from the Russo-Turkish war. The desired territorial limits for Greece included the Morea, Attica, and the adjacent islands.[101]

Guilleminot did not arrive in the Turkish capital until June 26. Gordon traveled to Besika Bay on the "Revenge," a British ship of the line; although it was deemed inexpedient to send that war vessel through the Straits, the remainder of the journey to Constantinople, where he arrived on June 20, was inexplicably made on the "Blonde," a frigate of forty-six guns, commanded by Captain Edmund Lyons. This vessel, accompanied by a war sloop, was ordered by Gordon to remain in Constantinople, being in the Bosporus continually until long after peace was concluded.[102] The strength of the allied squadrons near the theater of war at that time may be noted. The British squadron, stationed outside the Dardanelles, to assure "a ready and certain communication with the ambassador," numbered thirteen war vessels. The French fleet, temporarily under Rosamel, was composed of three warships and six smaller vessels, while the Russian unit, under Ricord, was made up of three ships of the line and one frigate.[103] Events will show that these British and French squadrons might possibly have played a decisive new role in the history of Turkey if Russia had occupied Constantinople in September, 1829.

Back at Constantinople, Guilleminot spent the month of July, 1829, negotiating on Greece, reporting no apparent alarm about the Russian military advances until the middle of the month. On July 27 Guilleminot tried to convince the Turks that it was time to make peace with Russia, but the next day he was informed that Turkey would not submit to the terms of Ackerman and London. This ended the hopes for peace at the moment. Two days later, Erzurum fell to Russia.[104]

10. RUSSIA ADVANCES

The Russo-Turkish War had entered a new phase in 1829 with the vigorous advances by General Diebitsch. The fall of Silistria in midsummer broke the military resistance of Turkey. Further defeats, suffered on all fronts, depressed the Turkish morale, especially at Constantinople. Gordon, on July 26, reported:

> The lower classes are beginning to murmur against the war. The Russian fleet constantly appears off the mouth of the Bosporus, within sight of the Sultan's palace [ten miles from Constantinople]; the Turkish fleet is not disposed to engage the superior Russian fleet in the Black Sea.

Within two weeks an "alarming apathy, pervading all classes," presented a danger to the continued existence of the Turkish government. The conduct of some Asiatic troops stationed in Adrianople infuriated the inhabitants, who "absolutely looked to the arrival of the Russians as a deliverance from evil." Turkey seemed "actually threatened with complete dissolution by the continual successes of the enemy." Guilleminot and Gordon joined in urging Turkey to accept the proffered moderation of Russia.[105] Still official Turkey continued its stubborn temper of resistance and made plans for a final desperate attempt to stem the tide of invasion.

Thus we have seen how and why the closing years of the Greek War had called for international interventions. Egypt aided Turkey in an attempt to subjugate the Greeks, while the Greeks found powerful support from three of the Great Powers of Europe. Although England, France, and Russia in 1827 collectively terminated the Egyptian interference, only Russia became involved in a war with Turkey. This occurred the following year. The Russian war was in part accounted for by the fact that Russian commerce, more than that of any other Power, was handicapped by the arbitrary restrictions placed by Turkey. Throughout the four years, 1825–1829, Austria refused to coöperate in the timely interventions which saved the Greek cause. The eastern policy of Great Britain was more directly applied after the dissolution of the Levant Company in 1825. Great Britain at first refrained from entering a European concert on the Greek question. France set the stage for her political penetration into Egypt. But British policy soon favored the negotiation of two important agreements which presaged the independent Greek state. The result was the Anglo-Russian agreement of 1826, which precluded any isolated political and commercial advantages by either Power, and the tripartite Treaty of London in 1827. In the second, France joined Great Britain and Russia. France participated in two major physical actions in favor of Greece, the naval battle of Navarino and the expedition to the Morea. Her policy throughout was evolved slowly. It represented a significant advance in the growth of a direct French governmental interest in all the affairs of the Levant. Its orientation toward Egypt had in part been brought about by commerce.

NOTES TO SECTION II

[1] Inefficiency was chiefly attributed, however, to the vice-consuls and consular agents, mostly foreigners, who served without regular salaries and all of whom engaged in trade.

[2] The fees of the Levant Company, for its expenses and profits, were authorized by various acts of Parliament. They amounted to from 1 to 2 per cent ad valorem. The annual expenses of the company amounted to about $75,000 by 1824, in addition to the fees applied as salaries by the consular agents. Active consuls, all under the company's direction, were stationed in the principal places of the Ottoman Empire, including Constantinople, Adrianople, the Dardanelles, Salonica, the Morea, Smyrna, Aleppo, Acre, Alexandria, and Cyprus, while vice-consuls served without regular salaries in many of the more remote parts of the empire.

[3] Cf. Liddell to Planta, October 10, 1822, FO 78 T 112.

[4] Planta to G. D. Clark, February 20, 1823, FO 78 T 119.

[5] Since the British mercantile establishments were scattered throughout Smyrna, this was really a proposal that the British police the entire city.

[6] Croker to Conyngham, February 10, 1823, FO 78 T 119. At that time the British government had no well-defined policy on the extent to which it would accord protection to the foreign commercial stations of its subjects, although British subjects domiciled abroad seemed to consider themselves as entitled to the protection of British warships against local risks and dangers.

[7] Conyngham to Liddell, August 15, 1823, *ibid.*

[8] Vice-Admiral Moore to Croker, September 15, 1823, *ibid.*

[9] T. Schiemann, *Geschichte Russlands unter Kaiser Nikolaus I* (Berlin, 1904–1911), I, 347.

[10] FO 78 T 191. This type of solution became European international law as a result of the decisions of the Congress of Paris in 1856.

[11] Canning to Grenville, January 29, 1825, FO 78 T 136.

[12] Hertslet, *Commercial Treaties*, IV, 484. A sketch of the history of the company appears in the foreign office archives, written by George Liddell, its last secretary (FO 78 T 136).

[13] Canning to Liverpool, November 5, 1824, in E. J. Stapleton, *Official Correspondence of George Canning* (London, 1887), I, 188.

[14] FO 65 R 144. Two secret ciphers were provided for the protection of his correspondence with London.

[15] Metternich to Ottenfels (in Constantinople), January 29, 1825, in Metternich, *Mémoires* (Paris, 1880), Doc. No. 777.

[16] FO 65 R 147. See S. Lane-Poole, *Life of Canning* (London, 1888), I, 164–172, for the indecisive discussions in March, 1825.

[17] This important reference was omitted by Lane-Poole, probably accounting for his careless repudiation of the notion that the mission of 1825 had anything to do with the dislike of later years (*Life of Canning*, II, 18). Lane-Poole's mistaken interpretation, repeated in almost the same words by E. F. Malcolm-Smith (*Life of Canning*, p. 93), argues that the dislike could not have been formed by the grand duke who became Tsar Nicholas I, Canning not having been presented to him. The reference given above shows the effect of the mission for what it probably was, Canning's winning of the dislike of the key figure, Nesselrode. As Canning himself put it, in retrospect, when recounting his complete failure regarding the Turco-Greek problem: "Count Nesselrode betrayed some little impatience at my continued silence about the mediation" (Canning, *The Eastern Question* [London, 1881], p. 166).

In 1832 Nicholas and Nesselrode refused to accept Canning as British ambassador to St. Petersburg after he had been appointed by Palmerston. The dislike of Nicholas and Nesselrode for Canning was well known; so much so that in 1852 Aberdeen heartily congratulated Brunnow when Canning was not permitted to fulfill his ambition by appointment as foreign secretary in the

Derby cabinet, an appointment which Nicholas would have regarded as an insult (S. M. Goriainov, "Secret Agreement of 1844," *Russian Review*, I [1912], iii, 112).

[18] Cf. Boyer to minister of war, December 1, 1824, AE Alexandrie 22.

[19] G. Douin, *Une mission militaire française auprès de Mohamed Aly* (Cairo, 1923), pp. 1–5, 30–31, quoting MG Egypte, carton 1677.

[20] See FO 78 T 112.

[21] Douin, *Une mission militaire*, pp. 25, 75–78.

[22] G. Douin, in *Les premières frégates de Mohamed Aly, 1824–1827* (Cairo, 1926), p. 35, suggests that the words "commercial speculation" figure in the documents only to save the government's face, the whole deal being a government-sponsored transaction which favored Mehemet Ali.

[23] *Ibid.*, pp. 25–26, citing MM, BB¹, carton 64.

[24] AE Alexandrie 21.

[25] AE Alexandrie 22.

[26] Douin, *Une mission militaire*, p. 31.

[27] AE Alexandrie 22.

[28] Cf. FO 78 T 179.

[29] AE Alexandrie 22. On May 20, 1826, a petition was signed by the French merchants of Alexandria asking the government to grant one warship convoy a month to French commercial ships as protection against the Greeks. In June there was recorded an escort by two warships of some commercial vessels loaded with oil from Crete (AE La Canée 24).

[30] Douin, *Une mission militaire*, p. 92.

[31] *Ibid.*, p. 65.

[32] FO 78 T 183.

[33] Imports from Egypt in 1827 amounted to nine million francs (Julliany, *Essai sur le commerce de Marseille* [Marseille, 1842], II, p. 315).

[34] AE Constantinople 83. Imports from Constantinople in 1826 were less than three million francs.

[35] Douin, *Les premières frégates*, pp. 43–45. Here Douin publishes a letter of that tenor from the Marseille Chamber of Commerce to the minister of the interior.

[36] Douin, *Une mission militaire*, pp. 79–81, 87, 107.

[37] AE Alexandrie 22. The second corvette did not arrive until May, 1827.

[38] *Ibid.*

[39] G. Esquer, *La prise d'Alger*, p. 93, gives the dey's version of what happened. According to this version, Deval had told the dey that it would be of no use to expect any further reply from the French government. The dey had answered, "Oh well, then, if your government does not think that I deserve a response from it, leave my house!" In making a gesture with his arm, he had touched Deval with his hand.

[40] See the account of the Drovetti Plan (pp. 112–134), which traces the Egyptian background of the French conquest of Algeria.

[41] The important role played by France in helping to convert England to a policy of coercion is usually omitted in traditional accounts; see the new treatment in the excellent monograph, G. Douin, *Navarin* (Cairo, 1927), pp. 31–57.

[42] AE Constantinople 83.

[43] The affairs of the allies at the Turkish capital were turned over to the minister of Holland. Guilleminot spent several months thereafter visiting various ports in the Mediterranean and receiving and analyzing reports from the Near East.

[44] Turkey announced that firmans for commercial ships would be issued but that she would have first choice, at her established prices, of their produce in transit through the Straits (AE Turquie 250). Several British merchants who held stocks at Odessa lost heavily (FO 78 T 187, 191), while some British grain ships were seized by Turkey (FO 78 T 181).

[45] MM, BB⁴, carton 488.
[46] CCM, Lettres pour Paris (December 21, 1827).
[47] FO 78 T 187.
[48] MM, BB⁴, carton 502. Crete was under allied blockade, to prevent its being used for further aid to the Egyptian forces in Greece.
[49] AE Alexandrie 23.
[50] MG, D², carton 1.
[51] G. Douin, *Les premières frégates*, p. 63.
[52] AE Alexandrie 23.
[53] La Ferronays to Mimaut, February 28, 1829, *ibid.*
[54] Professor Schiemann (*op. cit.*, II, 439) publishes a memorandum by General Diebitsch in 1827 (without day and month) which outlines two proposed distributions of the territory of Turkey in Europe. The provisions are similar to those which Nicholas proposed to England in 1853, Constantinople and the Straits being left unassigned.
[55] Previously, and in accordance with the terms of the convention, the privilege of the navigation of the Black Sea had been accorded by Turkey to Spain, Naples, and Denmark.
[56] AE Turquie 250.
[57] AE Turquie 251, 254.
[58] FO 65 R 227.
[59] Communication of April 30, 1828, in A. Maggiolo, *Pozzo di Borgo* (Paris, 1890), p. 300.
[60] AE Alexandrie 23.
[61] AE Turquie 251.
[62] La Ferronays to Guilleminot, May 28, 1828, *ibid.*
[63] La Ferronays to Guilleminot, June 12, 1828, *ibid.*
[64] AE Alexandrie 23.
[65] E. A. Betant, ed., *Correspondance du comte Capodistrias* (Paris, 1836–1837).
[66] E. Jurien de La Gravière, *La station du Levant* (Paris, 1876), II, 266.
[67] AE Turquie 251.
[68] La Ferronays to Guilleminot, July 20, 1828, *ibid.*
[69] MG, D², carton 1.
[70] AE Turquie 251.
[71] The French marine declined this service (*ibid.*).
[72] AE Alexandrie 23.
[73] FO 78 T 184.
[74] The return of the slaves proved a troublesome problem. The affair was finally concluded with the aid of a French agent, M. de Gros.
[75] AE Alexandrie 23. Mehemet Ali, according to Drovetti on August 25, counted on the support of the allies against any recriminations of the sultan because of his signature of the convention.
[76] Report by Louis Castagne, August 21, 1828, AE Turquie 252.
[77] *Ibid.*
[78] Ibrahim returned to Alexandria on October 9, 1828, after an absence of three years.
[79] Modon was made the administrative headquarters during 1828–1829 (MG, D², carton 3).
[80] AE Athènes 4. See also below, pp. 99–100.
[81] FO 78 T 182. In accordance with the decision of the allied conference at London, in January, 1829, Crete was to be left to Turkey (FO 78 T 184).
[82] FO 78 T 178. The entire volume is devoted to the problem.
[83] In January, 1829, Portalis substituted for La Ferronays; on May 14 he became French foreign minister in his own right.
[84] Drovetti was forced to retire because of ill health but still played an important part in the pro-Egyptian policy of France later in the year. Mimaut arrived at Alexandria on June 26, 1829.

85 AE Alexandrie 23.
86 *Ibid.* To aid Cerisy Mehemet Ali asked for some twenty-one French masters and workers.
87 Note by Guilleminot (AE Constantinople 83).
88 AE Turquie 253.
89 CCM, dossier, Evénements politiques, 1828–1869.
90 FO 78 T 182, 186. Lesur of the French foreign office staff considered international law as opposing such an interpretation (AEMD Turquie 19).
91 Petition by the "Mediterranean and Levant Association," May 18, 1829, FO 78 T 186.
92 Gordon to Aberdeen, June 30, 1829, FO 78 T 180; AE Turquie 252.
93 Aberdeen to R. W. Brant, June 27, 1829, FO 78 T 185.
94 Aberdeen to Heytesbury, May 22, 1829, FO 65 R 178.
95 FO 78 T 187.
96 Gordon to Van Lennep, June 9, 1829, FO 78 T 180.
97 Aberdeen to Stuart de Rothesay, June 30, 1829, FO 27 F 389.
98 Heytesbury to Cowley (in Vienna), February 20, 1829, in Schiemann, *op. cit.*, II, 455.
99 Aberdeen to Stuart de Rothesay, February 20, 1829, FO 27 F 389. Prussia was acting as a strictly neutral power (FO 64 P 158).
100 AE Turquie 254.
101 Aberdeen to Gordon, April 9, 1829, FO 78 T 179.
102 S. M. Eardley-Wilmot, *Life of Edmund Lyons* (London, 1898), pp. 45–47; FO 78 T 187.
103 Malcolm to admiralty, June 16, 1829, FO 78 T 187.
104 AE Turquie 254.
105 FO 78 T 180.

III. FOCUS ON ADRIANOPLE

INTERNATIONAL RELATIONS AND THE PEACE OF ADRIANOPLE

PRECARIOUS INDEED was the position of the Ottoman Empire during the few weeks before the Russo-Turkish War was ended by the Peace of Adrianople (September 14, 1829). Dangers threatened within and without. Within, Greece was undoubtedly lost, the three allies holding their ground under the Treaty of London and the French expeditionary force in the Morea guaranteeing that Turkey could not return there; threats of anarchy at Constantinople were paralleled by reports of further potential revolts in the provinces. Serbia and the Principalities were sheltered by Russia; Bosnia and Bulgaria were ready to rise; Egypt sought French support to win Syria, while the Barbary regencies had further increased their autonomy. Externally, the war with Russia had entered the acute stage. Turkey had almost ceased to resist and, if she continued the war despite Russian military successes, must make additional territorial concessions and pay heavier indemnities; already the fighting was near her strategic heart. Other external dangers, projected without her knowledge, were a plan of partition approved by the French council and another probably under negotiation by Austria. Meanwhile, British officials despaired of her ability to survive.

Several factors, however, augured a measure of relief. Many statesmen in Europe, although admitting Turkey's weakness, were unwilling to see her disappear entirely from the map of Europe. Russia's proffered terms were moderate and had recently been confirmed. Peace might be signed on two principal minimum conditions: the freeing of Greece and the surrendering of the Turkish right to interfere with the foreign commerce that passed the Straits. Müffling and Küster of Prussia were on hand to serve as neutral negotiators, Müffling having just come from a conference with the tsar in Berlin. Gordon and Guilleminot, the French and British ambassadors, were not only sympathetic but were determined, if necessary, to do anything to prevent the actual fall of Constantinople; their fleets soon appeared before the Dardanelles. Another circumstance was the illness of large numbers of Russian troops, which, if it had been known in Constantinople, might have reduced the Turkish panic. Still another and more important favorable factor was the impending secret decision of Russia herself to uphold Turkey.

The outlines of the negotiations underlying the Russo-Turkish peace are well known, although much is lacking in detail and in the adequate interpretation of the policies and attitudes of the four most interested Great Powers. This part of our work will attempt, in recapitulating the conditions and negotiations, to add new and integrated documentary material. It will be readily observed that many of the factors discussed here either have not been sufficiently emphasized or have not been generally accepted by historians of the period.

1. POLIGNAC AT THE HELM

By August, 1829, the affairs of the Levant had produced many problems for France, including the maintenance of the French army in the Morea, the restiveness of Egypt, the continuance of piracy, and the new economic and political difficulties of Greece. Algeria, still under French blockade, might have been the best point of departure at the moment for fulfilling the known desire of French statesmen to expand the then small French empire. But the imminence of disaster to Turkey overshadowed all other matters.

France and Great Britain disagreed in interpreting Russia's intentions toward Turkey. The British cabinet seemed greatly alarmed by the Russian military advances, whereas the French, disturbed by a cabinet crisis, appeared "content to let the British allay their own fears."[1] The ministerial change called Polignac, the French ambassador to England, to head the ministry and to take personal charge of foreign affairs on August 9. Aberdeen hopefully expected Polignac's advance to effect a closer entente between Great Britain and France; instead, as events proved, it meant a greater divergence between the policies of the two Powers.

The last days of August were anxious ones for Aberdeen, who shared Gordon's belief that the Ottoman Empire might disintegrate. As soon as the new French cabinet was functioning smoothly, he pointedly inquired what attitude France would take if Russia destroyed the Ottoman Empire at a single blow by capturing Constantinople. To him reëstablishment of the Ottoman power, if once

[1] For notes to section iii, see pp. 108–111.

destroyed, appeared impracticable. There was therefore no time for delay before shaping new policies.[2] Ostensibly preoccupied with other problems but really formulating a pro-Russian policy, Polignac evasively replied that he had lacked time to study the matter carefully; but he did give England some indications. Satisfied with Russia's promises of moderation, he was willing to leave all necessary decisions to the ambassadors at Constantinople and favored a concert of the three allies (that is, including Russia) in all such important questions.[3]

As a matter of fact the military successes of Diebitsch, then about to occupy Adrianople, clearly had placed the whole matter beyond the reach of the cabinets at London and Paris. Even expedited service at that time required six weeks for an exchange of dispatches with Constantinople. Influenced, doubtless, by the British suggestion of the possible necessity of finding successors for Turkey, as well as by the new status of the Russo-Turkish War, Polignac sought a comprehensive Near Eastern policy for France.

2. Turkey Faces Collapse

Turkey's first genuine admission of her defeat occurred on August 15, when she finally agreed to recognize the independence of Greece. Presenting a tentative memorandum of conditions, she agreed to negotiate a treaty with Russia. Acting on the advice of Müffling, Gordon, and Guilleminot, she offered to enforce all existing Russo-Turkish engagements, especially that of Ackerman; to guarantee "in a most solemn manner" the unrestricted commercial navigation of the Black Sea; to liberate the Greeks on the basis of the Treaty of London; and to regulate other matters by common accord. She neither mentioned the indemnity nor agreed to cede any territory, either in Europe or in Asia.[4] The memorandum, which really sought the bases on which the Russian commander would end the war, did not disclose the maximum of the concessions Turkey was willing to make.[5] It simply gave the Ottoman interpretation of the well-publicized concessions demanded by Russia. It was forwarded by Müffling to Diebitsch on August 17, along with expressions of hope from Gordon and Guilleminot that the commander would make peace with Turkey.[6] The plan of the ambassadors was to attempt through offers and counteroffers to start negotiations before the Russian army came too close to Constantinople, for they evidently expected Diebitsch to reject this Turkish plan to avoid territorial and financial indemnities.

In his reply to the Turkish memorandum, issued three days after his occupation of Adrianople on August 20, Diebitsch stressed the obstinacy shown by Turkey when he himself had attempted negotiations in April and June and emphasized the present favorable position of the Russian armies. Although he controlled the Balkans to Adrianople, although Paskevich was in Erzurum, and although Turkish obstinacy deserved further punishment, he was willing, he said, to negotiate at his headquarters with properly authorized Turkish plenipotentiaries. The tsar, he said, wanted a "strong and solid" peace, with a guarantee of its duration. This reply, received late on August 24, was more than welcome since the fall of Adrianople had increased the consternation and foreboding at the Turkish capital. That evening the Turkish foreign minister held an important conference with Gordon, Guilleminot, and Küster.[7] The Reis Effendi announced that Turkey was willing to send negotiators and solicited the advice of these agents. Gordon and Guilleminot counseled Turkey to throw herself on the moderation and equity of the tsar rather than to advance any further specific bases for the negotiation.[8] When Turkey adopted this recommendation, Gordon and Guilleminot announced, in a joint letter to Diebitsch, that Turkey "subscribed in advance to the terms" he would dictate. They were convinced, they added, that, in view of Turkey's willingness to demand peace, Tsar Nicholas would not wish to continue the military operations. Such a continuance, they said, would immediately expose "to the fury of the revengeful populace the Christian peoples whose only hope and guarantee of safety, not being able to count on the protection of the Turkish government, was in the prompt cessation of hostilities."[9]

Gordon, without awaiting the result, at once wrote Admiral Malcolm of the British squadron concerning the nearness of the Russian armies and the collapse of Turkish resistance. "The capital," he stated, "is menaced, and the lives and property of foreigners might be in danger." Malcolm, receiving the letter on August 26, immediately ordered part of his squadron to the Dardanelles to give possible assistance to foreigners. As he wrote Rosamel on the same day, he considered it his duty to give assistance to Frenchmen; but he hoped such help would not be required, since negotiations had begun already. Malcolm considered that the Russians, if they accepted an armistice, might be trusted to sign a treaty of peace. All this was surprising news to Rosamel, who sent, however, one frigate, the "Atlante," and a brig toward the Dardanelles, besides writing Guilleminot that others would join the British and Russian squadrons if summoned by information from Constantinople.[10] The instructions of the French ministry of marine on August 28 directing Vice-Admiral Rigny to resume command of the Levant squadron, specifically stated that French policy with respect to the fleet had not changed.[11] Rosamel's intention, not yet known at Paris, was to follow the British if they actually passed the Dardanelles.[12]

The potential seriousness of a Turkish collapse was revealed by Gordon's letter to Aberdeen on August 26:

Nothing but an immediate cessation of hostilities can possibly save this empire from total destruction. The internal disorder is even more alarming than that from which it is threatened from without; disaffection and insubordination have reached the highest pitch.

So disheartened were the Turks, Gordon thought, that the sudden appearance of 10,000 Russians upon the heights above Constantinople would suffice for the capitulation of the capital; "in ten days more the Russians might be masters of both sides of the Dardanelles, from Tenedos to the Black Sea."[13]

3. SPECULATION AND POLICIES

After the departure of the Ottoman negotiators, accompanied by Küster, there was much speculation on possibilities. Müffling thought that the best way to assure the freedom of the commerce of the Black Sea, Russia's *sine qua non* for peace, would be to make Turkey responsible not only to Russia, but to England, France, and Austria as well. Gordon was sympathetic to such a plan because subsequent guarantees would then not be exclusively Russian.[14] Guilleminot agreed that the matter was of general interest, especially since the Great Powers enjoyed most-favored-nation status in their commercial relations with Turkey; French vessels under the Turkish rules might not, for example, ship timber for naval construction from southern Russia to France.[15] The territorial limits for Greece not having yet been fixed, although Turkey had accepted the principle of an independent Greece, Gordon advised

Aberdeen against forcing Turkey in that matter "at a time when an enemy whose power cannot be resisted is at the very gates of Constantinople."[16] Müffling proposed that the Porte send an ambassador to St. Petersburg to seek less onerous terms than would be likely in dealing with Diebitsch. Although Diebitsch might sign an armistice, would he sign a treaty of peace without special instructions from the Russian capital? On August 29 Gordon suggested that Guilleminot and himself protest to Russia if Diebitsch, after the Porte's acceptance of the bases of peace announced by the tsar, continued his march on Constantinople. In that event, he told Müffling, the British fleet might come to Constantinople. Guilleminot added that, if the British fleet came, he would call the French fleet also, "but with the single object of assuring a way out for all Europeans in the event of a popular rising in Constantinople." Gordon, also preoccupied with the idea that the Russians would occupy Ottoman territory for a long time, thought that Diebitsch should evacuate immediately after signing the armistice; but, according to Guilleminot and Müffling, evacuation would be proper only after the signing of the treaty. Constantinople was now quiet, many considering that peace had come already.[17]

At Paris, meanwhile, Polignac wrote his first detailed instruction to Guilleminot (September 6). The French ambassador at the Porte, whose reports down to August 10 had been received, had been without special orders since the cabinet change in France. The instructions reflected, without disclosing, the new secret proposal for a partition of Turkey which Polignac was now submitting to Russia, as will be shown below. Guilleminot must make all subsequent communications at Constantinople in a reserved manner and must exemplify the friendship that united France and Russia. The communications must not indicate any desire of France to act as mediator or to have a peace concluded in accordance with all her own views. Polignac then gave special directions respecting the problem of Greece, now nearing solution.[18] At the same time the ambassador was urged to adopt a policy of closer connections with Egypt, including special concessions for Egyptian commerce in French ports.[19]

A more pointed statement of French policy for the pressing Levantine problems of the moment was made by Polignac on September 10 in answering the questions of Rigny, newly ordered to resume command of the Levant squadron. The admiral must not permit Capodistrias to pass the territorial limits fixed at London on March 22, even if the Russian successes excited further Greek insurrections. As to sending the squadron through the Dardanelles, with or without the consent of Turkey but in the wake of England, Rigny was directed to confer with Guilleminot and "to follow his directions." If the Turkish troops were withdrawn from Athens, no part of the French force in the Morea was to be sent to occupy the Greek capital.[20]

At London, prompted by a report that Russia might help to detach the Ionian Islands and include them in the new Greek state, Aberdeen made it clear that Great Britain did not intend to give up her Ionian protectorate.[21] He also answered the repeated complaints of British subjects engaged in trade on the Black Sea. Although he excused the original detention of their vessels and cargoes at Constantinople as politically justifiable, he admitted that the Turkish method of evaluating the cargoes was open to criticism. In his opinion, the only way of preventing subsequent abuses of that kind would be to grant a firman for every commercial ship passing the Straits; then the owner could decide whether to utilize the Turkish market or not.[22] This was essentially an adoption of the Russian policy on commerce.

It was reported in London that Tsar Nicholas had twice expressed his dissatisfaction with Great Britain, and particularly with the Duke of Wellington, charging that England did not wish to coöperate with him. On September 4, to prove the contrary, Aberdeen assembled the diplomats at the Foreign Office, where, in the presence of Lieven, Wellington made a long statement indicating a desire to act with Russia.[23] As a matter of fact, he agreed with Russia on the question of Greek independence but opposed her in the dangers that beset Turkey elsewhere. This we know from his published letter to Aberdeen on September 11. Although admitting that the tsar was at least precluded from a separate negotiation on the Greek phase, Wellington thought that Diebitsch should stop his advance if the tsar really desired peace with Turkey; otherwise, Constantinople lay at the mercy of Russia. In his opinion, even if Prussia and France agreed with Russia on the terms of peace, the tsar's armies would settle the whole matter without their interference. Safety would be found, however, if Diebitsch halted to negotiate. In the event that Russia occupied Constantinople and caused the downfall of Turkey, the best basis for a reconstruction of Europe would be found, he thought, in the coöperation of England and France "if the French government has a will of its own."

My opinion [he added] is that the Power which has Constantinople and the Straits ought to possess the mouth of the Danube and that the sovereign of these two ought not to have the Crimea and the Russian Empire. We must reconstruct a Greek empire, and give it to Prince Frederick of Orange, or Prince Charles of Prussia; and no sovereign of Europe ought to take anything for himself except the Tsar a sum for his expenses.[24]

At Berlin the French minister, Hector d'Agoult, repeatedly declared in diplomatic quarters that the Powers must now arrange for the succession to the Turkish provinces in order to prevent controversies in the otherwise inevitable scramble for the spoils. Internal weakness, independent of external aggression, would, he thought, soon destroy the Ottoman Empire.[25] At Vienna there was frank pessimism about the efficacy of negotiations. Metternich seemed convinced that the Russian armies would decide the two pressing phases of the Near Eastern question simultaneously, and that the negotiations at Constantinople were thus of little value.[26]

4. THE POLIGNAC PLAN

The reflections at Constantinople, London, Berlin, and Vienna, foretelling the dissolution of the Ottoman Empire as a possible result of the Russian conquest of Constantinople or of internal revolution in Turkey were, however, academic in character. Polignac, insistent that France take account of her interests in the problem, now planned concrete action. Already French policy had been oriented to favor Russia rather than England, and upon this basis he now developed a partition scheme for the Ottoman Empire which proved to be the most pretentious official nineteenth-century French plan for solving the Near Eastern question. To take full advantage of Turkey's reverses in the Russo-Turkish War, Polignac not only would have partitioned Turkey but would have remade much of the map of Europe as well. Having seen what Napoleon had done to the small states of Europe, the French cabinet of 1829 might have considered the remaking of Europe a fairly simple operation; but the indispensable requirement, as Napoleon had admitted in 1808, would be the coöperation of Russia. Anyway, if

Turkey were completely crushed by Russia, the terms of peace would probably become a general European matter, while internal conditions, independent of the wishes of Nicholas, might lead to the downfall of Turkey.

After considering these factors, Polignac expressed to King Charles X the positive conviction that the fall of Turkey might well be combined with a general reorganization of Europe. This idea being accepted by the king, a deliberation in council was ordered on the details which Polignac might submit. Accordingly, and apparently in haste, Polignac and his assistant in charge of political affairs, Baron Boislecomte, drew up a memorandum embodying many features of the French and Russian discussions of 1808. The memorandum was read to the council, debated, and approved as the tentative basis for negotiations to be opened with Russia if the Russo-Turkish War did not end too soon.

In outline, the Polignac memorandum proposed the following changes: Holland would be entirely eliminated but the king of Holland would reign at Constantinople as a Christian monarch, having territories composed of Turkey in Europe except those detached for Russia and Austria. France would acquire the Belgian provinces to the Meuse and Rhine rivers and would recover from Prussia the Alsatian frontier she lost with the fall of Napoleon. Prussia might also surrender her other Rhineland provinces; the king of Saxony might be transferred to rule the provinces between the Rhine and the Meuse, while those to the east might be given to Bavaria.[27] Prussia would be compensated by the acquisition of all Saxony and of Holland from the North Sea to the Rhine. At least part of the Dutch colonial islands would be assigned to Great Britain. Russia would acquire Moldavia and Wallachia, with as much Turkish territory in Asia as would be deemed expedient. To balance the Balkan acquisitions of Russia, Austria would receive Serbia and Bosnia. It is significant that Polignac, like Napoleon in 1808, was unwilling to assign Constantinople and the Straits to Russia. He did, however, guarantee the unrestricted navigation of the Straits upon payment of moderate duties to be regulated by common agreement. The Turks would be compressed into Anatolia, while Greece would be given the Asiatic banks of the Dardanelles and the Bosporus.[28]

After approval of the plan, Polignac on September 4 dispatched a lengthy secret instruction to the Duke of Mortemart, French ambassador at St. Petersburg, which directed the opening of negotiations with Russia on the partition project, provided Mortemart found peace still unsigned and conditions favorable. "In that case," Polignac instructed, "you will make no use of all that I have written today, and regard it as null and void." The king of France had full confidence that the tsar would show moderation to Turkey, continued the instruction; but the internal dissolution of Turkey, over which the tsar had no control, might prevent the execution of the promise. If the Turkish Empire in Europe were destroyed, no one expected its restoration. In that event, what could be done? Polignac did not think that the Balkan peoples, left to themselves, would form stable governments. Nor could the Turks, having only one-fourth the numbers of their non-Turkish subjects, reëstablish their own empire. There remained two alternatives. The first was the possible Russian determination of the succession by right of conquest. "That," said Polignac, making use of the Russian thesis phrased by Kochubei in 1802, "clearly is inadmissible; Russia cannot appropriate Constantinople for herself without a war against almost all the other Powers of Europe; and such an acquisition, located so far from the center of her power, would disquiet her other provinces without really adding to her strength." The other alternative was for all Europe to assist in forming a new Christian state, with Constantinople as its center. If Russia thought of addressing any Powers on such a subject, Polignac suggested that France would prove most amenable to the confidence of the tsar, especially since her interests and those of Russia appeared, in this question, to be identical. Mortemart was directed to proceed slowly in making this communication and to outline the proposed partition only if invited by Nicholas to make known the disposition of France. If conditions warranted a discussion of terms, Polignac indicated the arguments to be employed in support of his plan. Russia should not object, said he, to French acquisitions that would give security against her powerful neighbors. If the claims of France appeared too large, the tsar must be reminded of her sacrifices in the Greek War—the military expedition to the Morea, financial and other support. Then, under the "theory of permanent hostility," which Napoleon had cited advantageously in the negotiations with Alexander at Tilsit, Mortemart must suggest that

France's geographical location might later make her politically useful to Russia. He must also emphasize that France did not ask for territorial cessions on the Italian frontier. She could not feel secure so long as Belgium offered facilities for an invasion and so long as Prussian armies occupied the Rhineland. Prussia's compensation in Holland north of the Rhine would make her a naval power, a result which ought to be welcomed by both France and Russia. If Russia thought her own part too small, Asia rather than Europe might well be represented as important for Russian expansion. If a congress were proposed, the obvious difficulties (France and Russia being better treated than Austria and Great Britain in the Polignac scheme) would seem to make preferable a preliminary secret agreement between France and Russia and the adhesion of Prussia and Bavaria to the plan. Then Austria would be forced to accept the provisions made for her. England, abandoned by the Continent, would not risk a war. If Mortemart could agree with Nicholas on terms, the project might then be submitted to Berlin and Munich, after which communications would be made to Vienna and London. Finally, discussions were authorized on the number of troops which each Power should place on a war footing to enforce the arrangements; France promised 200,000. Mortemart was cautioned to promptness and secrecy in the undertaking.[29]

After sending his instructions to Mortemart, Polignac marked time for three weeks. Then news arrived in Paris which changed the whole situation. Guilleminot's report of August 24 indicated the approaching end of the Russo-Turkish War. Although Adrianople had fallen, Diebitsch had indicated willingness to negotiate, and the Ottoman commissioners had been appointed. The plan would not be used because the conditions for its application would then not exist. Hence, on September 24, Polignac began considering an important new and alternate French policy for the Levant, that of arranging a concert with Egypt. We have thought it advisable to reserve that policy for detailed discussion as the principal problem of our section called "Shift to Egypt" (pp. 112–134).

5. An Alleged Austrian Plan

Whether the imminent downfall of Turkey was the only reason for the sudden emergence of the Polignac project is not known. According to French explanations given the British in 1856, another reason operated—namely, Polignac had received information that Metternich in 1829 was negotiating with Russia and Prussia to partition Turkey, a partition from which France would have been all but excluded.[30] We may therefore interrupt our recital of events in order to analyze briefly the available information on the alleged Austrian plan, to show that all French discussions of it were of later date than would have been likely if it had been a motivating influence for the Polignac plan.

Although, as we shall show, the alleged Austrian project of partition was disavowed by Metternich, Professor Schiemann believed that an Austrian plan had undoubtedly existed.[31] There are ample speculative considerations to support his conclusion. Metternich certainly disliked the Treaty of London; many times he so expressed himself. Russia, furthermore, was winning over Turkey; and none of the other Powers seemed to be interfering—not that it was their concern, in point of strict right. Presumably, Metternich would have wished to discuss the future of the Turkish territories bordering on Austria, since they were then in jeopardy. If so, the logical Powers with which to discuss the question would have been Austria's big neighbors—Prussia, because she was the other great Power nonsignatory to the Treaty of London and because she was closely associated with Austria in German affairs, and Russia, since her war with Turkey provided the immediate key to the problem. We may suppose that Prussia, if so approached, might have discouraged the discussion as lacking urgency, in view of her repeated expressions of full confidence in the tsar's intention to treat Turkey moderately. We shall see that Russia was hardly approachable at the time because of her secret decision to uphold Turkey. We know, despite contrary assertions, that Metternich and Ficquelmont feared lest Nicholas change his moderate views in the treaty to be signed with Turkey, especially after the notable successes of his armies.[32] Furthermore, the Polignac project had not included Austria in its scheduled principal negotiations, so that Metternich, if he had chanced to learn of it, might have planned a similar exclusion of France—provided always that any official Austrian plan were devised at all.

The archives of the interested Powers apparently reveal nothing factually conclusive on the Austrian plan. No such project appears among the regular instructions to the Austrian ambassador at

Berlin,[33] and this investigator found no substantiating documents in the Prussian archives in Berlin-Dahlem. Since material of that kind would doubtless not have been handled with routine business, documents may later be discovered among the miscellaneous papers. The archives of Paris and Vienna, however, contain several dispatches covering the alleged project with special reference to the French reactions.

The documents available seem to start with an account of a discussion at Berlin on September 4, which happened to be the same day Polignac addressed his own instructions to Mortemart, as we have seen above. Agoult, as he later reported to Polignac, had asked Ancillon whether Austria was seeking a *rapprochement* with Russia to prevent being excluded from the benefits of the Russo-Turkish War. The Prussian minister had not confirmed the report. A lengthy ciphered dispatch from Agoult two weeks after the Peace of Adrianople presented circumstantial evidence on the details of the project. The principal source of information, an unnamed German diplomat on intimate terms with the French minister in Berlin, led Agoult to fear that Metternich intended "to provoke a partition of Turkey." A special messenger, apparently, was en route to St. Petersburg with an Austrian brochure—not, however, written personally by Metternich—stating that the time had come to expel the Turks from Europe and to partition their provinces. According to the informant, Prussia had refused to sanction the scheme. G. H. Seymour, British chargé at Berlin, also had heard of the project and had pointedly questioned Ancillon about it. According to Agoult's relayed report, Ancillon denied that such a proposal had been made to Prussia at all. This Seymour told Agoult, who in turn relayed the report to Polignac. The other evidence was Agoult's recollection of conversations a few weeks earlier suggesting that Austria favored the creation of a group of independent Balkan states. Apparently Bernstorff of Prussia had opposed this plan, believing that such states would be dominated by their powerful neighbors, Russia and Austria; he had also doubted whether the Balkan states could maintain stable governments even without external interference. Berlin, reportedly, then decided to maintain Turkey as long as possible.[34]

Polignac's reaction to this evidence, all circumstantial, was to instruct his chargé at Vienna "to seek to penetrate the secret designs" of the Austrian cabinet on the plan. The answer was that nothing observed or heard at Vienna gave credence to the report, either before or after the Peace of Adrianople. Metternich, however, had seemed reticent on the subject. Polignac then took up the matter with Apponyi, Metternich's envoy in Paris, on October 13. The partition plan, suggested Polignac, had doubtless come from the belief that Russia was about to cause the fall of Turkey. After detailing his reports on the subject, he pointedly commented on the alleged exclusion of France from the scheme. "France does not want to remain outside," he stated, "in great questions of European policy which are common to all the Powers, and whose solution must come from an understanding between all the cabinets. You know the violence with which French opinion is attached to the affair of the East." He requested a formal explanation from Metternich.[35]

Polignac also directed Agoult to renew his efforts "to penetrate the secret." Bernstorff, however, when directly questioned at the end of October, appeared embarrassed and quickly changed the subject, suggesting only that the tsar, not wishing additional territory, had even refused to exchange the forthcoming indemnity for some lands which Turkey had offered. Agoult decided that the secret could be obtained only from Metternich.[36]

On October 28, accordingly, Metternich sent Apponyi a long reply to Polignac's request for an explanation. "Not only is the partition of Turkey entirely foreign to our thoughts," he wrote, "but still more repugnant is the idea that it should originate in Vienna." Austria would oppose such a plan, no matter from which cabinet it came. Metternich presumed that the idea had reached Paris from Berlin, whence he had heard similar reports about a month before, when everyone was excited about the advance of the Russian army. He had attempted in vain to find the source of the "invention" implicating Austria. Perhaps it had been some political club, where such matters were agitated constantly. The story, he declared, should rank with reports like those that Austria planned to dismember Sardinia or sought to aggrandize herself at the expense of the Papal States. Metternich said that he had not distrusted the moderation of Nicholas but had seen a sound basis for the fear that internal revolt would follow the occupation of Constantinople by Russia. Yet, he remarked, he had correctly predicted that the war would end on the Danube or at Adrianople.[37]

After hearing this dispatch read, Polignac admitted never having seen a copy of the alleged Austrian brochure, thus officially closing the Austro-French discussions of it.[38]

Nevertheless, Polignac directed Mortemart to check up on the story.[39] Nicholas told the French ambassador that before the Peace of Adrianople Austria had suggested to him a plan for the partition of Turkey in which France had been excluded but that he had not given it serious consideration.[40]

6. Negotiations and a Plea

The Ottoman envoys and Küster, arriving at Adrianople on August 26, appeared satisfied with the first statements by Diebitsch. Küster, who was cordially received, frankly explained the situation at Constantinople. Diebitsch at once announced his readiness to negotiate for peace and promised, meanwhile, not to advance farther toward Constantinople.[41] One powerful reason for this agreeable disposition of the Russian commander was the almost tragic condition caused by illness within his army at that moment. The sickness extended from the servants to the highest ranks; at headquarters all were ill except Diebitsch and a few minor officers, and the disease was spreading rapidly. "We were slinking around like ghosts," wrote a Russian adjutant later, "so merciless was the fury of the fever." Over four thousand were in hospitals, and forty died each day. The artillery were so ravaged that the infantry manned the cannons. At Varna there was a plague also. This state of things precluded an immediate advance upon Constantinople. Diebitsch, however, cleverly concealed this condition from the negotiators, revealing neither the weakness of his army nor his own intense concern.[42]

The first official discussions between the Turkish and Russian negotiators took place on August 29, but the more important ones opened with the arrival of Orlov and Pahlen from St. Petersburg and the Russian presentation of the first draft treaty on September 2. Turkey objected to the war indemnity and to the provision that hostilities would continue until the treaty was ratified. Finally her envoys requested ten days' delay for communication with their government. Although this was granted, Diebitsch declared positively that, if a satisfactory answer was not then forthcoming, his army would resume its advance toward the Turkish capital. Meanwhile, he would stop at Silivi, some fifty miles from Constantinople. He refused to dispatch a previously promised messenger to Paskevich to halt hostilities in Asia pending the negotiations. Because it appeared too late to halt the move, Diebitsch did not prevent Admiral Greigh from occupying Midia and, in fact, sent soldiers to aid at that point. During the interim of ten days he considered his alternatives of action. It was seemingly within his power, as far as Turkey was concerned, to annex Moldavia and Wallachia, provinces already regarded at Constantinople as lost. But that would create new problems by placing Russia on the Austrian frontier in the Balkans; the tsar's promise to annex no territory of Turkey in Europe had been widely publicized in Europe. Balkan national problems confronted him. Should he act on his discretionary power, accorded by the tsar in June, to arm the Bulgars if necessary to bring the Turks to terms? Prince Milosh of Serbia was restive, witness his written statement to Diebitsch that, upon word from the Russian commander, Bosnia and Albania would rise against Turkey and Bulgaria would follow.[43] On September 4 Diebitsch wrote Müffling, accepting the tentative arrangements for exchanging prisoners of war with Turkey.[44]

At Constantinople the receipt of the Russian draft treaty, with the notification of the ten-day period for its acceptance, threw an entirely new light on the problems, which now became more pressing than ever. Gordon believed that any and all conditions proposed by Diebitsch would be accepted by Turkey. Russia's method for guaranteeing the freedom of foreign commerce through the Straits was at last known: she stipulated that any violence or interference by Turkey with "any merchant vessel whatever" would in the future be considered "a legitimate cause for war."[45] Matters were brought to a head on September 7, when the Turkish foreign minister, in conference with Gordon, Guilleminot, and Royer, the minister of Prussia, disclosed that official Turkey was in despair. Turkey disliked the required indemnity, the territorial cessions east of the Euxine, the Russian military occupation of the Balkan provinces until the indemnity was paid, and especially the provision omitting an armistice and continuing hostilities until the ratification. Apparently Turkey accepted without question the independence of Greece, autonomy for Serbia and the Principalities, and the commercial provisions, for no objections to these points were reported by Guilleminot or Gordon. The purpose of the conference was to solicit something more than advice. The Porte wanted some modifications before the expiration of the deadline on September 12. Gordon and Guilleminot were asked to go personally to Adrianople to try to win the modifications; but both ambassadors refused this request and also the alternate proposal of sending their first secretaries instead. Royer finally agreed to go provided the Porte made a written request, while Gordon and Guilleminot promised to entreat Diebitsch not to enter Constantinople.[46]

The joint plea by Gordon and Guilleminot, later characterized by Baron Brunnow as among "the most precious documents in the Russian archives"[47] and by Diebitsch as a "glorious compensation" for the campaign of 1829,[48] was signed on September 9. The ambassadors informed the Russian commander of the "infallible consequences" of a march on Constantinople:

The Sublime Porte has formally declared to us, and we do not hesitate to attest the truth of the declaration, that in that case it will cease to exist; and in annihilating its power the most terrible anarchy will strike indiscriminately, without means of defense, at the Christian and Muslim populations of the Empire.

In making known this state of affairs they had discharged a duty for which all Europe would hold them responsible. As for their actions, they had concerned themselves only with the means that might yet be taken to preserve the Christians of Constantinople from imminent disaster. This letter and the orders for the Turkish plenipotentiaries to sign the treaty were borne by Royer, who left in haste the same day for Adrianople. Royer also was to seek two changes in the draft treaty: (1) the cessation of hostilities with the signing of the armistice or treaty, without awaiting ratifications, and (2) the simple stipulation of Turkey's obligation to pay the expenses of the war without specifying the precise amount of the indemnity.[49]

The fatalist views at Constantinople were in part voiced elsewhere. Polignac believed—or so reports indicated—that the political role of Turkey had been "effaced for always."[50] Sharing the opinion of Metternich, he thought that Diebitsch could solve the problems of both Greece and Turkey "long before the deliberations of the allies could be followed by any demonstration." Concerning the fate of Constantinople, Polignac was willing to state only that

France would concert with her allies. Though he did not know the British intentions, he presumed that there would be little divergence between French and British views.[51] On September 28 word was received in Paris that Nicholas would not take Constantinople but would hold to his moderate views despite the occupation of Adrianople.

7. THE FLEETS SUMMONED

Four years later, during the excitement incident to the Treaty of Unkiar-Iskelessi, Tsar Nicholas was quoted as having said that the key to the Ottoman Empire had been in his hands when his army was at Adrianople. His statement was based on the joint Gordon-Guilleminot plea to Diebitsch.[52] Whether he actually possessed such complete power is doubtful considering the readiness of the British and French ambassadors to summon their squadrons to Constantinople in the crisis of 1829. Especially is it doubtful when we consider the admitted attitude of Gordon, whose directions affected the movement of twenty-one formidable vessels; his plans for action, he reveals, were calculated to save the Ottoman Empire as well as to protect the foreigners in the Turkish capital.

The archives present new light on this aspect of the problem. According to Gordon's dispatch the Russian army was reported as actually marching on Constantinople. Hence on the same day when the plea was dispatched to Diebitsch the ambassadors of Great Britain and France thought the time ripe for expressing to Turkey their willingness to order their fleets to Constantinople[53] even though the part of the French squadron not yet dispersed was still at Smyrna. The two ambassadors agreed between themselves to ask the Porte to admit the British and French squadrons into the Dardanelles and, if judged necessary "one day or another," to call them also to Constantinople. Their written request to the Turkish minister of war made clear that they desired, not to intervene in the Russo-Turkish War—a step not sanctioned by their instructions and hence contrary to their intentions—but solely to protect helpless persons of all religions and nationalities. The request was granted and secret orders to cover the contingencies indicated were issued.[54] To prevent further danger of disturbances the minister of war also agreed not to execute some convicted non-Muslim prisoners.[55]

Gordon even considered not waiting for the outcome of Royer's trip to Adrianople or for the arrival of the French fleet before ordering the British squadron into the Sea of Marmora. In his opinion the British government would sanction such a step to prevent "the approaching dissolution of the Ottoman Empire." A practical difficulty, which he no doubt appreciated, was that the Russian squadron was watching the British. Although in a naval encounter the Russians would have been beaten, they and the usual adverse winds might block the British passage long enough for the success of Diebitsch, if his purpose had been to march on Constantinople.[56] That Gordon fully understood his personal responsibility and the danger inherent in this plan we know from his letter to Aberdeen on September 10. If peace were not signed, he said, the passage of the Dardanelles might involve the British in a war with Russia, which in that event might seize the castles of the Dardanelles and close the exit to the British warships.

Still [he added], the pretext of security not only to British subjects but to Christianity at large might suffice to disarm the opposition of Russia, while the presence of the British fleet would serve the double purpose of encouraging the Sultan, thus upholding his cause, and of producing great caution, if not delay, in the advance of the Russian army.

Believing, as did David Urquhart four years later, that British control of the Black Sea would entirely change the fortunes of the day, he was determined to act without authority if circumstances seemed to warrant it.[57] Guilleminot, in contrast, simply did not wish to be left out.

In his ingenious attempt to present Stratford Canning as an almost unqualified pacifist, Professor Temperley has vehemently assailed the thesis of the moral influence of British warships at Constantinople during critical periods. Gordon's letter, however, concisely states the point of view of other British ambassadors, especially Canning, concerning the employment of the fleet. Canning knew very well that the sultan was indisposed "to every kind of foreign interference unaccompanied with a moral or physical coöperation in his favor."[58] The important point, always, was not so much the strategic factors involved (only a few of which have been yet analyzed), as the moral influence on Turkey of the support of British warships and their probable physical force when acting in concert with the Turkish navy. In short, we are no more concerned than were the ambassadors with the technical question whether or not the fleet could have accomplished the objectives sometimes enthusiastically set for it. The question is whether its mere presence was not more encouraging to Turkey than any test of its physical prowess. Certainly Gordon's letter proves that Canning was not the only British ambassador who relied heavily on the British squadron as a check against the Russians at Constantinople, with or without the authorization of the home government. Gordon's opportunity in the Russo-Turkish War came too late for us to judge the probable outcome, whereas Canning's opportunity preceded the next Russo-Turkish War (1853).

The sultan was pleased by Gordon's attitude, especially in view of the promises that, if the fleet entered the Dardanelles, it would not come all the way, crossing the Sea of Marmora, and appear at Constantinople until requested by the sultan.[59]

The desire for this naval maneuver was apparently predicated on the assumption, featured by Gordon, that Diebitsch would menace Constantinople even after the signing of the treaty. The assumption of course was justified by the provision to that effect included in the Russian draft treaty. Although Guilleminot did not fully share this view, as he wrote Rosamel on September 10, the latter was nevertheless requested to concentrate his fleet near the Dardanelles. The move indicated no desire to take hostile action but it seemed warranted by conditions. "Major political considerations combined with the powerful humanitarian motives in case of the continuation of the war and the occupation of the capital by the Russian armies," he wrote, "would require the presence of the two squadrons." The precautionary move to the Dardanelles was dictated not by the despair of peace but, as stated, by the fear that even the treaty would not stop the Russian advance. If Royer failed to have that part of the draft treaty eliminated, said Guilleminot, it was easy to predict the disastrous consequences. "I also think," he added, "that the French fleet should not remain far away from the theater of action of such powerful interests." It was not necessary for the French to have ships numerically equal to the British.[60] Indeed, on orders from Toulon, Rosamel had dispersed most of the French ships. According to Guilleminot's report to Polignac, the British fleet had been at Tenedos for ten or twelve days, whereas France had only a brig and a frigate there.[61] The remainder of the French squadron left Smyrna on September 15.[62]

8. Peace of Adrianople

When Royer arrived at Adrianople, the political situation was tense. The Russian army threatened to advance toward Constantinople in one more day; the Black Sea fleet under Greigh was already in sight of the Bosporus; Turkish resistance had collapsed; there were threats of provincial revolts and the menace of insurrection at Constantinople; the British fleet was poised for action before the Dardanelles; and the remainder of the French fleet had been ordered on the way. Relief came suddenly. On September 11 Royer transmitted the communication of the western ambassadors and the Turkish acceptance of the Russian requirement for an indemnity. When he guaranteed to Diebitsch the immediate ratification of the treaty by Turkey, the general accepted the two desired modifications.[63] Before the signature of the Peace of Adrianople on September 14 Diebitsch knew, having been informed by Royer, that the failure of the negotiations would be followed by the appearance of the British and French squadrons at Constantinople.[64]

The terms of the peace were more liberal than those which the political situation might have suggested to victorious Russia: the independence of Greece was acknowledged, the practical autonomy of Serbia and, to a less degree, that of the principalities of Moldavia and Wallachia was granted, claims on Georgia and other disputed provinces of the Caucasus were surrendered to Russia, the exclusive jurisdiction of Russian consuls over Russian traders in Turkey was stipulated, other contested points arising from the Treaty of Bucharest were clarified, an indemnity was stipulated with Russian occupation of points on the Danube until its payment, and, lastly, the freedom of commerce through the Straits was positively established. In signing the treaty Diebitsch had acted on the tsar's original instructions, although he sought special instructions considering the new conditions after his occupation of Adrianople.

9. New Bases of Russia's Policy

Turkey's ratification of the treaty had been guaranteed, as we have seen. Ratification by Russia was the next question. To find the answer we must treat the important development in St. Petersburg before September 23, when news of the treaty arrived there.

Mortemart on September 11 reported from St. Petersburg the occupation of Adrianople and the collapse of Turkish resistance. The military successes had not changed the tsar's announced intention to treat Turkey with moderation, and the Russian armies would enter Constantinople "only in the last extremity."[65] The date of this report is significant. It was sent before receipt of the contingent instructions for Mortemart to begin negotiations on what we have termed the Polignac plan. More important, it represented an advance announcement of Russia's new policy, adopted a few days later, for her subsequent relations with Turkey. Despite the report, the ultimate policy was still uncertain; the instructions to Diebitsch on September 13 disclose that Nicholas had probably learned of the approach of the British and French squadrons and that Russia anticipated occupying, at least temporarily, Constantinople and the Dardanelles. Diebitsch was directed to advance on the Turkish capital and to make himself master of the Dardanelles in order to prevent any outside naval interference.[66] We know, of course, that at that moment the negotiations at Adrianople had been concluded; the treaty, without the intervention of a formal armistice, was signed on the following day.

With the capitulation of Adrianople a new policy had obviously become imperative. Two questions had confronted the tsar: (1) Could the Ottoman Empire be reëstablished in Europe? (Or, from the Russian point of view, would the maintenance of Turkey in Europe be more advantageous than its dissolution?) (2) What supplemental instructions should be issued to Diebitsch to cover the contingency of the occupation of Constantinople and other points as well as to outline the method of handling this problem before the other Powers?

These problems were submitted by Nicholas to a selected secret committee of important members of the State Council—Kochubei, Golitsyn, Tolstoi, Nesselrode, Chernyshev, and Dashkov. The decisions were taken on September 16 at the official session of the committee. Sketches of the work of the committee have long been at the disposal of historians. Now available for the first time are the text of the protocol of the session and its correct analysis, both being the contributions of Professor Kerner, giving us a clear picture of what actually took place.[67] The session was opened by Kochubei, head of the committee, who stated that its purpose was "to deliberate on the political complications" of the possible collapse of the Turkish Empire in Europe. Nesselrode then summarized the principles and views that had guided the Russian cabinet during the war and the explanations made at various times to the allied courts on the possible results of the conflict in the Near East. His memorandum argued (1) that it was to Russia's interest not to desire the destruction of the Ottoman Empire, advantageous as a neighbor because of its weakness, and (2) that Turkey, once dissolved, could never be restored. Energetic measures, therefore, should be taken to safeguard the interests of Russia; and, if the empire should definitely collapse, an international congress should be called at St. Petersburg to decide the fate of its peoples and its territories.

Supporting these opinions and the recommendations of the ministry of foreign affairs, extracts from various dispatches, instructions, and memoirs were presented and read. Judging from certain of the instructions, Great Britain had been assured that Russia had no desire to expand her territories, no intention "of keeping Constantinople or any part of the Ottoman Empire, the acquisition of which would upset the equilibrium of Europe." Among the memoirs was a plan by Capodistrias of March 30, 1828, including the essentials of the project which, as we have seen, had been recently attributed to Austria. It called for the creation of five independent states in Balkan Europe, these to be confederated and centered in the free city of Constantinople. Among the dispatches read was one wherein Pozzo di Borgo suggested that, if Russia did not desire to drive the Turks out of Europe, peace should be made on the basis of dismantling the fortresses on the left bank of the Danube and at Shumla and Varna; or, if the Turkish Empire in Europe was destroyed, on the basis of the occupation of Constantinople and other important points on the Straits, the establishment of Constantinople as a free port, and the call for a conference (presided over by the tsar) to decide the organization of European Turkey.

Dashkov supported Nesselrode's conclusions in a memoir sketching Russo-Turkish relations and criticizing Capodistrias' plan.This, in the opinion of Professor Kerner, was probably the decisive document. Its principal thesis was that the destruction of the Ottoman Empire would inevitably cause a general European war. What was of importance to Russia was not new territorial acquisitions but rather "their security in the midst of neighboring peoples." Russia "could most easily attain that by prolonging the existence of the Ottoman Empire under certain conditions." The compression of Turkey into Asia Minor would lead to a Turkish revival and endanger the Russian territories in the Caucasus and Transcaucasus. But, if Turkey went to pieces "by the force of circumstances," her empire might be either partitioned among the Powers or divided into independent states. Both solutions presented difficulties. The time had passed when Russia might adopt the plan of partition: the part of Turkey which would be really useful to Russian commerce—the Bosporus and the Dardanelles—could then be obtained only by enormous sacrifices; and the other Powers could make more advantageous acquisitions[68] than Russia, leaving her afterwards to face "dangerous enemies instead of indifferent Turks" at the south. To consent to the plan of Capodistrias, on the other hand, Russia would have to obtain territories on both banks of the Bosporus and fortify them to protect her commerce.

The committee carefully considered the recommendations of Nesselrode and the impressive support given by Dashkov. Then it unanimously agreed:

That the advantages of the maintenance of the Ottoman Empire in Europe are superior to the disadvantages which it presents; that its fall henceforth [dès lors] would be contrary to the true interests of Russia; [and] in consequence it would be wise to try to prevent it, taking advantage of all opportunities which might yet present themselves to conclude an honorable peace.

The special committee then applied these principles to two different sets of conditions: first, those falling short of the collapse of the Ottoman Empire; next, those resulting from its downfall by the force of circumstances and contrary to the desire of Russia. These we shall not analyze here. Some were made contingent upon the occupation (not necessarily the possession) of Constantinople, the Dardanelles, Vidin, and perhaps other points. Of special interest was the decision to make peace with any Mohammedan sovereign who still ruled in Turkey. Finally, the committee agreed that upon the tsar's approval of all these decisions, the protocol of the session would be transmitted to Diebitsch to serve as his principal instruction.

Tsar Nicholas accepted the policy as laid down by his secret committee. The policy of contingent maintenance, not partition, of

Turkey; of contingent occupation, not ownership, of the Straits—in short, a policy just opposite that generally assumed heretofore by historical writers—was basically established in 1829. The conclusions then reached became the fundamental basis of Russian policy in the Near East for over two decades. Such is the new evidence which Professor Kerner has made available through his significant contribution.

In communicating to Diebitsch the tsar's approval of the new policy as outlined by the committee, Nesselrode stated that reports from London were satisfactory. He added, "The affair is in our hands. Those officious ambassadors can do no good in the negotiations, and very little harm, when one considers the magnificent attitude in which we are placing our victories."[69]

The Peace of Adrianople having been signed in advance of the committee's decision, the significance of the new policy in our immediate problem was its guarantee that Russia would ratify the Peace of Adrianople. Indeed, the treaty by its liberal terms had already placed the new policy in operation. The celebration which we shall note as occurring at Constantinople on November 5 followed the news of the ratification by Russia.

10. The Commercial Article

The Treaty of Adrianople was one of the most important treaties in the history of the Near East. Since most of its provisions are well known, only the commercial article, which aroused the greatest contemporary interest and the most British criticism, need be analyzed here. By this Russia for the first time won complete liberty for her commerce as far as Turkey was concerned, with the liberty guaranteed in a unique manner. The article specifically provided the free and unrestricted commercial navigation of the Black Sea, the Straits, and the Danube, unimpeded by Turkish formalities, the merchant ships being of every size and tonnage; the right to unmolested trade throughout the Ottoman dominions upon payment of the usual tariffs; the right to extraterritorial jurisdiction of Russian traders in Turkey; the full protection by Turkey of Russian subjects, ships, and merchandise in Turkey; the right to transship merchandise in Turkish waters and to warehouse it in Turkish ports; the abolition of two long-vexing abuses to commerce, the Turkish inspection of ships within her ports and the Turkish right to preëmpt any produce, especially wheat, found within the Straits. The same privileges were likewise expressly extended to all Powers in commercial relations with Russia. The guarantee was as follows:

> If any one of the stipulations contained in the present article should be infringed, and the remonstrances of the Russian minister thereupon should fail in obtaining a full and prompt redress, the Sublime Porte recognizes beforehand in the Imperial Court of Russia the right to consider such an infraction as an act of hostility, and to have immediate recourse to reprisals against the Ottoman Empire.

In brief, the article meant the complete emancipation from Turkish restrictions of Russian commerce in and through Turkey and of foreign commerce with Russia. The positive stipulations admitted of little chance for misinterpretation or evasion. The abolition of preëmption immediately affected tallow, which, as we have seen, before the treaty had been sent through the Straits only by simulation;[70] although during the Greek War, as at other times, Russian wheat also had been preëmpted.

Gordon observed that the commercial article "in many respects denied to the Porte the exercise of those rights which essentially belonged to an independent government." Guilleminot, after considering carefully the analysis furnished him by Louis Castagne, enthusiastically wrote Polignac, "From this treaty must date a new era in the navigation of the Dardanelles and the Bosporus."[71] Castagne's analysis covered the effects of the article (1) on foreign commerce, (2) on Turkish commerce and finance, and (3) on Russo-Turkish relations. In his opinion there was no doubt of the benefits conferred upon foreign trade in the Levant by the provision Russia had stipulated. The question was whether or not the article as worded was the proper means to secure the desired extension of commercial privileges, for the effect on Turkey would be extensive, thought Castagne, and mostly detrimental. The roots of the problem went back to her acceptance of a 3-per cent customs rate, by which she had signed away a part of her sovereignty and prevented her own industries from developing. In the years just preceding the Russo-Turkish War, Turkey had sought to recover some of her independence, lost in the capitulations, by making a distinction between foreign and domestic commerce. Now her hands were tied. Castagne feared that the granting of a blanket right to warehouse grain in Constantinople, for example, would destroy her monopoly of retail trade in grain. Now, probably, she would have to use her administrative power to hold her own regions as a market for indigenous produce against Russian competition. All this would affect Russo-Turkish relations. Castagne regarded the provision for reexport of produce as satisfactory, but feared that the door had been opened to Russian abuse of the privilege; the Porte "probably would nourish a secret desire to revoke the concession." Though the phrases of the article sounded simple enough, the problem, he said, was that of extensive interpretations later.[72]

11. AFTER THE TREATY

Gordon continued to show his friendship for Turkey in numerous ways. After the signature of the treaty he justified his attitude with respect to the squadron by writing Aberdeen that his sole desire had been to save Constantinople. "All hopes of defending it were abandoned by the Turks," he said, "and in the present state of disturbance among themselves, the loss of the capital in my opinion would have involved the ruin of the Ottoman Empire." Fearing that Turkey would not live up to the engagements taken, he advised her ministers to observe the treaty scrupulously, giving Russia no reason to renew the war.[73] He drafted a letter for Halil Pasha, the new Ottoman minister to Russia, to carry to St. Petersburg. The letter, which sought to have the terms somewhat modified, was essentially a protest against every article of the treaty.[74]

The fleets, at Tenedos, awaited further orders. Their commanders, in communicating with their embassies more or less regularly by means of war vessels, attracted unfavorable attention. Ottenfels, the Austrian internuncio, showed some jealousy of the British, French, and Dutch. Upon his request Admiral Dandolo stationed a frigate at Tenedos and placed it at the disposal of the internuncio. Ottenfels thereupon inquired of the Turkish government whether the Straits were open or closed; if open, he would like a firman for the passage of an Austrian war vessel. The Turkish foreign minister replied that the Straits were as usual closed to foreign warships; the only vessels sent through by England and France had been in the service of their ambassadors, a privilege which Turkey would not refuse to Austria in similar circumstances. Ottenfels, though not in need of a warship, was glad to have the principle established so that Dandolo might make a pleasure trip to Constantinople if Metternich would agree.[75]

About September 30, when the Russian blockade of the Dardanelles was lifted, Guilleminot notified Rosamel that the French fleet was no longer required at the entrance of the Straits. Gordon did not follow in this move. Guilleminot's reserve in his communications to the Turks, which was in accordance with his instructions, annoyed Gordon, who reported to London that the French ambassador was apparently not acting as the friend of Turkey. Malcolm was presented to the sultan on October 14.[76]

For Mehemet Ali the peace had come rather unexpectedly. Although he considered it would last only three months, it appeared so humiliating that he expected Sultan Mahmud to leave him alone for the time being.[77] Soon, however, the sultan called upon him to return the eighteen Turkish and two Algerian war vessels blockaded by the allies at Alexandria since the battle of Navarino and also to station the Egyptian fleet of nineteen vessels in the Bosporus. Mehemet Ali, incensed at the sultan's interference in Egyptian attempts to secure proper timbers for constructing new war vessels, at first refused to send the Turkish squadron. He took care, moreover, to publish his refusal, suggesting that Great Britain and other Powers might use their resources if Turkey were to be defended.[78] Gordon negotiated a little on the possibility of British protection for the Turkish vessels in their voyage to Constantinople,[79] but Guilleminot gave himself the principal credit for arranging for their return, which actually took place in November.[80]

12. Gordon and the Frigate "Blonde"

Even after the ratification of the peace, Gordon did not release the frigate "Blonde," which had been stationed at Constantinople early in September. He planned to transport the Ottoman minister on it as far as Odessa but was dissuaded by his colleagues from doing so.[81] High Turkish dignitaries were entertained on November 5 at his party on board the "Blonde" in celebration of the peace. Virtually every important person in Constantinople was invited also, including the diplomatic corps. Guilleminot, not to be outdone, entertained the same guests brilliantly at the French ambassador's palace on November 25.[82]

The most conspicuous cruise of the "Blonde" while its headquarters were at Constantinople began six days after the British party. The steamer entered and remained in the Black Sea for over two weeks, visiting Sevastopol, Odessa, Varna, and Sinope "much to the irritation of the Russians."[83] The call at Sevastopol presented a rare opportunity for an official check-up on the naval equipment there. Finding Admiral Greig away at Nicolaïev, Captain Lyons made notes on the Russian warships and recorded angles, bearings, and other information about Sevastopol, all serviceable to the British admiralty. A map of the harbor "sufficiently correct for all useful purposes" was made.[84]

Aberdeen disapproved of the cruise on several grounds. It would offend Russia; it was an action which England had sought to prevent Russia from taking; it might even give Russia the right to claim that Turkey had permitted an infringement of the dangerous commercial clause of the Peace of Adrianople, by which only commercial vessels might pass the Straits without search or visit.[85] Russia was notified of this disapproval.[86]

Gordon, when defending himself to Aberdeen, did not mention the Treaty of the Dardanelles, by which Great Britain had agreed to conform to the Turkish regulation excluding from the Straits all foreign war vessels except those in the service of the missions. He was unaware, he wrote, of any treaties between Russia and Turkey that would preclude Turkey from admitting foreign war vessels if she wanted to do so; discussions at Constantinople had seemed to imply that the regulation was purely a Turkish precaution for the security of the city. In addition, he considered that Russia had no more right to close the Black Sea than to close the Baltic.[87]

Russia did not permit the cruise to pass unchallenged. Indeed, she exaggerated its importance, in the opinion of Metternich.[88] Orlov protested against the facility with which the "Blonde" had been admitted into the Euxine, in contrast with the difficulties made for Russian vessels. Probably, however, he blamed Gordon more than the Turks.[89] Nesselrode's report to the tsar suggested that Gordon had arranged the cruise because he felt humiliated by his part in the closing events of the war and was anxious to convince the English of his value. The cruise, said Nesselrode, would be regretted by the Porte because Russia would seek a reciprocal privilege of navigating the Bosporus.[90] In Metternich's opinion the British had given the Russians ample grounds for insisting on reciprocity.[91] True, a Russian war vessel called at Constantinople to wait upon Orlov in February, 1830, while another transported Ribeaupierre back to his post as minister to Turkey; both these were in the Bosporus at the same time.[92] To combat such arguments as those used by Gordon may have been one purpose of the unique provision in the Treaty of Unkiar-Iskelessi (1833) closing the Dardanelles to the enemies of Russia.

Perhaps to increase British prestige but more likely to await the departure of Orlov, who did not leave until June, Gordon kept the "Blonde" at Constantinople until August, 1830. Only short cruises into the Sea of Marmora were permitted, however, none being taken in the other direction.[93] Lyons and his aides utilized the opportunity for further services to the admiralty, drawing detailed maps of the Dardanelles, the Bosporus, and the Sea of Marmora, and advising against any attempt to force the Dardanelles because of the adequate defenses then found to be installed.[94]

13. PARTIAL EVACUATION BY FRANCE

The Turkish forces remaining in Attica were ordered evacuated ten days after the signing of the Peace of Adrianople. The French soldiers were still in the Morea. While the peace was yet under negotiation, Great Britain and France had exchanged terse comments about them. Aberdeen requested their recall. When Polignac evasively replied, "The King of France is always ready to fulfil the engagements he has taken," Aberdeen countered with a sharp threat "to suspend British relations with the government of France in that which concerns Greece" if the troops were not withdrawn. Polignac thereupon offered to have the matter considered by the allied council, which, reflecting his own pro-Russian policy, would have permitted Lieven to approve the wording of a memorandum on the subject.[95] With the news of the peace in Paris on October 9, Polignac notified Guilleminot that the French expeditionary army was to be recalled.[96]

The notification for Turkey said nothing of a merely partial evacuation of the Greek fortresses by France; but the official orders of the ministry of war and the ministry of marine, dated October 14, covered the recall of only 4,600 men, leaving 5,300 in the Morea.[97] The reason is not clear from the documents. Probably, however, Polignac hoped to use the complete withdrawal of the expedition as a bargaining point with England in his newly adopted venture, the Drovetti plan, which sought to employ Egypt in conquering the Barbary regencies. The Drovetti project was announced to Guilleminot on October 10. At any rate, against the pressing solicitation of the Greek government, Polignac did not order the complete withdrawal of the army. Not until November 26 did he notify Guilleminot that the French government now thought best to recall the troops in two installments, of which only one was coming out at the time.[98] As a matter of fact, part of the French army remained in Greece until 1833. It had been reduced gradually.[99]

14. France Approves

During the succeeding months of relative quiet in Turkey, all of the Powers peacefully considered the problem of commerce in the Levant which the Treaty of Adrianople had placed so forcefully in perspective. England established new British consulates in the Levant and surveyed the potential routes through this region to India. Austrian commerce in the Levant, heretofore conducted with little governmental support, was given new encouragement by a series of consular reforms; Russia, her southern commerce now secure, looked toward the Middle East for new markets; and France, inspired by the aggressiveness of others, studied official memoirs and made plans.

The French Bureau of Commerce and Colonies on October 7, 1829, notified the Marseille Chamber of Commerce of England's "very great activity" in preparing to resume and expand her Near Eastern commerce because of the favorable situation after the Russo-Turkish treaty. Should not France do likewise?[100] Detailed studies were ordered by Paris, the result of which was a series of some thirty analytical memoirs, totaling over 500 manuscript pages by March, 1830.[101] Most of them pronounced the capitulations inadequate for the needs of French commerce. As the historical sketches indicated, the system had shown inherent weaknesses all along; and, although the treaty of 1802 had for the first time made it nonrevocable through unilateral Turkish action, the French had then missed a great opportunity to secure a comprehensive commercial treaty with Turkey. In practice, as the criticisms showed, the capitulations were receiving divergent interpretations, sometimes contradictory. Despite the right of extraterritorial status, for example, Frenchmen still lacked an effective security for their persons and property throughout the Ottoman Empire in times of peace. The memoirs at least analyzed the origin and nature of the capitulations, giving forceful criticisms based on the facts of a long history.

That France had accepted the Peace of Adrianople without reservation was implied by Polignac's communications to Turkey, to Russia, and to Great Britain in mid-October, 1829. To Turkey, the peace was the best way out of a pressing situation. "No matter how difficult for the Porte to accept some of the conditions imposed," wrote Polignac in commending Guilleminot for having advised the Turks to yield, "in the desperate position to which it had been reduced it had become indispensable to sign." Perhaps Russia would make other concessions besides the one in which Diebitsch had left the amount of the indemnity for later determination.[102] To Russia, despite the "lively irritation" about the treaty reported from London,[103] France approved of the treaty, requesting Russian support for the secret Drovetti plan.[104] To England, however, she showed a seemingly hesitant approval.

Aberdeen inquired through Rothesay how Polignac liked the terms; he had heard, he said, that France objected only to Russia's right to interfere in religious affairs. That, Aberdeen pointed out, was not a new right but rather a "vague one capable of almost any interpretation," dating from the Treaty of Kuchuk Kainardji in 1774.[105] In the conference Polignac refrained from direct comments, but he did give Rothesay the impression that the treaty would prove favorable to French interest. He revealed that French commercial houses had been encouraged to avail themselves without delay of the benefits of the treaty. A few days later Polignac frankly praised Nicholas for not utilizing his excellent opportunity to seize Constantinople; he did not object specifically to any part of the treaty. French interest in the Greek question now appeared lethargic, France usually concurring in whatever was done by Great Britain and Russia in the negotiations at London.[106]

15. ABERDEEN THINKS TURKEY WILL CRUMBLE

The British withheld their comments to Russia until they had checked the attitude of France. Then, reluctantly, they accepted the peace, Aberdeen admitting that "the fortunes of the war might have enabled the Tsar to exact still harder terms."[107] At first Aberdeen regarded the precise terms as immaterial:

However advantageous they are in appearance to the Turks, considering the relative condition of the belligerents, and even if the moderation of the Tsar had been more conspicuous, the possibility of all successful resistance is destroyed for the future, and henceforth it is incontestable that the Sultan will reign only by the sufferance of Russia.[108]

Wellington resented particularly the provision respecting commerce which he incorrectly said called for "immediate hostilities" if the Turks visited a single Russian ship in a Turkish port. Turkey, he thought, might justifiably inspect every ship that passed the Straits to see whether it was a warship or to ascertain, for a merchant ship, "the amount of the duty to be claimed under the treaty of commerce." (This was a misinterpretation, for commerce now passing the Straits was subject to no duty at all.) He therefore considered the elimination of the right of visit "a subversion of the independence of the Porte." To justify his view, he even compared the Bosporus and the Dardanelles to the Thames. "These Straits and the intervening sea," he said, "are in fact a closed sea in the possession of the Porte, over which that power always has exercised and must always exercise dominion."[109]

The interpretative British reaction, a quite general condemnation of the treaty, was dispatched to Russia at the end of October. "The treaty appears to affect vitally the interest, the strength, the dignity, the present safety and the future independence of the Ottoman Empire," stated Aberdeen, drawing his reasons from an analysis of several of its provisions. Possession of the eastern shores of the Black Sea seemed to give Russia the keys to Asia Minor and Persia. Turkish administrative control in Moldavia and Wallachia was virtually terminated by the abolition of the right of preëmption there, while the permission to establish quarantines at the navigable delta of the Danube had seemingly placed the control of the navigation of the river exclusively in the hands of Russia. The existence of Serbia and Greece as states would naturally be "incompatible with the security of Turkey." Finally, "the commercial privileges and personal immunities . . . were calculated to invite and justify the renewal of hostilities," war thus becoming contingent upon "the capricious extortion of a Turkish officer or the unauthorized arrogance of a Russian trader." Wellington's comments on the abolition of the former Turkish right to inspect ships were repeated and emphasized,[110] but with no indication of what Great Britain might do even if these interpretations were entirely justified.

By now Aberdeen was convinced that the Ottoman Empire was near its end. At the outbreak of the Crimean War, when he justified his contingent agreement in 1844, along with Wellington and Peel, to coöperate with Russia in a later partition of Turkey, he dated his views on the impending dissolution of Turkey from the Treaty of Adrianople.[111] The documents for 1829 substantiate the opinion he expressed in 1854. In one dispatch he stated the case in almost the same manner as Tsar Nicholas in 1833, in 1844, and in 1853. To Gordon he wrote on November 10, 1829:

> In looking at the state of anarchy and disorganization of the Turkish Empire, as well as the total change of national character exhibited in the apathy, the disaffection, or the treachery of a great proportion of the population, we may perhaps be tempted to suspect that the hour long since predicted is about to arrive, and that, independently of all foreign or hostile impulse, this clumsy fabric of barbarous power will speedily crumble into pieces from its own inherent causes of decay. . . . We cannot reasonably look for any long continuance of its existence.

Turkey, he said, would fall by further revolts of her subjects; or by an overwhelming invasion; or "even by a mutual understanding, and consequent partition, between rival states," perhaps with Austria joining, for the sake of her own defense, "in the commission of an act which she was unable to prevent." At present Turkey existed only "upon the absolute will and pleasure of Tsar Nicholas." But that was not all. Whenever the Turkish Empire ceased to exist, Great Britain should not attempt to restore it:

> Our object ought rather to be to find the means of supplying its place in a manner the most beneficial to civilization and to peace. . . . We cannot be blind to the detestable character of Turkish tyranny. Every day renders more and more certain the impossibility of any European sympathy with a system founded upon ignorance and ferocity.

Great Britain, concluded Aberdeen, should be glad to see independent Greece ready to supplant Turkey after the demise.[112] Those who scoff at the idea of any responsible Englishman's having considered replacing Turkey by concert and partition or by permitting internal dissolution might well ponder the concise opinions in this really remarkable state paper left by Aberdeen. Even after discounting expected overstatements inspired by the occasion, we still have a clear picture of his profound convictions. His agreement with Nicholas in 1844 and his views on Turkey in 1853 are more comprehensible in the light of his 1829 pronouncements.

The British pessimism reflected in the dispatches to Russia and Turkey was soon whispered about the chancelleries of Europe. Metternich complained that Great Britain did not wish to maintain Turkey. Aberdeen replied that the British government was "most anxious to avert the dangers to which the destruction of Turkey would expose the peace of Europe." Nevertheless, he held that the new relationship with Russia deprived Turkey of any important part in an effective balance of power and that Turkey's internal condition was "fully calculated to deprive all rational persons of any confidence in its stability." She had only weakness and submissiveness with which to oppose a foreign enemy.[113] Gordon sought to convince Aberdeen that the Peace of Adrianople was not by any means the last straw for Turkey. Peace was welcome, but its terms did not mean her disintegration. British policy, he urged, should be to maintain Turkey in spite of the treaty; dismemberment would certainly produce a general European war, with further aggrandizement of Russia.[114]

Although the decision of the Russian government to uphold Turkey was of course not known at Constantinople, the developments soon convinced even Gordon that Russia was not such a menace as she had been popularly considered in September. By the beginning of 1830 he no longer feared a second Russian invasion of Turkey. He reported, moreover, that internal conditions had improved, partly because the subjects of the sultan had learned a lesson from the methods used in dissolving the janissaries in 1826. He did not wish to change the British policy of supporting Turkey, because all the other Powers, including Russia, were then actually upholding the sultan.[115] Aberdeen also, not indifferent to the preservation of Turkey, wrote that Great Britain "would readily coöperate in any practical and rational means for giving additional security to her existence." Yet that desire, he added, did not preclude the consideration of her probable dissolution and of "the consequences which might be expected to ensue from that event." Although the internal causes for Turkish decay were obvious, the British government was "never more anxious for the preservation of the dominions of the Sultan against foreign attack."[116] Throughout the remainder of his long career Aberdeen upheld Turkey as a public duty, convinced that there was no suitable alternative from the point of view of British imperial and commerical interests.

16. Polignac Foresees Turkey's Collapse

After Russia's apparent confirmation in November of the alleged Austrian plan for partitioning Turkey, Polignac wrote Guilleminot. He stated that the proposal had been founded not upon the desire to crush the Ottoman Empire but upon the belief that Turkey could no longer survive. In Austria's opinion, said Polignac, the weakness came from several causes: the discontent of the subject peoples; the hasty launching of reforms by Turkey without careful consideration; the "pitiful" means of executing them; the recognition of Greek independence, which had raised the hopes of other discontented subjects; the doubtful obedience of the pasha of Egypt; the devotion of the Serbians to Russia and the submission of the Principalities to Russia; and finally the new conviction that the Balkan states had ceased to be a barrier between Russia and Turkey. Although there had been no result to the overture from Vienna, the proposition had been founded, thought Polignac, on an opinion well worth study. He solicited Guilleminot's views concerning the ability of Turkey to survive.[117] The reply was delayed several months, after which the opinion was transmitted that "the sickness of Turkey, though severe, was not incurable." What Turkey needed, said Guilleminot, was wise government. The weak-willed Sultan Mahmud was a Turk who desired to be nothing more and was not a reformer at heart. Turkey, having not even one statesman who really understood the evils of his empire, was desperate because "she had neither army nor treasury, her provinces were devastated, her agriculture and industry practically did not exist, and a spirit of hatred and revolution was common among her subjects." Other causes of decay were the religious fanaticism and the "ruinous and humiliating restrictions" placed on Turkey by her commercial treaties with Europeans.[118]

17. Polignac Is Pro-Russian

Writers have commonly fallen into the error of ascribing to Anglo-French relations an entente or even an alliance basis from the

Treaty of London to the crisis on Near Eastern affairs in 1840. Such a conclusion has doubtless been drawn from the concert on Greece and the close coöperation of the two Powers against Russia, especially from 1833 to 1838. It is not warranted for the period of Polignac's ministry. Indeed, the divergent French and British policies on Russia came into the open with the signing of the treaty.

These divergent policies had been indicated in the first comments of the representatives of London and Paris at St. Petersburg, even in advance of information of the opposite official views to be taken by the two governments on the merits of the peace. Mortemart acted on the general trend of Polignac's policy when, upon reading the treaty, he thanked Tsar Nicholas especially for including the commercial clause. He suggested also that the benefits to other nations would be complete if piracy could now be eliminated from the Barbary States. In reply Nicholas stated that piracy was the especial concern of France; any expedition launched against it would have the support of Russia. Mortemart remarked that doubtless all the nations except Great Britain would approve the commercial freedom of the Black Sea, although Russia would be the principal beneficiary.[119] Heytesbury, in contrast, assumed that Russia by the treaty had become the protector of Turkey, whereas the true interests of what he called "Europe" demanded a strong state at Constantinople against Russia. He stated with an attitude of resignation that the only thing now left was for a strong Greek state to be constructed instead.[120]

A better illustration of their divergent views is found in the policies now adopted by France and England for the squadrons which they had moved to the Dardanelles.

French policy in reference to the squadron in the Levant had not been clear-cut. Polignac, himself without pronounced opinions on the subject, had given great latitude to Guilleminot and had not restricted the ambassador. He had seemed greatly concerned about the Greek rather than the Russian phase of the Near Eastern question at the time. In this sense, also, Rigny had viewed the presence of the squadron; at the beginning of October he wrote that it might have influenced the early determination of the Greek question. Rigny regretted that the question of Greece had not been settled before the Russian treaty with Turkey and that the French ships had not appeared before Constantinople with that object in view.

Had the treaty not intervened, he said, the British squadron would have passed the Dardanelles. In that event his purpose would have been "to calm the irritations and impatience of certain groups, and to make the démarche one favorable for Greece," thus maintaining the "good relations" of France.[121]

Guilleminot's order for the squadron to move was approved, like Gordon's, by the home government, Polignac regarding it as justified by the conditions reported. But the danger having ceased with the end of the war and no revolution having occurred at Constantinople, the French government was pleased that the two squadrons had not passed the Dardanelles. Their presence on one side and the pressure of Russia on the other would, observed Polignac, have made serious complications for Turkey.[122] The return of the French squadron was now ordered. Great Britain alone kept her squadron at the Dardanelles to await subsequent developments. "Notwithstanding peace having been concluded," the admiralty ordered Malcolm on October 9, "you are nevertheless to remain, with the battleships under your orders, in the Levant until you receive further instructions from London." The anchorage would depend upon consultations with Gordon "in reference to the season and other circumstances."[123] This order was not revoked until December 4. Concrete evidence also appears in the dispatch of November 30, 1829, addressed by Polignac to Guilleminot. The French ambassador was commended again for all his services since his return to the Turkish capital, and Gordon was severely criticized. Gordon's plan to transport the Ottoman ambassador to Odessa on a British war vessel would have been an action "which nothing would have justified." It would have "produced a very bad effect" and might later have been invoked as a precedent. Gordon, in Polignac's opinion, flattered the Turks and, by bad will or inertia, encouraged their opposition to the "just demands of Russia." Such an attitude impeded the granting of more moderate and generous treatment to Turkey by the tsar.[124]

The best proof of Polignac's pro-Russian feeling was in the desired coöperation of the tsar in both the Polignac and Drovetti plans. Russia, as we shall see, was the only Great Power whose support was sought in the Drovetti scheme until after the intended secret negotiations with Turkey and Egypt had been generally disclosed. Although the documents do not prove that the Polignac plan was ever discussed at St. Petersburg, some preliminary discussions must have taken place, for the dispatch of November 3, confirming the alleged Austrian plan, contains some interesting comments by the tsar. Nicholas told Mortemart that he would never consider a partition of Turkey without including the king of France. At the same time, France was invited to weigh the possible results of an unexpected fall of the Ottoman Empire, which might occur "some day or other" despite Nicholas' precautions. The tsar felt sure of the coöperation of the king of Prussia in the views which he would concert with the king of France.[125] Although the instructed ciphered correspondence on the Polignac plan, if any was sent by Mortemart, was soon destroyed, there is available one private dispatch, characterized by Douin[126] as a poorly disguised refusal of Russia to coöperate in the Polignac plan. Here Mortemart stated that the health of the tsar and the weakness of Russian finances after the war with Turkey made the time "most inopportune for a very delicate overture." He suggested, therefore, that the negotiation be deferred until after he had visited Paris to get new instructions, and predicted that Prussia would refuse to cede the left bank of the Rhine.[127]

Aside from the general concert on Greece, established in 1827 and continued by Polignac but inharmonious because of the French expedition, there was apparently only one important evidence of a unity of action between Great Britain and France after the Peace of Adrianople as long as Polignac remained foreign minister. Austria suggested, as the means to help Turkey pay the Russian indemnity and to secure the evacuation of the Danubian provinces, a jointly guaranteed loan by the Rothschilds to Turkey. This Polignac opposed,[128] and Wellington also declined to participate.[129]

By December, Aberdeen was much concerned about the attitude of Polignac. The latest action of the French foreign minister was to permit the publication of certain secret correspondence prejudicial to Great Britain.[130] Throughout the eleven years that followed, British and French interests always clashed where Egypt was concerned. This tendency, as we shall see in the next section, was manifest during the remaining months of the Polignac period.

NOTES TO SECTION III

[1] Roth to Portalis, August 7, 1829, AE Angleterre 627.
[2] Aberdeen to Rothesay, August 21, 1829, FO 27 F 390.
[3] Rothesay to Aberdeen, August 28, 1829, FO 27 F 395.
[4] T. Schiemann, *Geschichte Russlands unter Kaiser Nikolaus I* (Berlin, 1904–1911), II, 503.
[5] Gordon to Aberdeen, August 17, 1829, FO 78 T 180.
[6] AE Turquie 255.
[7] Küster substituted for Müffling, who fell ill at the time.
[8] FO 78 T 179.
[9] Guilleminot to Portalis, August 24, 1829, AE Turquie 255.
[10] Rosamel (from Smyrna) to the ministry of marine, August 29, 1829, *ibid.*
[11] MM, BB[4], carton 510.
[12] Dupré (French consul at Smyrna) to Polignac, August 29, 1829, AE Turquie 259.
[13] FO 78 T 180.
[14] Gordon to Aberdeen, September 1, 1829, *ibid.*
[15] AE Turquie 255.
[16] FO 78 T 180.
[17] AE Turquie 255.
[18] *Ibid.*
[19] AE Alexandrie 23. This recommendation was made by the famous Juchereau de Saint Denys, who previously had sought an important appointment in the Levant from Richelieu and Portalis. He now sought an appointment as inspector of French commerce in the Levant and later as consul general for Egypt. The latter title would permit his headquarters to be wherever the pasha might be, thus duplicating the office created for Greece. Polignac accepted the idea but assigned the title to Mimaut in October.
[20] AE Turquie 255. These are marginal directions in Polignac's own writing. The British squadron in Levant waters at that time included eight ships of the line, six frigates, and seven other vessels, while the available French squadron included only two ships of the line, two frigates, one corvette, and one brig.
[21] Aberdeen to Heytesbury, August 28, 1829, FO 65 R 178.
[22] Aberdeen to Gordon, September 2, 1829, FO 78 T 179.
[23] Aberdeen to Heytesbury, September 8, 1829, FO 78 T 178.
[24] Wellington, *Correspondence on the Eastern Question* (London, 1877), pp. 32–34.
[25] Seymour to Aberdeen, September 1, 1829, FO 64 P 159.
[26] Metternich to Ficquelmont, September 1, 1829, HHSA Russland varia 18.
[27] The Dauphin opposed the decision of the French council not to ask for all of the Rhineland; he would have sacrificed Belgium to get the Rhine provinces. Polignac successfully defended this part of his plan in a supplemental memorandum (AE Russie 178 and Schiemann, *op. cit.*, II, 517–519).
[28] FO 27 F 1140 (1856). Napoleon III in 1856 communicated to England the text of the Polignac memorandum of 1829, with explanatory comments, when he sought British aid for his Moroccan policy after the Crimean War. These papers have been utilized for this part of the section. The principal dependence, however, is the series of four documents on the problem deposited by Boislecomte in 1829 (AE Russie 178). The secret instructions to Mortemart were not transmitted to England in 1856; they have been published by Schiemann (*op. cit.*, II, 511–517), under the incorrect date of July 4, 1829. Many summaries of the Polignac plan have been published, most of them inaccurate in details.
[29] AE Russie 178.
[30] FO 27 F 1140.

Puryear: France and the Levant

[31] Schiemann, *op. cit.*, II, 384.
[32] On September 12 Laval reported that, although Metternich was then of the opinion that the Russian terms would be moderate, the Austrian statesman also believed that the Ottoman Empire had already been killed spiritually (AE Autriche 411).
[33] Cf. HHSA Preussen 133.
[34] Agoult to Polignac, September 25, 1829, AE Prusse 272.
[35] Apponyi to Metternich, October 13, 1829, HHSA Frankreich 388.
[36] Agoult to Polignac, October 28, 1829, AE Prusse 272.
[37] Metternich to Apponyi, October 28, 1829, HHSA Frankreich 389.
[38] Apponyi to Metternich, November 13, 1829, HHSA Frankreich 388.
[39] AE Russie 178.
[40] Mortemart to Polignac, November 3, 1829, *ibid.*
[41] Report by Küster, AE Turquie 255.
[42] Report on September 29, 1829, by a British officer, *ibid.*, and Schiemann, *op. cit.*, II, 357.
[43] Schiemann, *op. cit.*, II, 357, 360.
[44] AE Turquie 255.
[45] Gordon to Aberdeen, September 5, 1829, FO 78 T 180.
[46] AE Turquie 255.
[47] A. M. Zaïonchkovskii, *Vostochnaia Voina* (St. Petersburg, 1908–1913), App. I, p. 44.
[48] Schiemann, *op. cit.*, II, 361.
[49] AE Turquie 255.
[50] Apponyi to Metternich, September 24, 1829, HHSA Frankreich 388.
[51] FO 27 F 396.
[52] Bligh to Palmerston, December 21, 1833, FO 195 T 114.
[53] FO 78 T 181.
[54] Memorandum by Guilleminot, AE Turquie 255.
[55] Guilleminot to Polignac, September 10, 1829, *ibid.*
[56] Cf. A. Slade, *Turkey, Greece, and Malta*, II, 57.
[57] FO 78 T 181.
[58] Canning to Palmerston, December 19, 1832, FO 78 T 211, published in C. W. Crawley, *The Question of Greek Independence* (London, 1930), p. 239. See also the Appendix to the present work, pp. 219–222.
[59] Gordon to Aberdeen, September 12, 1829, FO 78 T 181.
[60] AE Turquie 255.
[61] There were six Russian vessels there also and one Dutch frigate (Malcolm to admiralty, September 6, 1829, FO 78 T 187).
[62] AE Turquie 259. Rigny did not arrive at his post until October 12.
[63] Royer to Gordon and Guilleminot, September 13, 1829, AE Turquie 255.
[64] Schiemann, *op. cit.*, II, 359.
[65] AE Russie 178.
[66] N. K. Shilder, *Imperator Nikolai Pervyi* (St. Petersburg, 1903), II, 460.
[67] For this paragraph and the five paragraphs to follow we utilize a part of the significant analysis and documentary publication by Robert J. Kerner in the *Cambridge Historical Journal*, VI (1937), pp. 280–290, as noted in the Bibliography of the present study (p. 229).
[68] Dashkov's suggestion of the possible allocations through seizures was quite general. He thought that England and France could seize Egypt, Crete, and the Greek islands; but he did not stipulate which part France might take.
[69] Shilder, *op. cit.*, I, 548. Chernishev also plainly stated that the tsar had approved the new policy (*ibid.*, p. 549).
[70] Gordon to Cartwright, December 4, 1829, FO 78 T 181. Turkey at first was a little hesitant about extending the benefits of the treaty to Powers other than Russia. Not until December, for example, did she agree to pass British ships containing every kind of produce.
[71] Gordon to Aberdeen, September 19, 1829, *ibid.*; AE Constantinople 83.

[72] AE Turquie 255.
[73] Gordon to Aberdeen, September 19, 1829, FO 78 T 181.
[74] Schiemann, *op. cit.*, II, 509.
[75] Ottenfels to Metternich, September 25, 1829, HHSA Türkei 21.
[76] FO 78 T 181.
[77] Acerbi to Metternich, October 26, 1829, HHSA Alexandrien, fol. 1.
[78] Barker (at Alexandria) to Gordon, October 12–23, 1829, FO 78 T 181.
[79] Gordon to Aberdeen, October 25, 1829, *ibid.*
[80] AE Turquie 255. Mehemet Ali held and repaired the two Algerian vessels. They were claimed by France by right of conquest of Algeria in 1830 but were given to Mehemet Ali in 1831.
[81] *Ibid.*
[82] Ottenfels to Metternich, November 26, 1829, HHSA Türkei 21. Metternich strongly disapproved of the proceeding (AE Autriche 411).
[83] AE Turquie 255.
[84] S. M. Eardley-Wilmot, *Life of Edmund Lyons* (London, 1898), pp. 47–50.
[85] Aberdeen to Gordon, January 25, 1830, FO 78 T 188.
[86] Aberdeen to Heytesbury, February 9, 1830, FO 65 R 184.
[87] Gordon to Aberdeen, March 2, 1830, FO 78 T 189.
[88] To Ottenfels, December 19, 1829, HHSA Türkei 21.
[89] Ottenfels to Metternich, January 25, 1830, *ibid.*
[90] Schiemann, *op. cit.*, II, 510–511. No matter what Gordon thought, it was Lyons who became politically prominent in England as the result of the cruise of the "Blonde." He became British minister to Athens from 1835 to 1849 and followed Dundas as commander of the British squadron in the Black Sea during the Crimean War.
[91] Metternich to Ottenfels, February 3, 1830, HHSA Türkei 21.
[92] Gordon to Aberdeen, February 11, 1830, FO 78 T 189.
[93] Gordon to Aberdeen, June 15, 1830, FO 78 T 190; Eardley-Wilmot, *op. cit.*, p. 114.
[94] Lyons to Malcolm, October 14, 1830, FO 78 T 195. In 1839 there were 416 heavy guns arranged to fire upon passing ships from every angle of the Dardanelles.
[95] AE Angleterre 627.
[96] AE Turquie 255. Guilleminot was instructed to see that the territorial settlement for Greece conformed to the decisions of the allies.
[97] MG, D², carton 3; MM, BB⁴, carton 510. Schneider had succeeded Maison as commander of the French expeditionary force in the Morea by orders of October 5.
[98] AE Turquie 255.
[99] Another evidence of the desire of Frenchmen to capitalize on the expedition was given by the recommendation of Schneider just before he was replaced by Gueheneuc on October 28, 1831. Schneider proposed to the Duke of Dalmatia, then the French foreign minister, that France officially establish a colony in Greece. Dalmatia refused to have the government sponsor such a colony but stated that no objection would be raised if French families moved to Greece on their own initiative and on their own risks (MG, D², carton 5).
[100] CCM, dossier, Evénements politiques, 1802–1855. During the Russo-Turkish War French trade with southern Russia had been virtually halted.
[101] AEMD Turquie 34; the principal reports were by A. J. DuLaurron, attached to the embassy staff at Constantinople.
[102] Polignac to Guilleminot, October 9, 1829, AE Turquie 255.
[103] Polignac to Guilleminot, October 12, 1829, *ibid.*
[104] Polignac to Mortemart, October 14, 1829, AE Russie 178.
[105] FO 27 F 390. This statement by Aberdeen in 1829 about the treaty of 1774 was not supported by the British cabinet under Aberdeen's leadership in October, 1853.
[106] Rothesay to Aberdeen, October 19 and November 2, 1829, FO 27 F 396.

[107] Aberdeen to Heytesbury, October 31, 1829, FO 65 R 178.
[108] Aberdeen to Gordon, November 10, 1829, FO 78 T 179.
[109] Wellington, *Correspondence on the Eastern Question*, pp. 38–47.
[110] Aberdeen to Heytesbury, October 31, 1829, FO 65 R 178.
[111] V. J. Puryear, *England, Russia, and the Straits Question, 1844–1856*, pp. 40–75. Wellington's approval of the Nesselrode Memorandum may not have been solicited, but all the sources agree that he took part in the verbal agreement with Tsar Nicholas.
[112] FO 78 T 179.
[113] Aberdeen to Cowley, November 14, 1829, FO 7 A 211.
[114] Gordon to Aberdeen, December 15, 1829, FO 78 T 181.
[115] Gordon to Aberdeen, January 5, 1830, FO 78 T 189.
[116] Aberdeen to Gordon, February 26, 1830, FO 78 T 188.
[117] Polignac to Guilleminot, November 29, 1829, AE Turquie 255.
[118] Guilleminot to Polignac, March 4, 1830, AE Turquie 260.
[119] Mortemart to Polignac, September 29, 1829, AE Russie 178.
[120] Ficquelmont to Metternich, September 30, 1829, HHSA Russland 17.
[121] Rigny to the ministry of marine, October 3, 1829, MM, BB[4], carton 510.
[122] Polignac to Guilleminot, October 12, 1829, AE Turquie 255.
[123] PRO Admiralty Secret Orders 1694.
[124] AE Turquie 255.
[125] Mortemart to Polignac, November 3, 1829, AE Russie 178.
[126] In the preface to G. Douin, *Mohamed Aly et l'expédition d'Alger*.
[127] Mortemart to Polignac, December 22, 1829, AE Russie 178.
[128] Apponyi to Metternich, October 29, 1829, HHSA Frankreich 388. French bankers were already asking for support by the government to get the liquidation started for the Greek loans contracted at London (AE Athènes 4).
[129] The first internationally guaranteed loans to Turkey were made during the Crimean War. Their aftermath proved the wisdom of these statesmen, from a financial point of view, in declining the suggestion in 1829.
[130] Aberdeen to Rothesay, December, 1829, FO 27 F 390.

IV. SHIFT TO EGYPT

THE DROVETTI PLAN

THE AUTOMATIC cancellation of the Polignac plan led to a sharp shift of French policy for the Levant, although the pro-Russian tendencies were continued. Almost immediately after news at Paris of the Peace of Adrianople, France launched her challenge for empire in Algeria. The story of the direct conquest need not be repeated here. But the initial project, of indirect action through Egypt, has been portrayed only in outlines. Only in recent years, indeed, have all the pertinent documents been made available. Many are now in print in the lengthy series of the Société Royale de Géographie d'Egypte; the others have been opened for inspection in the French archives. The interesting details of that phase of the problem of Algeria may well be recounted, as well as their effects on Anglo-French relations. This section will be limited in scope and in period to the negotiations on those phases of the background of the conquest. Two subdivisions will attempt to clarify briefly the French commercial interests in Egypt after Adrianople and the contemporary British plans for a Near Eastern route to India.

1. EGYPT AND FRENCH POLICY

The French policy, begun in 1824, of strengthening Egypt within well-defined limits had been temporarily contradicted by the battle of Navarino and its aftermath. With the coming of the Russo-Turkish War the activity of Egypt was still narrowly circumscribed. Its development was to be carried on within the vague formula of the Powers of preserving the Ottoman Empire. The original French idea of the desirability of a strong Egypt had not changed, however, and peace brought it to the front again. After Adrianople, Turkey was supported by Great Britain and Russia. Considering the weakness of Turkey, France might now either play a role secondary to Great Britain and Russia or assert her former leadership by taking an independent attitude in support of Mehemet Ali. In the latter case, three seemingly conflicting tendencies must be reconciled. The problem was how to limit the territorial and strategic power of Egypt in a manner satisfactory to Egypt, desirous of expanding, to Turkey, important for the equilibrium of

Europe, and to France, seeking new outlets for empire. France attempted to work out a solution in her new North African policy. Little progress had been attempted in the French war with Algeria, legally in effect since 1827. The blockade of Algiers still continued; but the affair was discussed in the French Chambers only in connection with budget matters. Judging from published reports in February, 1829, France was at last about to prepare an expedition to chastise the dey;[1] debates were animated. In the address from the throne, however, the unfinished business had been treated lightly: King Charles, having reaffirmed his solicitude "for the honor of France and for the protection of her commerce," mentioned the need of making "a prompt and satisfactory reparation" and of eliminating piracy. Pending the settlement of the Greek and Russo-Turkish questions a dilatory attitude had, indeed, been inevitable. Yet some further attempts had been made for a settlement with Algeria, the last one being the Bretonnière mission of August, 1829, which had resulted in the dey's positive rejection of the French propositions. Drovetti, who was in Paris at the time, now came forward with his favorite plan.

2. The Project

The project was one by which France would aid Mehemet Ali to conquer the three Barbary regencies of northern Africa and would settle with Algeria into the bargain. Its genesis, aside from the imperialistic tendencies of Polignac and his advisers, was both the special status of Egypt in relation to French policy and the zeal of Drovetti. We may, for convenience, term it the Drovetti plan.

Before leaving Alexandria on June 20, 1829, Drovetti, on his own account, had undertaken preliminary negotiations. His enthusiastic discussions of the project, and also those of his successor Mimaut, had not failed to catch the ears of the other consuls in Egypt. According to Barker, who on August 18 reported the essence of the plan to London, Drovetti had gone to Paris to urge the government to adopt his ideas, had already promised French support to Mehemet Ali whenever needed, and was the sole originator of both project and promise.[2]

Drovetti submitted the details to Polignac in a memoir dated September 1. France was in duty bound, stated the memoir, to

[1] For notes to section iv, see pp. 144–146.

terminate her quarrel with Algeria in a dignified manner. The means hitherto employed had proved ineffective. A military expedition to the Barbary shores would present difficulties. The greatest danger (as Drovetti had learned from his personal knowledge of Bonaparte's expedition) was clearly that of exposing the expeditionary army to the chances of provisioning by sea routes. Even if successful, a military expedition to Algeria would be expensive. The establishment of a permanent colony would arouse the jealousy of rival nations; the hostility of England might be presumed in advance. A better plan, suggested the memoir, would be to let the Egyptian coreligionists of Muslim Algeria perform the task. Mehemet Ali might advance all three regencies to the same state of civilization and dependence upon Turkey that Egypt then enjoyed. As an added advantage, simply through monetary sacrifices Mehemet Ali might make use of the Bedouin tribes in the intervening deserts. Drovetti was certain that Mehemet Ali would win, once he started the campaign. The military resistance of Tripoli and Tunis would not stop him, nor would even the defenses of Algeria hold for long. (This confidence, as will be seen, was not shared by military men in Europe.) The Porte would see the advantage, thought Drovetti, of such a conquest. Its authority in the regencies was only nominal, and the tribute usually went unpaid. To Mehemet Ali, eager to regain the sultan's favor, such an expedition would appeal, especially since it would win the approval of Europe. The pasha had long desired to extend his territorial authority; now that the Greek War was almost over, he feared retaliatory measures from the sultan; this would be the means of making the Porte forget the Egyptian evacuation of Greece. England, Drovetti concluded, would not oppose openly.[3]

3. THE COUNCIL CONSIDERS

From our preceding discussion of the Peace of Adrianople we remember that when the project was submitted on September 1, no reports in Paris had indicated the nearness of the peace between Turkey and Russia; all speculations, on the contrary, had been based on the probable dissolution of Turkey. Hence the expected happened. Polignac for the moment refused to consider Drovetti's proposal; within the three days his own and Boislecomte's "Polignac plan" were dispatched to Mortemart at St. Petersburg.

Three weeks later, however, conditions had entirely altered. All reports now indicated an early peace in the Russo-Turkish War. This seemed a practical certainty after Guilleminot's dispatch of August 24 announcing the capture of Adrianople, the willingness of Diebitsch to negotiate, Turkey's decision to throw herself on the mercy of Russia, and the appointment of the Ottoman commissioners to treat for peace. Not yet received were the reports two weeks afterward describing the subsequent tension and excitement at Constantinople. These, dispatched on September 10, reached Paris almost simultaneously with the news of the actual signing of the Treaty of Adrianople. With the report of August 24 at hand, Polignac and his advisers now began considering the Drovetti scheme, apparently in order to have an alternate plan before the council.

Consideration began on September 24 when Polignac, through a long list of questions to Drovetti, sought the history and further details of the plan. Analyzing the most important questions and Drovetti's answers, we learn the following details: Drovetti had not intended to propose a union of the French and Egyptian squadrons in the venture. That step was not regarded as necessary for success; and it would be better to give an all-Muslim character to the enterprise, especially to prevent the jealousy of England. If Mehemet Ali asked for subsidies, ten million francs or more might be proposed. The idea went back to 1826, and the plan combined Mehemet Ali's and Drovetti's ideas of 1827. When Mehemet Ali had wished to go into Syria, Drovetti had advised an advance into the Barbary regencies as more likely to win European approval and to awaken less jealousy at the Porte. It was supposed that Mehemet Ali still had the idea, because the matter had been broached after Navarino. At that time also, the ambassador of Russia had promised to support the plan.[4] Turkey could probably be handled by offering her the advantages of the reconquest of the regencies, together with an annual tribute of four million francs, duplicating the amount paid by Egypt; she would lose more if the plan were not approved, because France would conquer Algeria and Egypt would take Syria.[5]

If an alternate plan were to be ready, time was now pressing; and Polignac did not wish to await an exchange of notes with Egypt before submitting the matter to the French council. To inform himself further regarding the probable dispositions of Mehemet Ali at that time, he studied the most recent reports from Egypt. Judging from the last one received (from Mimaut, dated August 10), the pasha's attitude was unchanged. In addition, Mehemet Ali wanted to move toward Syria because Russia had occupied Erzurum; he had plainly expressed his belief that the proposed French conquest of Algeria would be impossible without the concert of Egypt, which possessed both the geographical location and the means to make the attack successful.[6]

To the council, late in September, were submitted documents for the project: Drovetti's proposal of September 1; the questions and answers of September 24; and a note, presumably by Polignac, arguing for the utility of the scheme. According to the note, the approaching conclusion of peace had brought the quarrel with Algeria to the front again. The best plan would be for France, without compromising her own army, to win her desired objectives in Algeria by letting Mehemet Ali do the fighting. France should inform Turkey that she would much prefer to see the sultan himself chastise his vassal and that the means might be found in the military resources of Egypt. Europe would be glad to see a happy and productive commercial country replace the piratical regencies; the Porte would find a counterpoise for its losses to Russia and would get an added proper tribute from Mehemet Ali. As for Mehemet Ali, he had proposed the scheme in 1827 and had since apparently changed neither his concepts nor his willingness.[7]

Still there was hesitation, doubtless to await news of the actual conclusion of the Russo-Turkish peace, especially important at that moment because of the attitude of Pozzo di Borgo. The latter was reported on September 25 to have exhibited "a spirit of hostility which was almost personal as regarded the principal members of the [French] cabinet."[8] This, presumably, was his personal reaction to information that the French and British fleets had been ordered to the Dardanelles.[9] With official news at hand, on October 5 Pozzo spoke of the "unfavorable impression" in Russia of the decision to anchor the fleets before Constantinople. Because of Pozzo's energy in his references to the movement of the fleet, Rothesay concluded that the Russian ambassador must have acted on instructions.[10]

The news of the peace was followed at once by a new analysis prepared by Baron Coehorn of the French foreign ministry. His memorandum interpreted what should be the new policy for the

Levant. France, he urged, might well let Great Britain and Russia alternate in political preponderance at Constantinople and Athens while she herself restored her former Levantine leadership by developing her sphere of influence at Alexandria: Mehemet Ali was continuing his aggressive tendencies, and Egypt would emerge as a real competitor for both Turkey and Greece if he extended his power either into Syria or into the Barbary regencies. France should be particularly interested in the extension into North Africa—a move quite significant in respect to the potential new commercial routes through the Levant. Mahmud and Mehemet Ali each held keys to the great commercial and maritime routes there. Mahmud, though forced to free the Straits for the passage of all commerce, held the Syrian route to the east, while Mehemet Ali held firmly the region connecting the Mediterranean with the Indian Ocean. It was important, continued Coehorn's memorandum, that Mehemet Ali be strong enough to prevent this route's falling into the hands of a single Power, whether commerce there was restricted or thrown open to all nations; "Mehemet Ali must always hold the isthmus of Suez." Egypt had offered its resources to France. France might make Mehemet Ali her lieutenant in the Levant and depend upon his son to continue his policies. Piracy, injurious to commerce in general, would be in itself ample justification before Europe for taking action against the regencies.[11]

4. Orders Are Issued

The French council adopted the Drovetti plan and began its execution with secret instructions for secret negotiations at Constantinople, St. Petersburg, and Alexandria. Guilleminot was to present the problem tactfully to the Porte; Mortemart was to solicit Russian support; Mimaut was to open negotiations with Mehemet Ali; Captain Huder, aide-de-camp of Guilleminot, was to carry on the negotiations at Alexandria; and Rayneval was cautioned to special watchfulness at Vienna.

The first order was to Guilleminot on October 10, the day after Polignac had written of the decision (later modified) to recall the French army from the Morea. The ambassador was directed to solicit a firman placing Tripoli, Tunis, and Algeria under the authority of Mehemet Ali. The explanations and arguments authorized to support the application were much the same as those submitted to the council. It was to be stated that the French government had fixed its attention on Mehemet Ali's repeated offer to help punish the dey of Algeria. The offer provided a means not only of settling with the dey without compromising French arms but also of destroying the piracy that was a disgrace to Europe. Under Mehemet Ali the three regencies would flourish, and commerce would be extended. The Porte, saved the trouble of administering those provinces, would receive a proper tribute. This projected Egyptian activity would, moreover, probably divert Mehemet Ali from his plan of conquering Syria. France would coöperate with her fleet at Algiers or through subsidies. If the Porte refused the firman, three points were to be suggested for pressure: Turkey might anticipate the permanent loss of the regencies; in any event, France was determined to avenge the insult of the dey; and the possibility of direct negotiation with Mehemet Ali was not to be excluded. A postscript to the instruction detailed the steps already taken and stated that "the interests of Russia on this point" were "entirely in accord with those of France." Guilleminot was authorized to confide, if necessary, in Count Pahlen (a signatory of the Peace of Adrianople, who was then in Constantinople) but not to solicit the aid of the representatives of Great Britain and Austria.[12]

Polignac's hopefulness with respect to Russia probably resulted from a conversation with Pozzo di Borgo, the Russian ambassador, whom he took into his confidence and reminded of his original support of the proposal in 1827. As Polignac notified Mortemart, Pozzo now appeared to be writing his cabinet to the same effect. Polignac backed up his conversation with Pozzo by instructing Mortemart to endorse the Treaty of Adrianople and to solicit Russian aid in negotiating for the Turkish firman. It was to be remarked at St. Petersburg that Great Britain and Austria had shown displeasure with the Russian terms of the peace with Turkey, whereas France was sensible of Nicholas' moderation toward the sultan. Secrecy was desired because of England, said to be always "indifferent to the question of concerting measures against the Barbary states." The friendship of France and Russia and the similarity of their views on Algeria led Polignac to believe, he stated, that the tsar would order his envoy at Constantinople to support Guilleminot if requested.[13]

Unknown to Polignac, Russia's approval of the chastisement of

Algeria had already been expressed to Mortemart in a conversation of October 6. When Mortemart mentioned to Nicholas the desirability of purging the Mediterranean of Barbary pirates, the tsar suggested that France might do it, thus terminating her quarrel with Algeria. Mortemart replied that France might pay the necessary costs but would not do so unless jealous neighbors could be prevented from making the expedition "ephemeral" and thus permitting the resumption of piracy on the first good occasion. "That is what I intend, and what Europe must desire," said the tsar, "and you may be sure that any decisions taken by the King of France in this regard will be supported with all my influence." In the tsar's opinion French occupation of Algeria would benefit the civilized world "even if it displeased some persons."[14]

Polignac made no pretense of awaiting the outcome of Guilleminot's negotiations for the firman. Indeed, in the absence of telegraphic facilities, six weeks would be required for the arrival of the first report of Turkish reactions. He simply delayed ten days to give a chance (which did not materialize) for the negotiations at Constantinople to precede those with Egypt, before writing the instructions for Mimaut and Captain Huder on October 9.

Mimaut was directed to inform Mehemet Ali that the Peace of Adrianople had cleared the way for action on the pasha's proposal as submitted through Drovetti. The French government now approved and supported the plan for Mehemet Ali, under French auspices, to conquer the three regencies and destroy piracy. Although France "accepted the offer which the pasha had made," Polignac, doubtless acting on Drovetti's advice, authorized the opinion that the conquest might be made easily "by the armies of Mehemet Ali alone." France would support with her fleet before Algiers and subsidies would be advanced if necessary. Because France insisted upon the prompt punishment of the dey, acceptance by Egypt was made conditional upon the pasha's prompt execution of the plan. Mimaut was authorized to offer a loan of ten million francs, payable in installments as the conquest progressed. France had already instructed Guilleminot, at Constantinople, to seek a firman that would unite the three regencies with Egypt. The pasha must judge for himself whether the failure to win the firman would be "a real obstacle to the success of his arms and expose him to the serious and permanent resentment of his sovereign." Polignac expressed, however, the belief that the Turkish government would be much influenced by *faits accomplis*—another reason for prompt action by Egypt. Polignac apparently had adopted Drovetti's reasoning in respect to the attitude of the other Powers for he told Mimaut that all Europe except England would support the move because of the anticipated destruction of piracy and that probably no Christian Power would openly oppose such an enterprise. The negotiation was to be kept secret as long as possible. This important instruction was entrusted to Huder; and a brig of war, the "Eclipse," was placed at his disposal for delivering the message and for returning the answer of the pasha. A second instruction directed Mimaut to open the discussion and sign the convention regarding the subsidy only, the actual negotiation to be handled by Huder.[15] Nowhere in these dispatches do we find any instructions on the particular promises or obligations which Mehemet Ali might fairly have been expected to assume in reference to France. That point, presumably, would be left for further negotiation after Mehemet Ali was actually proceeding in the manner that Polignac had intimated to Drovetti.

The documents have disclosed that Polignac had weighed carefully the possible roles of Russia and Great Britain respectively in the new venture. As for Austria, Polignac presumably feared a liaison with Great Britain through the operation of one phase of "the theory of permanent hostility." This assumption is justified by the initial instructions to Rayneval, the new French ambassador to Vienna: "Of all the great Powers, England is the only one on which Austria can count; these two Powers have the same adversaries, and there does not exist between them any point of contact of a nature to place their interests in collision." Their natural alliance was practically indissoluble. Economic rivalry alone might give unrest in London respecting Austria. One aspect of this was the development of shipping and commerce through Trieste while the British continued to hold the Ionian Islands. The role of the French embassy at Vienna was stated to be one of observation, but rarely one of action. Rayneval might study closely the coöperation of Great Britain and Austria regarding Turkey, follow "the uncertainties of Russia and the systematic variations of Prussia," and incidentally observe the possible effect on Austrian commerce of Greek shipping in the Levant.[16]

5. First Negotiations

The successive developments in the problem at Alexandria and at Constantinople may be examined in their order. The impressive arrival of Huder on the "Eclipse" on November 16 attracted considerable attention in Alexandria,[17] especially since Mehemet Ali had just named certain French officers to the command of four of the best Egyptian war vessels and since Cerisy was actively directing the naval construction there.[18] As Mimaut later reported, the Drovetti plan was already known in the Levant, and the coming of Huder amounted to a public announcement of it.[19]

Details of the first negotiations are disclosed by the reports of Mimaut and Huder. The two French agents conferred with Mehemet Ali, Ibrahim, Boghos, and Osman Bey for a fortnight. The proposal was distinctly submitted that Egypt alone undertake the conquests, with French support before Algiers and a subsidy in the form of a loan if the expedition took place promptly. The question of Turkey was disposed of without difficulty. Mehemet Ali expressed his willingness to proceed, with or without the firman. He requested the suspension of the French negotiation at Constantinople, lest it develop an Anglo-Turkish entente, but agreed that the request might be acted upon as Guilleminot saw fit. In the event of a conflict with the sultan, the pasha appeared disposed to let the Muslim world decide the issue. Mehemet Ali agreed to offer the Porte not only the annual tribute suggested by France but also a special contribution to help Turkey pay the war indemnity to Russia. The proposals relating to foreign Powers did not satisfy Mehemet Ali: in the conferences he always insisted that France accord "efficacious support" against England if interference came from that quarter.

The negotiations were stalemated on the question of the subsidy. Here Mehemet Ali set his own terms, a loan of twenty million francs, repayable four years after the conquest of Algeria, and the pure and simple donation of four ships of the line, each carrying eighty cannons. When Mimaut declared himself without authority to grant the ships, Mehemet Ali expressed surprise. According to him, Drovetti had indicated such terms to be acceptable to France. As Huder later reported, Drovetti had apparently known of the clause concerning four vessels, and Mimaut had therefore not mentioned it in his dispatch of August 10. Upon the pasha's request, Mimaut and Huder submitted a succinct written statement of the French proposal. The zealous arguments of Huder could not change Mehemet Ali's unrelenting demand for four large war vessels to give the venture a more purely Egyptian color and to provide added protection against the Turkish navy. The pasha apparently had a fixed idea that a formidable navy was necessary to his position. Since Huder and Mimaut believed that he would repay the loan even if the expedition were unsuccessful, they tentatively agreed to double the amount and to reduce the repayment period to half that originally proposed by France. Mehemet Ali, however, would not proceed on the mere promise of a double loan; the outright cession of the four war vessels became an absolute condition. On November 29, accordingly, Huder sailed for France on the "Eclipse" to secure new instructions.[20]

That the project was known, at least before Huder's departure, is shown by the Russian consul's report. Many believed, he said, that Huder's trip had concerned a project of subjugating the Barbary regencies with French help and with the consent of the sultan and the Christian Powers. Afterward, the regencies would be controlled by Mehemet Ali. The scheme was regarded as a vast enterprise for the pasha; but, confident of his own ability, he was hastening his preparations.[21] Barker's reports on the Huder mission indicated the same opinion. His first account was received by Aberdeen on December 18, when the foreign secretary directed the British ambassador at Paris to make judicious inquiries.[22] There Polignac denied the existence of the negotiation.[23]

Guilleminot's negotiations on the problem began on December 1. For some reason the instruction did not reach Constantinople until November 19; then the ambassador had not been able to discuss the matter of the firman with the Turkish foreign minister until December. The first conference, lasting some three hours, was quite successful from the French point of view, the Turkish foreign minister appearing quite enthusiastic and his objections being quickly brushed aside by Guilleminot's logic. It was agreed that the matter be submitted to the sultan. When asked whether preliminary negotiations had been undertaken with Mehemet Ali, Guilleminot responded that he did not know. In a formal note transmitted next day, he urged a prompt decision because France was determined to proceed with the conquest of Algeria if the plan for Egypt to do so failed. After a week of consideration, however, the attitude of the Reis Effendi had changed. In the conference Guilleminot had apparently met all the new objections now raised. But the Porte submitted a counterproposal—the sending of a special Turkish negotiator to Algiers to straighten out the differences with France and the appointment of a special French agent to accompany this envoy. Although Guilleminot could accept this proposal only *ad referendum*, he nevertheless expressed his opinion that it was now beneath the dignity of France to negotiate with the dey. When the Porte then asked for French approval of the suggested method, Guilleminot neither admitted nor excluded this as a possibility. By December 10 it was known in Constantinople that Mehemet Ali was willing to proceed with or without the sultan's consent. Thereupon Turkey rejected the request for the firman. Guilleminot had not utilized his contingent authority to concert with the Russian envoy because he expected the Porte to regard such coöperation as a menace. Thus the negotiations at Constantinople had expanded the problem to three possibilities: for Mehemet Ali to proceed with the conquests; for France to conquer Algeria; or for Turkey to negotiate with Algeria in behalf of France.[24] Characteristically, the Turks did not keep the secret. A report of the negotiations for the firman was soon sent to London by Gordon,[25] who, as Guilleminot later learned, had been instrumental in the Porte's refusal.[26]

6. The Counterproposal

Because of inclement weather, the "Eclipse" did not dock at Toulon until December 21. Then Huder was forced to remain on board during the usual period of quarantine. His and Mimaut's reports were forwarded to Paris, along with the request for new instructions on the character of the convention to be concluded with Mehemet Ali. These items were in Polignac's hands on December 26. Without awaiting the premier's reactions, Huder wrote Boghos at once of the difficulties that would probably be encountered on the request for the cession of four warships.[27]

Polignac seemed inclined to gratify Mehemet Ali despite the hint from England and the opposition of some of his colleagues. The matter was debated for several days. Strong ministerial opposition developed against donating four vessels without any guarantee of the success of the enterprise. Haussez, Bourmont, Gueron-Ranville, Courvoisier, and Chabrol all thought it hardly honorable to turn French warships over to a foreign Power, and all preferred to supply money rather than ships. The principal opposition came from the minister of war and the minister of marine: Bourmont impatiently advocated a direct expedition by France; Haussez flatly told the king that he would resign sooner than cede the ships. In fact he opposed the entire Drovetti plan, declaring it beneath the dignity of France to ask anyone else to avenge her injuries.[28]

In the face of such strong opposition, a compromise had to be worked out. The result was a counterproposal—to lend Egypt twenty million francs without interest and to give Mehemet Ali eight million francs toward the purchase or construction of the desired war vessels. This new proposal was accepted by the council on January 3, 1830, and approved by the king. For four days thereafter Polignac busied himself with the instructions for Mimaut and Huder and with the draft of the convention which Mehemet Ali would be asked to sign. Ready on January 7, they were carried to Toulon by Drovetti, who was also to consult with Huder on various aspects of the problem.[29]

Quite significant was the language instructed to be used to cover the protection Mehemet Ali had sought against England. Protection was refused, but the "good offices" of France were promised. The pasha was to be told that nothing would so soon provoke England's opposition as to see the French marine take an active part in the expedition. Polignac, though inexplicit with respect to support other than moral, again assured Mehemet Ali that all Europe would approve the venture. One moral advantage for Egypt was to be emphasized—namely, that the willingness of France to sign a convention with the pasha amounted to a virtual recognition of his independence. Mimaut and Huder were cautioned against signing any engagements obligating France to make war against England if the latter should interfere with the pasha's campaigns. To make doubly sure, Polignac explicitly excluded any modification of the draft article extending to Egypt the "good offices" of France in relation to other governments. As a safeguard against paying for services which might not be rendered, the draft convention also stipulated that the expedition should be personally commanded by Ibrahim Pasha, should consist of not less than 40,000 men, and should be continued by land if England interfered by sea. As for the ships, France did not think that Mehemet Ali would need them, for two reasons: his would be primarily a land expedition, and France could give naval support at Algiers under cover of the continuance of her blockade.[30]

The refusal to grant protection against England may be partly explained by the concern shown by France at that juncture about the inferior size of her Mediterranean squadron as compared with the British.[31] Aberdeen in reply informed France that the large British squadron was necessary to protect British commerce and the Ionian Islands because Greece appeared hostile to England and because the Russian squadron was still in the Levant.[32]

If Mehemet Ali accepted the counterproposal, France expected to win part of the Tunisian coast, together with an indemnity. In the draft convention, which Mimaut was authorized to sign if only minor changes were made, appears the first tabulation of the specific French objectives. The reduction of Algiers was to be the principal object of Mehemet Ali's expedition; piracy was to be abolished; the persons and property of foreigners in the three regencies were to be protected; the privileges already acquired by foreign commerce were to be preserved; all exclusive commercial advantages for France were barred; but France herself was to hold the Tunisian coast from Seybas to the Red Cape, and reparations for the financial losses to the French and Roman subjects were to be provided. Other points covered by the draft convention were as follows: French artillery officers would be provided if requested; under no circumstances need France supply war materials; the subsidy would be paid in installments beginning in February; and, if possible, some Egyptian guarantees for repayment of the loan might be inserted.[33]

Polignac became more insistent upon treating Mehemet Ali as virtually independent when five days later a special messenger appeared in Paris with Guilleminot's dispatches concerning the failure to win the firman and the offer of the Porte to send a special negotiator. In view of this information, supplemental instructions were issued to Huder. Polignac, whether he actually believed it or not, directed Huder to inform Mehemet Ali that the Porte appeared unlikely to sanction the expedition: the Turks, he said, had little confidence in its success and feared that to approve it would needlessly compromise their relations with the regencies. Mehemet Ali, however, was left free to assess these Turkish considerations at whatever value he liked. The French agents were to tell the pasha that "the refusal of the Porte and the information it probably already has given to the other Powers was a very pressing motive for hastening the departure of the expedition." The Turkish proposal to send a special envoy to Algeria was regarded in Paris as unimportant. On the same day, January 12, Huder wrote Boghos again to suggest that the pasha abandon his request for four war vessels.[34]

7. Notifications to the Great Powers

The premature disclosure of the plan by the Porte destroyed the resolution of secrecy which Polignac had kept until that time. He broke his official silence toward England on January 12, when he confidentially revealed to Rothesay that he had just received the direct overture from Egypt. Three days later almost identical confidential communications were drafted to inform Russia, Austria, Prussia, and Great Britain of some of the French negotiations with Egypt, to justify the venture, and to prepare them for the possible later French conquest of Algeria. The communications sketched the French attempts at conciliation with Algeria and attributed the basic difficulty to the type of government in Algeria. Only the destruction of the Algerian regime, stated Polignac, could give France satisfaction for the past and guarantees for the future. Since the city of Algiers had been fortified, an army must be sent to reduce it. But Mehémet Ali's proposal would effect the same result "in a manner equally advantageous for all the Powers of Europe." Mehemet Ali wished to conquer all three regencies, ending piracy there. France was in peaceful relations with Tunisia and Tripoli but could aid against Algeria. Hence France would be willing to leave the whole matter to Mehemet Ali to attain the general European objective of abolishing both piracy and the enslavement of Christians in the regencies. According to Polignac, the Turkish foreign minister had first approved, then disapproved, the venture. France did not think that the absence of the Turkish authorization would stop the pasha. Finally, he stated, if this negotiation failed, the king of France would "terminate the Algerian affair in the manner which seemed most convenient to him."[35] The approval of the several Great Powers was sought. In his communication to Russia,

Polignac acknowledged Pozzo di Borgo's assurances that Russia had "completely adopted" the project.[36] The laying of the foundation for independent negotiations with Egypt as well as for the subsequent direct French action against Algeria was more strongly emphasized in Polignac's reply to Turkey's refusal of the firman. The Porte was now to be told that its refusal to coöperate had left France free to follow her own course of conduct; notifications to this effect were being dispatched to the principal Powers. Huder was to return to Alexandria, and presumably the expedition would soon start. Assuming that the Porte would oppose the project, Guilleminot was to meet that contingency in his comments with Turkey. Although France would not promise in writing to make war in support of the enterprise, she was ready "to declare in a most formal manner that she would view with extreme displeasure any measure taken by the Porte against Mehemet Ali while that prince was engaged in an activity in which France, so to speak, was associated." France would protect Mehemet Ali against Turkey if Egypt signed the convention, and Rigny's squadron would prevent an encounter between the Turkish squadron and the Egyptian squadron and convoys. Guilleminot was directed to use a language of quiet reserve toward all the diplomats except the Russian envoy, confining his remarks to the explanation as officially communicated to the Powers.[37]

8. REACTIONS

The military classes, especially those of Austria and Russia, expressed skepticism of the feasibility of the plan. Metternich reflected the advice of the Austrian militarists when he doubted Mehemet Ali's ability to execute the undertaking.[38] At St. Petersburg, where numerous militarists, like Muraviev, knew the ways of Oriental warfare and where the tsar always consulted the commercial classes before undertaking military operations, the plan evoked two opinions. To the militarists the scheme "seriously discredited" France; the idea of sending a large Egyptian army along the relatively barren African coasts made the entire operation impractical. Because of their views Nicholas appreciated the ephemeral phases of the projected expedition. He supported it, however, for two reasons, his regard for France and the preference of his commercial classes. The expedition, if successful, would eliminate piracy and thus safeguard Russian commerce in the Mediterranean. The new guarantees won from Turkey at Adrianople might be jeopardized if Mehemet Ali met reverses in the attempt (because of non-support by any European Power?) or if the Barbary regencies won their independence.[39]

Although both Prussia and Austria disliked the idea of adding the three regencies to the administrative responsibilities of Mehemet Ali, the Prussian reaction was in general favorable. Bernstorff told Mortier that the Prussian government would indicate through its Egyptian consul an interest in the expedition. The gains, he observed, would be worthwhile provided Mehemet Ali would promise to remain true to the sultan.[40] Bernstorff instructed the Prussian consul at Alexandria to state confidentially but positively that Prussia "was perfectly in accord with France on the spirit and the principle of the projected expedition."[41] Metternich, on the other hand, assumed toward France an evasive attitude;[42] but he agreed with Aberdeen that the projected alliance between France and Egypt could not be considered "regular and legitimate."[43]

Although Austria showed reserve, the only prompt and vigorous objection came from Great Britain. The reasons for the British opposition seem obvious. They were something more than the jealousy superficially attributed to England by Drovetti. Strategically, England did not want French establishments in Tunisia; Wellington and Aberdeen requested explanations from Polignac on that score.[44] Commercially, there were two reasons. The British were just beginning their economic rediscovery of the eastern Mediterranean;[45] and, as we shall see, their projected new route to India had just been placed under serious study. Politically, the French plan seemed to oppose the British thesis of the desirability of maintaining the Ottoman Empire. The policy had been formally announced at the time of the Peace of Adrianople. England upheld Turkey as the lesser of two evils, Aberdeen not knowing any other way to postpone solution of the Near Eastern question and at the same time to provide a reasonably tolerable status for the inevitable international rivalry in the Levant. According to the British view Turkey needed to be stronger in order to hold her own against Russia, whereas she could only be weakened by the French plan of independent action through Egypt. Given Russia on one side and France with a pro-Egyptian and pro-Russian policy on the other,

Turkey would be wedged in between the imperialism of two Great Powers, making the British policy of maintaining Turkey more difficult to apply. Great Britain did not know of Russia's secret determinations in favor of Turkey; she did know that her own prestige in the Levant would be jeopardized by the French project.

The first official discussion at London in rejoinder to the notification took place on January 23 between Wellington and Laval. Wellington evidenced surprise that France would go beyond Algeria, into Tunisia and Tripoli, to get satisfaction. He emphasized the importance of the Turkish refusal of the firman; in his opinion that amounted to the formal disapprobation of the plan. "The alliance of Mehemet Ali with France," he said, "will be envisaged as a combination fatal for the Ottoman Empire." He invited the French government to renounce its design of a concert with the government of Egypt. Laval stated, in reply, that the hour of counsels was past and that France was determined to act. Personally Laval believed Wellington to be jealous of the French advance. Aberdeen's report to Rothesay of Wellington's comments to Laval added further details. Wellington had suggested to the French ambassador that the démarche would substitute French for Turkish control in the regencies—not a desirable method for eliminating piracy; in any event, France was strong enough to obtain satisfaction from Algeria without asking Egypt to aid. Aberdeen, on his own account, stated next day that Mehemet Ali's proposing the move had been quite irregular.[46]

But the British did more than refuse the request of France for their concert in the negotiations. Besides stationing Admiral Malcolm before Algiers, they sent two pointed instructions to their agents in the Levant which were to have telling effects—immediately, as an influence on the government at Paris, and later in the Near East. Barker was directed (January 29, 1830) to warn Mehemet Ali "to weigh well the serious consequences of the enterprise in which he seems disposed to engage" and to express the British opinion that France should settle her troubles with Algeria without recourse to so questionable an alliance as that proposed with Egypt.[47] Gordon was instructed to urge the Porte to secure amends from the dey to France, while the British government would try to check the French.[48]

Another reaction, quite minor, was the speculation at Constantinople on the origins of the plan. Gordon and Ottenfels agreed that it had originated not with Mehemet Ali but with the French agents in Egypt. Gordon suggested that the affair had not been so much a "secret" at St. Petersburg as at London and Vienna.[49]

9. An Abrupt Shift

Before the British rejoinders had gone further than the instruction of January 29, Polignac had appreciated the French error. From Drovetti on, he and his associates had based their assumptions on the unlikelihood of England's open opposition; they had not counted on her indirect action through Turkey and Egypt. Although doubts regarding Mehemet Ali's ability to complete the project and the disinclination of some of his colleagues in the council may have been important, England's attitude was the principal reason assigned by Polignac, in his note to the French council on January 29, for the abrupt shift in French policy which then occurred. The other reasons given were the Porte's refusal of the firman (previously regarded as unimportant) and the delayed execution of the plan. The shift to the policy of direct action against Algeria, though sudden, came logically, as the result of all the factors enumerated.

Judging by the note to the French council, the communications from Laval in London led to the belief that England would—through Turkey—oppose the venture. Hence it was now regarded as wise for the French to abandon the projected coöperation with Egypt and themselves to advance directly against Algeria. If the council approved, the projected convention with Egypt would exclude Algeria as a region for action by Egypt, would reduce the subsidies available to Mehemet Ali, and would require only 25,000 instead of 40,000 Egyptian troops. Besides Algeria, some of the Tunisian littoral might be reserved for France also. The French negotiators should state to Mehemet Ali that the difficulties of conquering Algeria necessitated the new decision. If the superseding instructions arrived in Egypt after the signing of the previously authorized convention, the French negotiators must tell the pasha that the convention could not be ratified. A new draft of the convention was made, and the council immediately approved this line of action.[50]

Next day, machinery was set in motion to transform the negotiations of Mimaut and Huder. The ministry of marine unsuccessfully attempted to have a war vessel overtake the "Eclipse," which had belatedly sailed on January 21, and halt the negotiations. New instructions, carried by Langsdorff, another special agent, notified Egypt that premature publicity had compromised the success of the project and that England had already sent Admiral Malcolm with two war vessels to wait before Algiers. France would therefore proceed alone with plans for conquering Algeria. Her first objectives would be Oran and Bône, the respective western and eastern ports, before attacking the fortified city of Algiers. Meanwhile, as if confident that Mehemet Ali would accept the modified project, Polignac directed the ministry of finance to prepare to pay the newly apportioned subsidy of ten million francs upon the signing of the modified draft convention.[51]

Two days after the decision, Aberdeen expressed to Laval more strongly than had Wellington the reasons for British disapproval of the scheme, suggesting again that France renounce it. None of Laval's explanations sufficed to disarm the British suspicions. France, stated Aberdeen, had shown a lack of confidence that justified British suspicions. Although he had received word of the Drovetti plan four months earlier, repeated questions at Paris had evoked only denials. The suggestion of the modified plan was now disclosed. "The British minister persists," wrote Laval, "in the opinion that an alliance of any kind, formed with a subject of the Porte and without the preliminary consent of the Porte, is an irregular negotiation." The plan had led to distrust among the Powers who had been kept in the dark. Laval suggested that probably Rothesay had overemphasized the "mystery" aspect of it.[52] Only upon learning from Vienna that Metternich shared his view of the irregularity of the transaction did Aberdeen show less aggressiveness. Both London and Vienna were confident that the Porte would never issue the firman, without which Mehemet Ali would not dare to make an expedition.[53]

According to a new report from Constantinople—a ciphered dispatch of January 6 from Guilleminot, received in Paris on February 9—the Porte had declared that it had nothing in common with Algeria but that it would send Tahir Pasha to Algeria to negotiate. This admission by Turkey simplified, in Polignac's opinion, the question of the projected French expedition.[54]

The next problem in applying the new policy was to prepare for the direct French expedition against Algeria. Various strategic aspects of the problem were discussed on February 6 in the French council, with naval officers present. Active preparations were launched on February 10,[55] Bourmont being named commander of the expedition. By this time the French military and naval officials agreed that the only effect of the Drovetti plan had been to delay action for four months. The approaching expedition was announced to the French Chamber on March 2. Since the Chamber was prorogued until September immediately after the address, there was no opportunity for parliamentary debates on the new policy. Much opposition was, however, voiced through pamphlets.

The rupture of the negotiations with Egypt was announced to England by Laval on March 12. Aberdeen expressed no surprise. To Laval, indeed, he seemed to take credit for the collapse of the scheme.[56]

In the change of policy France had in fact done nothing more than what Wellington in his conversation of January 23 had unwittingly suggested. In the long run Egypt was to be lost but Algeria won.

10. Huder Fails

Although stormy seas had delayed Huder's second departure from Toulon for Egypt, he had left eight days before the new decision of the council. Two factors foredoomed his new negotiations to failure—the unwillingness of France to cede the four large warships and the abrupt change in French policy. On the second trip there were two distinct periods during which Huder tried his persuasive qualities: the first included what was done between February 12 and February 17, or until the arrival of Langsdorff; the second, the month of the finale to the now hopeless Drovetti plan.

In the first period, Huder in Alexandria at once began lengthy conversations on the original French counterproposal with Boghos and Osman Bey, neither Mehemet Ali nor Ibrahim being there at the moment. Mimaut soon came down from Cairo to second him. The conversations were reported to Mehemet Ali, who, instead of coming himself, sent Ibrahim to Alexandria to carry on the negotiations. Contrary to the French expectation, Ibrahim took all the communications *ad referendum*. Mehemet Ali then refused the counterproposal.

For the second period, an impressive array of French power was displayed at Alexandria with the arrival of Langsdorff and the sharp modifications of the counterproposal. Three French warships, each having borne an official, were anchored there. The negotiations were kept secret from the other foreign consular establishments.[57] Since Mimaut and Huder had been convinced that Mehemet Ali could not be argued into accepting the counterproposal, Huder's first task was now to go to Boghos and Osman and retrace all that he had said in the conversations. When Ibrahim desired to have the modified French proposition submitted, Huder thought best to transmit it along with an explanatory note; Mimaut agreed, since Polignac's instruction of February 1 made mandatory substitution of the third plan for the other two projects.[58] Mehemet Ali definitely rejected the project which would have given him French coöperation with a loan-subsidy of ten million francs in his conquest of Tripoli and most of Tunisia. His decision was again conveyed by the otherwise noncommittal Ibrahim. Repeated attempts were made to reopen the matter on the new French basis. By March 8 the pasha's decision had become so unequivocal that the French agents were left in a daze. They could only report that the influence of Barker had been conspicuous on the day before the arrival of Mehemet Ali's refusal.[59]

That was when Barker impressively communicated to Mehemet Ali in person the British opposition to the project and their warning. He was reassured that the French offer would not be accepted without British concurrence. During the conference, the pasha revealed to him for the first time the full history of the negotiations with France and turned the tables on England by requesting an alliance with Great Britain. If England supported him, said Mehemet Ali, the sultan would soon have an Egyptian army of 125,000 to help against the Russians, while the British would find that army useful in keeping Russia out of Persia. Eventually, according to the pasha, the British must meet the Russians in Asia; Egyptian power alone provided adequate means of checking Russia in the Levant. Besides, Egypt might aid England in other ways, for example by supplying cotton in the event of another war with the United States.[60]

Huder, before departing from Egypt, held several further meetings with Egyptian officials. On March 20 was repeated the previous Egyptian request for the sale from the naval stores at Toulon of timber for constructing two war vessels. The ministry of marine refused the request on May 4.[61]

The epilogue of Huder's failure was Polignac's dispatch to Mimaut on May 6, stating that the disruption of the negotiations under the Drovetti plan had not altered the French favor for Mehemet Ali. Mimaut was chided for having communicated in writing both the drafted convention and an explanatory note before agreement with Egypt on the principal points, thus enabling Mehemet Ali to show the documents to the other Powers. Mimaut then had Boghos return the originals to him (on July 12).[62]

Although Franco-Egyptian relations had cooled for the moment, as illustrated by Mehemet Ali's overture for an alliance with England, Barker believed that the events set in motion by the negotiations had led the pasha still to prepare the people of Egypt for an eventual rupture with the Porte.[63] Aberdeen evaded a direct answer to the Egyptian overture. As we know already, such an alliance would have been contrary to the Wellington-Aberdeen policy of supporting a strengthened Turkey as a barrier against Russia. We shall see that Palmerston in 1833 preferred Turkey to Egypt as holder of the Syrian routes to India. Britain's later pro-Egyptian policy, in its various well-known aspects, came into force only with Disraeli—and after the Suez Canal had been opened.

Mehemet Ali, having learned of the British attitude, seemed inclined to turn back again to France. Late in April he told Mimaut that, if the expedition had taken place the previous November, he would have risked the sultan's disapproval: now he could not leave Egypt exposed to resentment from that quarter. Late in June he declared that France need depend only on him, and upon no other friends, for the control of Tunisia and Tripoli. He predicted that within a few years he would have "a flourishing commerce, twenty cavalry regiments, fifteen vessels of the line, and thirty-five frigates," Egypt then becoming the fourth naval power of the world. Mehemet Ali expected the early demise of the Ottoman Empire, describing its navy as too weak even to occupy Crete. He now—as Mimaut reported—awaited events "with great confidence, or at least with much resignation."[64] Despite failure, French Levantine policy had been oriented toward Egypt as against Turkey. The groundwork had been laid for the significant developments which were to come during the First Syrian War (1832–1833).

11. EXPERIMENT IN ALGERIA

With the analysis of the Egyptian background of the French expedition to Algeria completed, the details of diplomacy for this part of the section have ended. Aberdeen now attempted to circumscribe the French imperial experiment in Algeria, but that is another problem. The French challenge to empire in Algeria dates from the forced capitulation of the fortress of Casabana on July 5, 1830. Although the French government which had instituted the experiment there was overthrown in the July Revolution, the work was continued by its successors. It still continues. This is attested by the hundreds of cartons of documents on Algeria in the archives of the ministry of war in Paris. The Levant had contributed its part in the emergence of the new French empire even if the steppingstone of Egypt had only appeared to be well lodged and even if Drovetti in the original plan for Egyptian coöperation had not considered the possibility of open action by Great Britain through indirect means.

12. FRENCH COMMERCE IN EGYPT

With the collapse of the Drovetti plan, French interest in Egypt shifted to the commercial problem. As early as February, 1830, some French merchants petitioned Mimaut to correct the Egyptian abuses to trade. They wanted a new and better tariff agreement with the Ottoman Empire on the expiration of the old one in November and they wanted still more the enforcement of the Turkish capitulations in Egypt. For example, they could not count on the 3-per cent duty, even when trade was permitted at all. The rates in practice varied from 7 to 30 per cent, while the pasha's monopolies and farming-out system extended to the principal agricultural and industrial products. If allowed the virtual free trade provided by the capitulations, they estimated that Egypt might supply a million bales of cotton a year, together with increased quantities of indigo, sugar, and coffee. Mimaut, though acknowledging the justice of the claims of what he termed the "young French merchants," answered them only by recommending patience. He referred the problem to Polignac, remarking upon Barker's vain attempts to have the pasha institute some exceptions to the trade restrictions.[65] Then came the July Revolution in France.

The reply to Mimaut's recommendation of improving the legal

bases for trade in Egypt was deferred until several months after Sebastiani was called to the French foreign office in November, 1830. Sebastiani, whose intimate association with French policy in the Levant during the Napoleonic period had given him a keen insight into the general problem, sent a judicious reply suggesting the essential lines of French commercial policy toward Turkey and Egypt. France and the other foreign states, he wrote, already enjoyed in Turkey lower rates under the capitulatory system than those available in other countries. He therefore thought it prudent not to touch that "old monument." Indeed, he regarded even a discussion of it impractical at the moment because Turkey might ask for reciprocity, the granting of which could not be advantageous to France. As to the tariff, some changes would be desirable. Yet, as he pointed out, the old tariff was advantageous to French merchants because of the then depreciated Turkish money. French policy now did not permit the revision of the Franco-Turkish tariff in advance of the other Powers lest the latter secure better rates on certain items of trade. Special difficulties were obvious for Egypt. "It would appear doubtful," he observed, "whether the renewal of our tariff would have all the advantageous results in Egypt which French merchants expect, more especially since their idea seems to be the complete suppression of the handicaps to trade." The complaints against the Egyptian monopolies were not, he said, the consequence of tariff defects, nor were they due to the conduct of Turkey. "Therefore," he concluded, "we must ask Mehemet Ali for the redress of our grievances." If Mimaut wished, a direct démarche to Egypt would be made.[66]

There the matter was allowed to rest. Mimaut in reply did not suggest a direct approach. Although continuing to criticize the Egyptian system, he stated that there appeared, at least, to be some improvement; he had cautioned French merchants to use more prudence in their speculations. Mehemet Ali might change his custom of permitting cotton sales in advance of production, but Mimaut doubted the possibility of his changing the system of trade in general.[67]

The cotton of Egypt especially appealed not only to French traders in Egypt but also to manufacturers in France. Mimaut urged the pasha to favor French merchants and reported some "appreciable ameliorations" and tendencies toward regularization of the cotton trade. In 1830 Egypt exported cotton to the value of 10,000,000 francs, of which Marseille took 40 per cent. Speculation by traders on advance crops continued, and the pasha himself also used this resource as a means of financing his new naval construction program. One firm (M. Pastre) contracted in advance for some of the anticipated cotton but was unable to finance the agreement. Mimaut intervened with an arrangement that saved the contract. Besides the two most important French buyers of cotton and other produce, who speculated both for their own and the pasha's account, there were two other important operators. One was Boghos Yousouff, then chief of the Egyptian commercial administration. The other was Samuel Briggs of London, who spent some fifteen months in Egypt renewing his contacts and extending the activities of his famous company at Alexandria. A part of his activity concerned the purchase of cotton by anticipation. Briggs, so reported Mimaut, furnished all sorts of mediocre-quality naval supplies to the pasha at high prices, taking in payment the pledges of part of the forthcoming cotton production. There was danger, therefore, that the obligations thus taken by the pasha in advance would divert the cotton of Egypt from Marseille to Liverpool. An excellent cotton crop was reported for 1831, making considerable activity for the British and French shipping.[68]

The grain trade was watched with interest also. In December, 1830, Sebastiani requested detailed observations on the quantities, prices, qualities, and movements of Egyptian grains. Mimaut explained that the situation would not permit answers to some of the questions. There was, in fact, no public market in Egypt. The government, sole proprietor of the lands, took through purchase what was left to the farmer after he paid his taxes. All grain destined for general consumption or for sale was deposited in government warehouses. Ordinarily, the price was fixed for a full year. The import of grain was prohibited. Crop shortages in 1829 and 1830 led the government to permit the cultivators to sell. Little actually found its way to the consumers' market, however, the price being arbitrary and high. Early in January, 1831, a market was opened at Cairo and Alexandria with operations based on the officially established price. Some Egyptian grain was exported by way of the Red Sea to India in English boats.[69]

In 1831 came a gradual increase in the number of commodities which the pasha farmed out. By that time the danger of an Egyptian war with Turkey increased the uncertainties, and much French capital at Alexandria was unemployed. The ravages of a great plague almost suspended commerce at Alexandria in August, 1831. By October trade was again under way. F. de Lesseps was then commissioned as French vice-consul in the city. By November, with the abundant cotton crop, French merchants were concentrating on that staple. "Mehemet Ali well knows that the real resources of Egypt lie in her agricultural products," wrote Mimaut; but he, like other foreign consuls, called attention to the pasha's attempts to extend some of the forms of indigenous manufacturing. Especially was there new activity in the arsenal at Alexandria, where all Egyptian war vessels were armed or rearmed. Naval production in 1831 was illustrated by the completion of a vessel carrying 100 guns.[70]

Shipping at Alexandria fluctuated considerably. In 1829 there had been a diminution of the numbers and tonnage of European ships at Alexandria and an increase of Ottoman ships of commerce there. In 1830 the total shipping was represented by 1,573 vessels of 283,754 aggregate tons, approximately two-thirds of which were Turkish. France sent only 79 vessels, totaling 17,064 tons. The general movement of Egyptian foreign commerce showed a total of about 70,000,000 francs, the French part being 8,500,000 francs. Many Greek vessels sought French protection, and papers were freely accorded them at Constantinople and Smyrna. Mimaut obtained from the Egyptian government an understanding that they pay only the traditional 3-per cent duty instead of the 12-per cent usual for Ottoman merchandise. The arrangement was based on the fiction that the Greeks had transshipped the Ottoman merchandise at a Greek port.[71]

A new activity for Mimaut after 1830 was the handling of certain Algerian affairs. Egypt became a haven for refugees from Algeria. Some, on their own request, passed over to French protection.[72] The purchase of Algerian horses by Egypt, authorized by the French government in May, 1831, won the thanks of the pasha.[73] Deeper gratitude, however, was expressed when France, early in 1831, donated to Egypt two Algerian war vessels, a frigate and a corvette which had lain at Alexandria for four years. One month after the capture of Algiers France claimed the vessels by right of succession to the former dey's possessions. Turkey sought the same vessels but Mehemet Ali refused to deliver them to Constantinople. He meanwhile had repaired the vessels at his own expense. He sought refunds for the repairs if France took the ships. When Mimaut reported that the vessels were not worth the value of their complete repair, the French government in February, 1830, gave up its claim to the vessels in favor of Mehemet Ali.[74]

On July 21, 1831, Sebastiani instructed Mimaut to make representations against the pasha's commercial system in Crete, especially the prohibition against the free export of oil, the principal product of the island. The restriction was stated to be against the promises of the pasha. Mehemet Ali should be asked to send orders to Crete revoking the measure, "justly complained against by the inhabitants and by foreign merchants."[75] The matter had already been discussed in Egypt, Mehemet Ali appearing disposed to meet the French suggestions. The measure had been instituted as a new means of raising Egypt's revenues.[76]

13. SPECTER ON THE HORIZON

Early in December, 1829, Mimaut had sent Polignac two reports on a new subject, one liable to hamper the seeming plan of France for making Mehemet Ali her lieutenant in the Levant. According to the first report (December 4) there was now much discussion of a projected new British route through Egypt to India. In Mimaut's opinion the British were laying the foundations for geographical, political, and commercial progress in Egypt. According to the second report, five days later, the plans for the route were further advanced than he had realized. There was at that moment a British corvette at Alexandria awaiting mail and passengers from India. Mehemet Ali, having evaded the suggestion for four years, appeared embarrassed by the new development.[77] Let us examine this specter on the horizon.

In the late twenties the Board of Commissioners for the Affairs of India (popularly known as the Board of Control) in London, actuated by the rising importance of steam, began studying the feasibility of steam communications with India by way of the Red Sea. Although this was an academic matter at first, the aid of the British consular organization in the Levant was later obtained to make surveys. The problem was to discover the relative merits of routes utilizing the Red Sea or the Persian Gulf. The establishment of a route through the eastern Mediterranean would greatly increase the importance of that area for British imperial interests and obviously would excite the jealousy of France.

In 1829 the warship "Thetis" of the East India Company was sent to the Red Sea to make investigations concerning depots for mail between Great Britain and India, the establishment of trading posts in Abyssinia and Arabia, and coaling stations.[78] In December another ship, the "Benares," was sent to Judda to survey that part of the Red Sea. In addition to passengers it brought mail consigned to Alexandria under care of Barker,[79] as Mimaut had learned. Before the "Benares" completed its work still another vessel, the "Palinurus," was sent all the way to the Isthmus of Suez to investigate. This had been the first merchant or other foreign ship to arrive at Suez for ten years. About the same amount of shipping was reported for Kosseir, except for occasional visits by grain vessels carrying supplies to Mehemet Ali's troops at Judda or an occasional Egyptian war brig accidentally there for repairs. About 120 small native coastal vessels were carrying on an unimportant trade between Judda and Gambu. Suez was considered a safe port.[80] In December the "Thetis" returned to the Red Sea, this time going to Kosseir with mail and passengers.[81]

A more expeditious transport of mail to India was the purpose of these surveys. At that time about five months was normally required for a voyage from London to India around South Africa. Early in 1829 James W. Taylor had asked the British government to establish a combination sea and overland route utilizing Alexandria, Cairo, and Suez, a journey to India by that route being estimated at less than two months. The matter had been referred to the postoffice department, where it was turned down. Aberdeen was dubious about the expediency of a change, especially since at that time mail for India required transportation without charge by boats going to India on the established route.[82] The government coöperated with the East India Company at the end of the year, however, by referring the question to its Near Eastern consuls. Memoranda from various sections resulted.

Barker believed that the existence of the strong government in Egypt under Mehemet Ali or his son Ibrahim would guarantee the unmolested transit of mail overland between Suez and Alexandria.[83]

Samuel Briggs shared this opinion, pronouncing Mehemet Ali strong enough to control the route even on the Arabian side. Yet Briggs pointed out the preponderance of influence then held by France in Egypt.[84]

Barker, having analyzed various routes, concluded that a Euphrates route utilizing Aleppo and Basra would be preferable to any Red Sea route, provided the river was navigable during all seasons. If a Red Sea route were established, however, Kosseir rather than Suez should be the terminal for steam vessels going to India, since land transport from Kosseir to Alexandria at all times of the year could be made in seven days. A Red Sea route by way of Suez to Lake Menzaleb was regarded as impractical.[85]

The British consul at Beirut recommended a route across the desert from Beirut to Bagdad or Basra rather than a more northern route through Aleppo, because it would be less subject to interruption and danger. He estimated that a journey of twenty-two days would be required from London, Marseille, or Ancona to Basra, from which point steamers would reach Bombay in five or six additional days.[86]

Clearly, the political status of Egypt must be weighed in determining any route through the Near East. In 1830, F. R. Chesney, later dominant in the British experiment with the Euphrates route, was commissioned by Gordon to travel in Egypt and Asia Minor to procure information. He found that Mehemet Ali desired complete independence as well as the annexation of either Abyssinia or Syria. Meanwhile, Egypt had aided the Porte with money and in terminating a rising in Crete. The pasha counted explicitly on France but feared Great Britain. From a military point of view, the Egyptian army was altogether too large in proportion to the size and population of the province. A Turkish attack on Egypt by the sea would be difficult, Chesney thought, whereas one by land through Syria would be relatively easy. Egypt was found to maintain many manufacturing plants, devoted mostly to arms and ships. These were operated with success, but expensively, as was also true of the cotton and silk establishments.[87]

Chesney attempted to discover what were the impediments to, and facilities for, steam communications with India. He visited Suez and Lake Menzaleb and sailed the Red Sea to Kosseir. He favored steam for the Red Sea because sailing vessels, to avoid coral rocks, must keep to the Arabian side. For steam it would be necessary only to establish coaling stations. The question of how high in the Red Sea the steamers should ascend was examined. As a terminus, Chesney preferred Kosseir, though he saw no difficulties to developing the terminus at Suez. The easier route would be Red Sea–Kosseir–overland to Qina—a journey of only thirty-two hours—and thence along the Nile to Cairo in small river boats. More difficulties would be found in crossing the Isthmus of Suez than from Kosseir to Qina, but either route would serve to connect the Red Sea with the Mediterranean. Chesney believed that Mehemet Ali would make trouble even though professing to coöperate. "It is natural," he said, "that he should not desire to make Egypt the channel of such an important intercourse as must draw the attention of Europe to that part of the world."[88] The Austrian consul at Alexandria made a trip to investigate the same problem on his own account in 1830.[89]

The practicability of navigating the Red Sea by steam was proved by four trips of an East India Company steamer from Bombay to Suez between 1830 and 1833. At that time, however, British steam service between Alexandria and Malta had not been opened, though the British squadron had sent steam packets between Malta and Gibraltar since 1825.

In England between 1830 and 1832 there was much public agitation for a Near Eastern route. The result was the appointment, in 1832, of a "select parliamentary committee" to investigate both trade and steam communications. Agitation for the Euphrates route continued. In September, 1830, James W. Taylor secured some commercial concessions from the pasha of Bagdad, including an exclusive grant of steam navigation of the Tigris for ten years. The plan was halted in its infancy by the sudden death of its originator.[90] Thomas Waghorn was another Englishman who sought to connect England with India through Egypt.[91]

The East India Company's interest in navigating the Red Sea was not paralleled at the outset by British steam services in the Mediterranean. The French, however, applied steam to the Mediterranean, establishing their first commercial steamboat service between Marseille and the Levant in 1830. Guilleminot in 1831 advised establishing regular steamer communications between Constantinople and Marseille because the route used in practice, through Austria, was inconvenient and subjected commerce to extra delays for quarantines.[92] Experience soon proved, however, that this kind of enterprise exceeded the resources of private capital and industry. On July 3, 1835, several French governmental lines were created for transporting mail and passengers to the Levant. Assigned to the service were twenty-three steam vessels commanded by officers of the French marine.[93]

NOTES TO SECTION IV

[1] Cf. *Courrier français*, February 19, 1829.
[2] Barker to Aberdeen, August 18, 1829, FO 78 T 184.
[3] AE Egypte 1.
[4] This apparently refers to the period just before Drovetti's return to Egypt at the end of 1827.
[5] AE Egypte 1.
[6] AE Alexandrie 23.
[7] AE Egypte 1.
[8] Rothesay to Aberdeen, September 25, 1829, FO 27 F 396.
[9] News of the orders had been quickly disseminated to the chancelleries of Europe. For example, cf. dispatch of September 15, 1829, *ibid*.
[10] Rothesay to Aberdeen, October 5, 1829, *ibid*.
[11] AEMD Égypte 19, quoted by M. Sabry in *L'Empire égyptien sous Mohamed Ali* (Paris, 1930), pp. 169–172.
[12] Polignac to Guilleminot, October 10, 1829, AE Turquie 255.
[13] Polignac to Mortemart, October 14, 1829, AE Russie 178.
[14] Mortemart to Polignac, October 6, 1829, *ibid*.
[15] AE Egypte 1. Rothesay at once sensed that some new development was in the air about what he termed the "ill-advised" war which Polignac's predecessors had begun with Algeria. He reported to Aberdeen (on the same day) that France was preparing for "decided measures" by the spring of 1830 (FO 27 F 396).
[16] Polignac to Rayneval, November 26, 1829, AE Autriche 411.
[17] The Austrian consul believed Huder was there to announce that France would aid Mehemet Ali to win his independence (Acerbi to Metternich, November 24, 1829, HHSA Alexandrien, fol. 1).
[18] AE Alexandrie 23. At Paris, Minister of Marine d'Haussez on November 25 authorized the recruitment on a volunteer basis of the naval construction workers requested through Livron.
[19] Dispatch of November 28, *ibid*.
[20] AE Egypte 1; AE Alexandrie 23. A little personal jealousy had been aroused between Mimaut and Huder; Mimaut thought Huder as a military man had handicapped the negotiations.
[21] Pezzoni to Heyden, December 3, 1829 in R. Cattaui, *Le Règne de Mohamed Aly d'après les archives russes en Egypte* (Cairo, 1931), I, 369. Mimaut reported on December 9 that the pasha had available 40,000 men for the expedition (AE Alexandrie 23).
[22] Aberdeen to Rothesay, December 18, 1829, FO 27 F 390.
[23] AE Angleterre 629.
[24] AE Turquie 255.
[25] Gordon to Aberdeen, December 15, 1829, FO 78 T 181.
[26] AE Turquie 260.
[27] AE Egypte 1. Huder also asked for a better clarification of the respective roles of himself and Mimaut. On December 31 Polignac directed Huder to second the negotiations of Mimaut, adding that the consul general alone would sign the convention.
[28] *Mémoires du baron d'Haussez* (Paris, 1897), p. 135; J. Travers, *Journal de Gueron-Ranville* (Caen, 1873), pp. 9–16 (which incorrectly gives December 19 as the date for the refusal of the pasha's offer); MG Algérie, carton 1.
[29] AE Egypte 1.
[30] *Ibid*.
[31] FO 27 F 406.
[32] Aberdeen to Rothesay, January 8, 1830, FO 27 F 405. The British fleet in the Mediterranean at that time consisted of thirty-five vessels carrying 1,220 guns and a combined crew of 8,894.
[33] AE Egypte 1.

[34] *Ibid.*
[35] AE Angleterre 629.
[36] AE Russie 178.
[37] Polignac to Guilleminot, January 16, 1830, AE Turquie 260.
[38] AE Autriche 412.
[39] Mortemart to Polignac, February 22, 1830, AE Russie 180.
[40] Mortier to Polignac, February 5 and 25, 1830, AE Prusse 273.
[41] Dispatch of February 3, 1830, AE Egypte 1.
[42] AE Autriche 412.
[43] AE Angleterre 629.
[44] FO 27 F 405.
[45] See Vernon J. Puryear, *International Economics and Diplomacy in the Near East* (Stanford University, 1935).
[46] Laval to Polignac, January 24, 1830, AE Angleterre 629; Aberdeen to Rothesay, January 26, 1830, FO 27 F 405.
[47] Aberdeen to Barker, FO 78 T 192.
[48] Aberdeen to Gordon, January 25, 1830, FO 78 T 188.
[49] Ottenfels to Metternich, February 25, 1830, HHSA Türkei 31.
[50] AE Egypte 1.
[51] *Ibid.* The decision was notified to Guilleminot on February 9 (AE Turquie 260).
[52] Laval to Polignac, February 1, 1830, AE Angleterre 629.
[53] Laval to Polignac, February 11, 1830, *ibid.*
[54] AE Turquie 260. On March 24, 1830, Guilleminot sent in some new regulations by Turkey which sought to attach the regencies more closely to the Turkish government.
[55] Travers, *Gueron-Ranville*, p. 17.
[56] AE Angleterre 630.
[57] Barker to Gordon, February 22, 1830, FO 78 T 192.
[58] All this was reported to Polignac on February 23, 1830 (AE Egypte 2).
[59] *Ibid.*
[60] Barker to Aberdeen, March 8, 1830, FO 78 T 192.
[61] AE Egypte 2.
[62] *Ibid.*
[63] (March 25, 1830), FO 78 T 196. Gordon at Constantinople took the opposite view. He even suggested that some of the loud talk at Alexandria might be attributed to strong drink (FO 78 T 190).
[64] AE Egypte 2.
[65] AE Alexandrie 24.
[66] Sebastiani to Mimaut, April 25, 1831, AE Alexandrie 24.
[67] Mimaut to Sebastiani, June 23, 1831, *ibid.*
[68] *Ibid.*
[69] *Ibid.*
[70] *Ibid.*
[71] *Ibid.*
[72] *Ibid.*
[73] AE Egypte 2.
[74] MM, BB⁴, carton 539, cited by G. Douin in *La première guerre de Syrie*, I, 11–18.
[75] AE Alexandrie 24.
[76] AE Egypte 2.
[77] AE Alexandrie 23.
[78] R. Moresby (a surveyor) to Barker, May 1, 1829, FO 78 T 184.
[79] Barker to Malcolm, January 18, 1830, FO 78 T 192.
[80] Moresby to Barker, January 7, 1830, *ibid.*
[81] Barker to Malcolm, January 14, 1830, *ibid.*
[82] Taylor to Backhouse, January 14, 1829, FO 78 T 186.
[83] Barker to Malcolm, January 23, 1829, FO 78 T 184.

[84] Briggs to Backhouse (of the Foreign Office), FO 78 T 195.
[85] Barker to Aberdeen, May 2, 1830, FO 78 T 192.
[86] P. Abbott to Aberdeen, May 8, 1830, FO 78 T 194.
[87] Chesney to Gordon, August 26, 1830, FO 78 T 191.
[88] Chesney to Gordon, September 2, 1830, *ibid.*
[89] Acerbi to Metternich, April 10, 1830, HHSA Alexandrien, fol. 1.
[90] H. L. Hoskins, *British Routes to India*, pp. 80–127.
[91] Cf. FO 78 T 267 (1835).
[92] AE Turquie 262.
[93] S. Charléty, *La monarchie de juillet*, p. 195. All lines terminated at Marseille. They extended to Naples, Constantinople (via Malta and Smyrna), Alexandria (via Greece and Malta), Ajaccio, and Bastia. Regular service every ten days was maintained, with more frequent voyages, to Corsica.

V. THE WAR FOR SYRIA

FRENCH POLICY AND THE FIRST SYRIAN WAR

THERE WAS comparative quiet in the Levant for several months after the French conquest of Algiers. Mehemet Ali, not satisfied with his mastery of Egypt, Crete, Arabia, and a part of the Sudan, continued to provide a question mark. Syria was the apex of his territorial ambitions, while his complete independence from the Ottoman Empire was considered the logical result of his successful administration of a modern Egyptian empire. His original plan of winning these objectives from Turkey as the reward for his coöperation against Greece had ended with the intervention of the allies in 1827; now he laid plans for an open assault on Turkey to win them.

The Great Powers were well aware of the menace of Mehemet Ali's ambitions. The significance of the establishment of an independent and vigorous Arabic empire on the ruins of a part of Turkey, or, indeed, to replace Turkey, was obvious. The diplomats commonly supposed that such an empire would be supported by the continued political liaison between France and Egypt, thus adding a new potentiality which was not liked by Russia, Great Britain, and Austria. The best of the various combinations, they thought, would be to maintain Turkey in her essential position as a part of the European balance of power. The problems of Turkey were great, even without an Egyptian question. Her weakness was quite apparent; Russia's easy victory over her had demonstrated that clearly enough. Hence, while the Powers utilized their light war vessels in the Straits in the service of their watchful legations at Constaninople,[1] they kept vigilant eyes turned toward Alexandria. Because Russia wished to consolidate her new gains, she was perhaps more alert after Adrianople than any other Great Power to help Turkey resist a possible attack by Egypt.[2]

But nothing happened at first. The pasha did not at once utilize his opportunity for striking Turkey before she had time to recover from the effects of the Greek and Russo-Turkish wars. The Powers then concluded that if and when it became necessary they might restrain Egypt by diplomatic pressure alone. Meanwhile, Mehemet

[1] For notes to section v, see pp. 179–180.

Ali proceeded with the rebuilding of his navy, almost ruined at Navarino, and strengthened his army. The coming of the First Syrian, or Turco-Egyptian, War (1832–1833) proved how unwarranted was the complacent attitude of the Powers and how utterly unprepared they were for its contingencies. Nor was the timely intervention of Russia to be the last chapter in the Turco-Egyptian antagonism.

The political outlines of the first Turco-Egyptian war over Syria have been published many times. Syria was won by Egypt in 1833 because of the military successes of Ibrahim Pasha and the help accorded by French diplomacy. Sabry's monograph for the first time utilized the Egyptian archives, adding excerpts from previously inaccessible French documents, in his sympathetic study of the career of Mehemet Ali.[3] Only recently have we been given a documentary publication of adequate significance to amplify and clarify the many heretofore hidden factors in both the military and diplomatic phases of the conflict[4] which, in the end, was to split the Muslim world temporarily into two administrative parts. Although these documents, drawn from the French archives, are fairly complete and textually accurate, not all of the pertinent documents on French policy are included in the collection. The much-debated French policy in the First Syrian War merits detailed consideration. Hence the primary purpose of the two divisions of this section of our work will be to trace the chronological development of French diplomatic and commercial policy in the Levant from 1831 to July, 1833, integrating it with the successive major developments in the Levant and with the essential features of the policies of the other principal Powers. Our basis will be the original documents, now made available by the more liberal policy of the keepers of the archives of the French ministry of foreign affairs.

1. Conversations at Choubra

Mimaut proved a good listener during the spring and summer of 1831. Mehemet Ali seemed quite concerned about the aggressiveness of Abdullah Pasha of Acre. In February Mimaut reported to Paris that Mehemet Ali had already proposed to the Porte that he be given the administration of Syria in exchange for a large annual tribute. The pasha stated that he thought France and England would be friendly to this arrangement and that meanwhile he was expanding his army and navy to reënforce thus the authority of the sultan. The pasha judged that France especially would concert with him, because Egypt later would be able to support Turkey against Russia. Mehemet Ali optimistically stated that his part of the Turkish Empire would "double the number of available men and quadruple the means of execution," if such necessity arose. Mehemet Ali even went so far as to suggest that he would like to have Algeria also, if the reported possibility of the withdrawal of France had any foundation. Mimaut in reply confined his remarks to vague expressions of French good will for the pasha, but declined to commit himself to any specific application.

The pasha's attention had been drawn sharply to Syria by reports of extensive projects credited to Abdullah. Moreover, Mehemet Ali charged that Abdullah sheltered Egypt's enemies, debauched Egyptian workers, and facilitated contraband trade with Egypt. In March Mimaut reported that the pasha considered the time opportune for an advance into Syria, because now an additional factor had appeared. Anarchy throughout the Ottoman Empire seemed to be presaged by the revolt of Mustapha, pasha of Scutari, and by the threatened revolts of the Bosnians and Rumelians and of the pasha of Bagdad. Mehemet Ali constantly repeated to Mimaut, every time something was said of his squadron, that his ambition was at some time to act in concert with, or under orders of, the French marine. Mimaut thanked him for his friendly expressions. The French consul general perceived that even then the pasha was thinking of an hereditary rule for his family in Egypt and the provinces which bordered Egypt if the Ottoman Empire should crumble. The pasha thought also of creating an Arabian Caliphate. It was at this juncture that some favor to the pasha was shown by France when the donation of the two Algerian war vessels, discussed above, was notified. The occasion also served as a slight to Turkey, which had sought the same vessels. Mimaut at the same time relayed to Paris the information of a new plan, which was described as an "approaching explosion" in Turkey because of the Albanian revolt. The plan was to depose Sultan Mahmud and establish the legitimate heir on the throne to rule under a regency. Mehemet Ali did not doubt the success of the conspirators if the coup d'état were attempted. In any event, with Bosnia and Rumelia reportedly aligned for coöperation with Mustapha, Mehemet Ali made his plans to claim an extension of his territories to balance what would remain to Turkey. Mimaut encouraged the pasha to persevere "in his sytem of circumspection."[5]

During this and later periods, Mimaut had an advantage over his consular colleagues in Egypt since he treated personally with the pasha, whom he saw frequently, whereas they did not. It was clear from the reports that three possibilities had now appeared, the success of the revolt of Scutari, the detachment of Syria from Turkey, and the establishment of a regency to replace the sultan. All these potentialities were discussed fully by the pasha in his conversations with Mimaut at the Egyptian palace of Choubra on May 18. A secret agent of Mustapha had been sent to Egypt to get the views of Mehemet Ali. It was believed that the sultan had already planned to seek refuge in Russia if the coup d'état were successful. Of especial interest, however, was the disclosure that Mehemet Ali planned a countercoup on his own account in that event, despite the recent request of the sultan for the pasha to reaffirm his often repeated expressions of loyalty. Mehemet Ali was confronted with the alternative of losing the good will of the sultan if he encouraged the revolutionists or of losing his chance of easily winning Syria if he continued his loyalty to the sultan. He decided to promise support to neither side, meanwhile consolidating his position and increasing his preparations.

The pasha had decided, however, on an expedition of 36,000 men to chastise Abdullah. Obviously it was now to French interest to assume an attitude opposite that of the Drovetti plan, which would mean turning Egypt's surplus resources toward Syria instead of toward the Barbary regencies. Mimaut had no doubt that Syria was the goal of the pasha's ambition and that none of the preparations were directed against Algeria. Mehemet Ali thought that no one would oppose his campaign against Abdullah, not even the sultan. He suggested that the European Powers might here find "a happy application of the principle of nonintervention." Mimaut was careful not to commit the French government in advance. But, now that there would be actually no time to interfere, Mimaut considered the pasha's project "an irresistible event and a *fait accompli.*" He agreed to expedite his confidential communication to the French government. As a recommendation of the policy he was about to pursue in the new venture, Mehemet Ali gave reassurances on the status of Christians and foreign nationals if he should occupy Syria and Damas (Damascus). Here he stated that his ideas were "liberal." Damas would not be included in the project until he heard the views of France. Especially did Mehemet Ali solicit the support of the French government with respect to the British reactions to the plan. The next day presumably reliable information was at hand which indicated that the end of the sultan's reign was near. "It is finished!" shouted the pasha.

An Egyptian warship was placed at the disposal of the special messenger commissioned by Mimaut to deliver the report of the conversations to Admiral Hugon, commander of the French station in the Levant, for transmission to Paris. Mimaut's ciphered postscript to the report stated that, although some of the Egyptian soldiers probably would see in the affair a chance to establish Mehemet Ali as the successor-regent, Mehemet Ali had stated that he would accept the regency only if it were tendered to him by the Ottoman chiefs and by law. The official gazette at Cairo at once published the grievances of Mehemet Ali against the pasha of Acre. Having been cautioned by Mimaut that Europe would be concerned with the possible extension to greater limits of his single punitive expedition against Acre, the pasha had promised to halt at Acre until he got the French reactions; meanwhile he seemed to entertain no doubts of the issue of events.[6]

By June the cholera appeared in lower Egypt and grew worse in August, temporarily checking preparations for the expedition. During the lull in activity Mimaut reported that the object of Mehemet Ali's land and sea preparations for the expedition was only to win Syria and not to take the sultan's throne at Constantinople, as suggested by travelers and pamphleteers. The pasha counted on the Egyptian fleet to beat the Ottoman squadron or even on the defection of the Ottoman fleet to his side. He expected "a beautiful conquest, probably not to be disputed by the Porte because it would soon be a *fait accompli*, to give him a good territory and a more numerous population, thus advancing the Arabian establishment."[7]

2. THE PEACE DISRUPTED

The plague paralyzed commerce and military activity at Alexandria during August and September, preparations for the expedition being resumed by October. Although the original plan was to stop at Acre to await also the reactions of the Porte, opinion at Alexandria was divided on that point; it was recognized that the enthusiasm of success might make it impossible for the pasha to halt there. Internal troubles in Syria continued, moreover, providing a pretext for extending the Egyptian campaign to Damas. The expedition was launched on both land and sea. Having embarked for Syria on November 14, Ibrahim Pasha debarked at Jaffa and occupied the city without resistance by the populace, the land troops meanwhile occupying Gaza. Back at Alexandria the new large Egyptian war vessel of 100 guns was rushed to completion and its command assigned to a Frenchman (Houssart) who had been in Egyptian service for a year.

Meanwhile, the Porte made concessions to Mustapha of Scutari and to the Bosnians, thus ending the possibility of their extending their revolt to Constantinople. These concessions, in the opinion of Mehemet Ali in November, revealed the weakness of Turkey. The pasha concluded that, when faced with the *fait accompli* of the conquest of Acre, the sultan would gladly arrange with his "true vassal" what the vassal deemed proper. Afterward, the Porte would find from him more support than from twenty such pashas as those of Acre and Damas. Renewed activity in Egypt contrasted sharply with the existing general lethargy throughout the remainder of Turkey.[8]

French representation at Constantinople changed just as the Syrian campaign got under way. Guilleminot, having continued as ambassador through the frequent foreign office changes at Paris under the July Monarchy, departed on November 2, 1831, leaving the embassy in the hands of J. E. Varenne, chargé d'affaires. Varenne reflected the Egyptian interpretation when on November 24 he reported that the pasha's expedition was not directed against the sultan directly but rather against Abdullah, to avenge personal grievances.

By the first week in December, Beirut, Syrian Tripoli, Seïd, Naplouse and Jerusalem were in the hands of Ibrahim Pasha. At that point (December 10) the sultan by firmans ordered Mehemet Ali and Abdullah to cease their hostilities. The firmans directed the warring pashas to submit their grievances to the sultan for adjudication, the Egyptian forces meanwhile being retired to Egypt and Abdullah ceasing his interference with the government of Egypt.

At the same time Abdullah showed surprising resourcefulness. He made an unexpectedly strong resistance at Acre, thus duplicating the precedent established by the defenders of the fortress against Bonaparte in 1799.

In his firmans the sultan evidenced especially strong resentment against Mehemet Ali, although they were directed to both pashas. Turkish forces were ordered mobilized. Two Ottoman commissioners were dispatched to Alexandria to carry the firman and an autograph letter from the sultan to the pasha. The commissioners held their conferences with Mehemet Ali on December 26. Convincing arguments were employed by the pasha, the principal point being that he intended to do homage to the sultan through the Syrian conquests.

After the conferences, Mehemet Ali related the details to Mimaut and asked whether France approved his policy and, in particular, if Mimaut was pleased with him. Mimaut replied that he did not doubt that the French government would welcome a development which would at least put down disturbances if at the same time it maintained the good relations of Egypt with Turkey. Personally, Mimaut repeated to Mehemet Ali what he already had said many times, that the pasha seemed to be conforming with the principles of moderation and prudence which would assure to him a merited and dignified success. It was reported that the commissioners had been convinced as much by financial payments as by argument. Further payments (five million francs) were promised at Constantinople. Almost simultaneously, the cherif of Mecca by proclamation announced himself as favorable to Mehemet Ali and against the sultan.[9]

Upon his assumption of governing authority in Jerusalem Mehemet Ali applied his previously announced principles of moderation. Protection was accorded to all Christian establishments there. Although the plan for a prompt capitulation of Acre had failed, Mehemet Ali's ideas of permanent success expanded as the siege continued. He would be content with nothing less than the conquest of all Syria and announced that he would hold the province for at least a year or two. Turkey continued her military preparations after the refusal of Mehemet Ali to withdraw his forces from Syria was reported.

A new interest in the problem was shown by England in January,

1832. Several vessels called at ports of the Levant to announce the return of Stratford Canning as ambassador at Constantinople.[10] One vessel, a war brig, called at Alexandria and its captain talked with Mehemet Ali and inspected the Egyptian arsenal. Mehemet Ali frankly expressed his belief that Turkey would soon begin hostilities against him. To Mimaut the idea was conveyed that, if war was begun, Egypt would attempt to revive the Arabian Caliphate.[11]

At the end of February the sultan announced his decision to punish the disobedience of Mehemet Ali.[12]

3. Does France Encourage the Pasha?

Early in March, 1832, Sebastiani approved the language and advice Mimaut had employed. "He [Mehemet Ali] knows how much we are favorable to him," added Sebastiani, "and with what friendly dispositions [France] learns of everything that conduces to his glory and prosperity." Yet France did not wish the expedition to Syria to cause a rupture with the sultan. To aid in preventing the rupture, Varenne had been directed to attempt to calm the irritation at Constantinople. Mimaut was to inform Mehemet Ali of this and to thank the pasha for the firman which had abolished the levies against the Christian pilgrims to the Holy Places and freed the churches and convents there from taxes and tributes. Mimaut was cautioned to a language of reserve, considering the delicate circumstances of the moment.[13] By interpretation, it would appear that this dispatch disapproved of nothing in the Egyptian campaign against Abdullah and found something in its results to commend; the restraint was to be applied in advices to the sultan, none being ordered at the time for the pasha. The same day, characteristically enough, Varenne wrote a report at Constantinople which told of the charges that France had encouraged the pasha to attack Syria and had favored him; and that England, at least through one agent, had done essentially the same thing.[14]

One month later, Sebastiani wrote Mimaut that the latest news from Constantinople reported the sultan as undecided and embarrassed by the opposition of so powerful a vassal as Mehemet Ali.

It is to be regretted, as you have suggested [wrote Sebastiani], that the strong defense of Abdullah at Acre has unduly prolonged the struggle, making it more difficult for the Sultan to close his eyes to the conduct of Mehemet Ali and to content himself, in appearance, with the pasha's protestations of submission and fidelity.

It was true also that, once the pasha was in Syria, it would be difficult to know where his ambition would strike next. But the sultan would better not have exposed himself to so powerful an adversary. Perhaps the last proposals of the pasha would lead to an arrangement. At any rate, France would work in their mutual interests to prevent a Turco-Egyptian war.

Sebastiani did not share Mehemet Ali's expectations of an easy victory over Turkey, which would have, in addition to its effective manpower, the added advantage of public opinion throughout the Ottoman Empire. Political and religious revolution, with the establishment of a new caliph, would not change the Turkish habit of thinking of the Caliphate as legitimate only with the sultan as caliph. Such a war would embarrass the Powers of Europe with respect to the pasha and might retard the development of civilization so well begun in Mehemet Ali's states. Mimaut was directed to express confidentially to the pasha the view that France would see with pleasure the disappearance of all subjects of friction with Turkey, in the interests of himself and of Egypt. France appreciated that the friendly dispositions of the pasha toward her had not ceased and that, in his worthy efforts to regenerate Egypt, Mehemet Ali had not forgotten his debt to France and her culture. The dispatch closed with flattery for the pasha:

You cannot better report your conversations with him than to give as textually as possible his own words, always so picturesque and often so judicious. With a man so remarkable as Mehemet Ali, this method [of reporting] is certainly the most expressive and most interesting.[15]

4. OBJECTIVES OF THE "REBELS"

The first encounter between the forces of Mehemet Ali and the sultan was reported by Mimaut on April 16, 1832. The Turkish army was repulsed. The pasha at once sought to strengthen his connections with France. He protested his devotion to France, pledging himself, his army, his fleet, and all that he possessed and would possess. Mimaut in reply stated that the French government had shown its regard for him by the attempt to bring the sultan into harmony with him, "the Sultan's illustrious and powerful vassal." After having said this, Mimaut asked Sebastiani for a new approval of his language, in view of the situation at the time of the remark. It was foreseen that the struggle might be long and costly, Mehemet

Ali believing the Turkish Empire to be on the brink of catastrophe. The pasha expressed his unlimited confidence in Mimaut. "The idea which dominates Mehemet Ali," wrote Mimaut, "is that only a powerful friend like France can impose its powerful mediation."[16]

France saw with regret that "the affair of Syria had degenerated into an open rupture." Mehemet Ali had not wanted this, stated the French foreign minister to Varenne, although the pasha felt that he could face the eventuality with confidence. Mehemet Ali demanded the free and entire possession of Syria, protesting at the same time his submission and devotion to the sultan. "In his interest, and perhaps still more in the interest of the Porte, we had sincerely desired that this unfortunate collision be prevented."[17] At the opening of the war French officers were found in both camps; two were in the Turkish army and a larger number served the pasha.

The decisive step was taken by the sultan on May 4. Turkey declared Mehemet Ali and Ibrahim, called the pasha's "pretended" son, to be rebels and punishable as such. A firman conferred the government of Egypt, Crete, and Arabia on Hussein Pasha, to whom command of the Turkish army in Syria had been assigned. The Porte expected that the foreign Powers in good relations with Turkey would not give any support, open or secret, "to the two traitors and their partisans." But because some individuals for speculative purposes might furnish munitions and provisions to them, foreign merchant vessels were forbidden to enter the port of Alexandria and the other ports of Egypt. The Porte requested that all foreign consuls, merchants, and other subjects be notified of this blockade by Turkey. Varenne acted upon the notification by transmitting it to Paris "for an appreciation of its merits"; he also directed the French consuls in the Levant to "dissuade" the French merchants and ships from exposing their transactions to "the inconveniences inherent in the present complication."[18]

Intimate conversations between Mehemet Ali and Mimaut became more frequent than ever. In one of them the pasha compared the English and French as his friends. The English were new friends; the French were old ones, who had elevated him, favored him, and protected him; only to France would he give his unlimited confidence. France, he added, had given him the genius (Cerisy) who in three years had formed his arsenal and his formidable marine. Other Frenchmen commanded two of the Egyptian vessels of the line. An Egyptian trained in France commanded another. France had aided in training his army. He spoke of the indissoluble connections between France and Egypt and offered again some day to aid France with all his resources. He suggested that after the war with Turkey, when he would have time to perfect his military system, he would ask the French government for general officers for instruction in comprehensive military tactics. He would request also a French naval captain of recognized merit to command one of his frigates, on which would be trained his young son Saïd and other Egyptians. No expressions of doubt accompanied these prophecies for the future of Franco-Egyptian relations. Mehemet Ali knew, according to Mimaut, that France would lose in commercial and political relations if Egypt fell. Obvious advantages for commerce, "besides the noble cause of humanity, of civilization, and of sciences which can only succeed under a regular government," made Mehemet Ali appreciate the fact that a great danger for France would result from a reversal of his power. Mehemet Ali thought that he would be much preferred by France to such pashas as Hussein and Tahir, "who would finish by selling out to the English and letting them quietly establish their dominion in Egypt."

Mehemet Ali suggested many historical precedents for the division of Turkey, one of which was the separation of the American colonies from England. Mehemet Ali's dual objective was to establish the limits for expanded Egypt and to form Egypt and Syria into a political unit which, "effectively separated from the Empire of Constantinople, would remain a tributary much the same as had been Algeria under its former dey." No matter how the separation was effected, the division could only serve to benefit French commerce. Mehemet Ali pointed out that, although the Turkish capitulations stipulated favorable grants, Egypt had not signed them and did not have to obey them; hence, so far as France was concerned, they were of no significance. But, if Egypt herself negotiated commercial agreements, it would be the duty of Egypt to enforce them, and the pasha would personally make them effective.

Mimaut transmitted these observations of the pasha to Sebastiani with the suggestion that it was for the French cabinet to judge whether the political considerations involved would be commensurate with the obvious economic reasons for a practical separation of Egypt and Syria from Turkey.[19] A report of Desuin, a French naval officer, to Hugon corroborated the impression that the objectives of Mehemet Ali were not so extensive as generally attributed to him. What he wanted was to extend his dominion over Syria and perhaps Aleppo, to form an hereditary government for his family, and to obtain his independence in fact under the suzerainty of the sultan.[20]

The Turkish firman of May 4 created only a mild sensation at Alexandria. It was recognized by the foreign consuls at once that the support for it would devolve upon the Ottoman fleet. The blockade of Egypt was quite generally regarded as impossible, and it was believed that shippers, especially of nations friendly to Mehemet Ali, would be the first to ignore it. Barker went at once to notify the pasha of the firman. In the conference Mehemet Ali showed his disregard of the firman by making a diverting comment about the good appearance of a new uniform.[21]

5. French Policy Modified

The enthusiasm of Mehemet Ali for the future of Franco-Egyptian relations was not fully reciprocated. The official French policy of strong favoritism for the pasha, obvious from the initial assault on Acre, was modified to neutrality with the coming of the Turco-Egyptian War. The policy of neutrality was authorized in Sebastiani's instruction of June 1 to Varenne, who was also directed to neglect no opportunity to destroy the opinion that France favored Mehemet Ali as against Turkey. The policy of strict neutrality was here stated to be perhaps more in the interest of Turkey than in that of Egypt, since Egypt was better prepared to fight. Turkey was to be told that, although Mimaut was in confidential relations with Mehemet Ali, the relations were self-explanatory. Sebastiani was convinced that "nothing could justify the ill feeling which they appear to cause the Turkish government." Mimaut's attitude had in fact been a balanced one, he said, whereas the attitudes of the consuls of England and Austria, hostile to Mehemet Ali, perhaps made a contrast appear which had led to the reported feelings of Turkey.[22]

In actual application, the official French policy of neutrality in the Turco-Egyptian War was fringed with a definite touch of benevolence toward Egypt. This is well illustrated by the French attitude toward the Turkish proclamation of a blockade of Egypt and by the negotiations through which Egypt now sought, as a tangible evidence of French support, a war loan from France.

Even before the beginning of the war with Turkey, Mehemet Ali had made known his desire to contract a loan from France to help support his eventual war with the sultan. Just as the war got under way (in April), he sought a commercial loan, under auspices of the French government, in an amount of ten to fifteen million francs (the figure previously discussed in connection with the Drovetti plan). Mehemet Ali referred to the previous generous offer of a subsidy, pointing out that there was more reason for it now. Egypt was virtually the work of France, he said; no Power had so much interest in the prosperity of the pasha as France; for France, reciprocal commercial relations were available in Egypt; and France might always find in Egypt a man, an army, and a navy available to aid French policy when needed. Boghos' written application for the loan stated that ordinarily a loan of that size could be secured from English and French mercantile houses; now the pasha did not want to expose himself personally to the possibility of their refusal, nor did he want to give publicity to the matter by that method. Three years was the term suggested for the requested loan; interest was to be stipulated, the rate to be fixed at the time the papers were signed. The loan would be guaranteed by the cotton crops of Egypt; the mode and form of its execution would be left entirely to France. In conversations with Boghos and the pasha Mimaut gave his personal opinion that the reaction to the request would be problematical, even if one considered only the question of its technical execution and not its political implications. It was this consideration which had led Mehemet Ali to give France carte blanche as to the conditions and methods of execution.[23]

The pasha's request was sent to Paris by Mimaut in duplicate. On the dispatch preserved in the archives the penciled ministerial marginal comment is for the most part illegible. But the ministerial exchanges show what happened to the request. Sebastiani on May 30 referred it to Baron Louis, minister of finance, and to C. d'Argout, minister of commerce. The transmitting note to these ministers, which accompanied a copy of Boghos' application, explained that Mehemet Ali had asked for a government-sponsored loan. It was not necessary to tell Egypt, further explained Sebastiani, that it would be impossible for France officially to make the loan because the pasha knew already that the French administration could not undertake such an operation ostensibly and directly, since it would arouse the antagonism of the Porte. But the pasha had suggested that the government might make the loan indirectly. The ministers concerned would know better whether private French funds were available for the loan and what very confidential usages might be made of Mehemet Ali's proposal. "Whatever is done," concluded Sebastiani, "I believe it superfluous to repeat that the government cannot intervene officially in any manner."

The replies were dated June 16 and 18 respectively. The minister of commerce "doubted whether the proposed guarantees were adequate in view of the existing state of relations between the Porte and Mehemet Ali; but the minister of finance might give an opinion regarding the capitalists." Louis replied:

I do not know fully what might be the reactions of French bankers and capitalists in regard to a transaction [of this kind] with the pasha, and I believe that in any case it will not be convenient for the government to make inquiries, directly or indirectly, in this regard. They would be even more ill-timed in the present circumstances, and when some credit operations are about to be opened to cover our own budget deficits. Prudence cautions me against any ministerial démarche relating to the transaction to which your letter relates.[24]

The official reply to Egypt was dispatched on June 23 in a note couched in friendly terms and softened by the announcement that France was refusing to recognize the Turkish blockade of Egypt. Sebastiani expressed surprise at the prolonged siege of Acre, the fall of which he had not yet learned. Sebastiani thought that nothing would be gained by Egyptian arms if that key to Syria did not fall into the pasha's hands. France would contribute, if possible, to the finding of an agreement with the Porte, "being animated by the most friendly dispositions toward Mehemet Ali." Although the French government could not officially grant the loan, it had considered the possibility of aiding secretly, by unofficial means. But it appeared little probable that French capitalists would be attracted to the loan considering the relationship of the pasha and the sultan at the moment. Even if they consented, it would be under conditions which the pasha could not accept. The problem had been referred confidentially to the ministers of finance and commerce, both of whom thought that the plan would have meager chances among French capitalists. Mimaut was directed to express regrets that France found herself unable on this occasion to give a more positive proof of her friendship for the pasha. On the other hand, Sebastiani stated, the Turkish paper blockade of Egypt's ports appeared to France to be completely inadmissible. Such a blockade would amount to nothing less than an indefinite suspension of commercial intercourse with Egypt and would apply legally only to those ports which were effectively blockaded by Turkey, not to those still under the control of the pasha. Having decided upon neutrality, France now invoked from Turkey the rights of a neutral. Varenne was directed to explain French policy in that sense to Turkey; Mimaut might make the same explanation to the pasha. Mimaut was told, however, that it would be proper to recommend to French merchants "a great prudence" in their trade with Egypt. They would understand their risks if their shipments of contraband of war were legally seized by Turkish vessels. They would understand, moreover, since the struggle was still uncertain, that it would be difficult, if not impossible, to procure their indemnification if Mehemet Ali lost.[25]

The instructions to Varenne (on June 21) respecting the Turkish blockade were even more explicit than the explanation sent to Mimaut. The directions which Varenne had dispatched to the French consuls in the Levant were stated to have been "much too positive," not conforming either to the system of neutrality which France now followed or to the rights of neutrals under international maritime law. The difference between ports effectively blockaded and others was explained. Even in effectively blockaded ports, Sebastiani pointed out, the ships attempting to enter might not be seized legally until their return after having been warned by the commanding officer. Hence, since no port of Egypt was thus effectively controlled by Turkey, the Porte was to be notified that France as a neutral could not conform to the paper blockade. Having thus explained the French position to Turkey, Varenne was to write again to the French consuls and state that the only restriction against French commerce with Egypt would be the real and effective Turkish blockade of Egyptian ports. Nevertheless, the consuls were also to recommend confidentially that French merchants employ a "very great circumspection" in the nature of their shipments, especially those for the service of the Egyptian government, because of the difficulty or impossibility of restitution. Munitions for the pasha would be subject to seizure by Turkish boats and by corsairs regularly armed in the name of the Porte.[26]

The French Levant squadron was ordered to enforce the neutral rights of France. Hugon was directed to act in conformity with the instructions to Varenne, using his warships as guarantees for French commerce "against acts of hostility feared through the pretentions of the Porte."[27]

The French answer to Egypt and the notification of the decision not to recognize the Turkish blockade were communicated by Mimaut late in August, after the successes of the Egyptian armies in Syria had changed the whole outlook. By that time Mehemet Ali's position had been consolidated, and previous fears of unfavorable reactions by the Syrians had disappeared. In communicating the decisions of the French government Mimaut told Mehemet Ali that France knew the duties of neutrals and also the way to insure that the rights of neutrals were respected. This seemed to increase the already great confidence of Mehemet Ali in France. Mimaut presented the refusal of the loan in a reserved manner, so that it was received without marked disfavor. It apparently did nothing to change the pasha's disposition toward France.[28]

6. Results of the Capture of Acre

The turning point in the Turco-Egyptian War was Ibrahim's capture of the fortress of Acre after a siege of almost six months, an achievement in which Bonaparte had failed in 1799. The capitulation, reported in Alexandria on June 1, came after Abdullah's original force of 8,000 had been reduced to 500 and when he was without money and munitions to continue the struggle.[29] It meant that the key to all of Syria was now in the hands of Egypt. Abdullah arrived in Alexandria on June 5, and was accorded courteous treatment by the conquerors.

The victory at Acre had great repercussions throughout the Ottoman Empire. It placed in sharp contrast the power of the pasha and the inherent weakness of Turkey. The question was that of an Arabian as opposed to a Turkish establishment. Mehemet Ali soon decided to act toward his objective and to demand the government of Syria under suzerainty of the Porte. His views had expanded with the victory, however. If the Porte would not cede Syria, the sultan might be deposed to prevent the dissolution of the Ottoman Empire. According to Mimaut (June 24, 1832), the Muslim world seemed to support the pasha.[30] An overture was dispatched to Turkey in September.

Mehemet Ali followed up the victory by consolidating his new position instead of attempting an immediate massed movement toward Asia Minor. Although the inhabitants of Syria philosophically accepted the new regime, the foreign merchants in Syria soon recognized the real import of it. A part of the restrictive trade system of Egypt was almost immediately extended to Syria as the pasha consolidated his new power. New regulations heavily taxed many articles of foreign commerce, including raw cotton, soap, oil, and grains from Russia and Greece. New supplementary levies were applied to interior commerce, from none of which were Europeans exempted. The consuls at Beirut filed a protest on August 7, declaring the new levies to be in violation of the capitulations granted their governments by Turkey. They also protested against the irregular methods of the new chiefs charged with enforcement of the regulations.[31]

Two alternatives were presented to Turkey as the result of the fall of Acre. She might either acquiesce in the demands of Mehemet Ali and end the war, or she might dispatch a new expedition to retrieve her losses. Varenne on July 23 advised the Porte to come to terms with the pasha. But Turkey was on the eve of a new campaign, the preparation for which had been quite costly, and she seemed to prefer to continue the war.[32] Confidence in Hussein Pasha, however, had vanished, especially with reports of the terror in Turkish ranks inspired by Ibrahim Pasha.

In August the military control of the remainder of Syria was abandoned by Turkey, and a new element, the possibility of foreign aid, was presented at Constantinople. Reports intimated that Stratford Canning, during his audience of leave on August 11, gave the sultan some hope of the help of British frigates. Varenne believed that misinterpreted or poorly translated remarks by the departing ambassador probably led to the new conviction that more substantial aid might be available from England.[33] Nevertheless, the idea resulted in the commissioning, against the advice of Varenne, of Namick Pasha for a special mission to London.

French reactions to the victory at Acre—aside from the indicated advice of Varenne to Turkey, which was later approved in Paris—may be treated briefly. Perhaps the most enthusiastic acceptance of the result of the battle by any French officer was that by Aubry-Bailleul, commander of the war vessel "Lamproie," who suggested that the government of Egypt should now be accorded de facto recognition, for he regarded as accomplished facts both the conquest of Syria and the independence of Egypt. The benefits of an independent Egypt for French commerce would be obvious.[34]

The friendly expressions of Mehemet Ali for France as reported by Mimaut on May 29 were not left unnoticed by Sebastiani. News of the fall of Acre provided a good occasion for a cordial reply, which was sent on July 20. The victory at Acre, Sebastiani stated, had created a sensation commensurate with its importance. It proved the superiority of French tactics; it would be of great moral influence for the Egyptian troops, giving them confidence and a military spirit; it suggested that the pasha really possessed a European-type army. Perhaps now the new offers of submission by Mehemet Ali would be taken into consideration at Constantinople. The sentiments of friendship which the pasha had expressed to France had been noted with pleasure. France, Sebastiani stated,

congratulated herself for having contributed in Egypt to the rebirth and the progress of a power capable one day of preserving against domination from Europe that rich debris of the Ottoman Empire, a power so naturally the friend of France, interested as are we in the liberty of the Mediterranean, and the development of which offers us advantageous political and commercial relations. In this connection we recognize that the consolidation of the order of things founded by Mehemet Ali promises us advantages. . . . We will be always ready to give to the pasha the same expressions of good will and friendship he has already received from France and from its government.[35]

To Varenne Sebastiani suggested that it would be now impossible for the Porte to conceal the advantages which the conquest of Acre gave the pasha "in addition to his already formidable and imposing position." Sebastiani thought that after "some demonstrations destined to save his dignity" the sultan would accept the means of arrangement and the submission offered him by Mehemet Ali.[36]

In mid-August, replying to Varenne's report of July 23 which detailed the advice tendered Turkey on coming to an agreement with Egypt, Sebastiani approached the problem more analytically. The special position of Egypt in the Ottoman Empire and in relation to Europe, he stated, was the result of several factors: its military and naval policy, its geographical location, and the nature of its resources. These for a long time had constituted Egypt as a really independent power, even though it was still held in some forms of vassalage to the Porte. The Turkish council had authorized this effective independence before Europe by its silence while Egypt progressively developed and by its frequent requests for aid. It was impossible for Turkey to nullify by simple decree the special relationships now established between Egypt and some of the Powers. Without accepting fully the reports of continued Egyptian victories, France "regarded the situation of the Porte as very critical." The advice France had tendered through Varenne had been dictated by a full recognition of the dangers to which Turkey exposed herself if she continued the war. The advice to come to terms was now renewed, Sebastiani believing that Mehemet Ali would be found willing to agree. According to Mimaut's report of June 24, said Sebastiani, the pasha asked only what he had wanted before the rupture, the government of Syria and Aleppo under the suzerainty of the Porte. It was to be emphasized that the Ottoman Empire was a matter of concern to the general equilibrium of Europe, hence Turkey must appreciate that later perhaps neither Mehemet Ali nor the Porte would be masters of the situation. Varenne must try again for an arrangement.[37]

A week later a terse dispatch to Mimaut suggested that the successes of Mehemet Ali in Syria made an accommodation between the Porte and Egypt desirable. Varenne had been instructed to express confidentially to the Turkish government the dangers inherent in the situation and to renew in a pressing manner the advice to negotiate. Replying to Mimaut's report of Egypt's terms, Sebastiani instructed the French consul to state to the pasha that France would be willing to name negotiators to help in the conciliation. Mimaut was to follow carefully the policy of England in respect to Mehemet Ali, especially since Stratford Canning had employed an English brig to expedite to Crete and Egypt the news of the Turkish firman of May 4.[38]

Sebastiani's suggestion of possible European intervention if the struggle were prolonged had an especial reference, doubtless, to the attitude of Russia. Unlike France, Russia must have seen in the Egyptian victory a possible danger to her own new policy of preserving Turkey as a weak neighbor state.[39] Mimaut observed that the Russian government, either because of the nature of its engagements to Turkey or because of private considerations, was hostile to Mehemet Ali. One report stated that the tsar would recall his consul from Egypt and that he "had forbidden any ship under the Russian flag to transport munitions, arms, and provisions to the rebels." Another stated that almost all the ships at Constantinople serving as transports were under the neutral Russian flag, a small number being under the Austrian. It was reported that Turkey employed no French and British flags. Mehemet Ali clearly understood the reactions of the foreign Powers, which may account for his increasing intimacy with Mimaut.[40] Varenne likewise transmitted circumstantial evidence on the attitude of Russia. The reports of military movements in Russia were of much concern to the Turkish public. Troops were reportedly being assembled in Bessarabia and additional armaments were arriving at Sevastopol. The troops might have been intended for use against either Greece or Egypt. If Russia wanted to send her fleet through the Straits, Turkey was thought too weak to refuse the authorization for its passage. A report of August 11 stated that Russia had offered her assistance to Turkey, proposing that an army be sent against Mehemet Ali through Erzurum and across Asia Minor into Syria.[41] Mimaut thought it significant that Butenev, while visiting Alexandria in October to inspect the naval arsenal, neglected to pay courtesy calls at the French and British consulates, although he did visit the consuls of Sweden, Holland, and Austria.[42]

Neither at Constantinople nor at Alexandria was one certain of the next development. Varenne reported at first that Turkey was disposed to treat with the pasha but did not want to make the first move. Later, Turkey seemed to have determined to continue the war. On October 6 Mimaut reported the result of the Egyptian overture. The Porte was found willing to consider the propositions of the pasha, based on the transfer of the government of Syria to him, but inquired what guarantees of his future good conduct the pasha was prepared to offer. The pasha would guarantee nothing more than his engagements and the renewal of his assurance of a desire to terminate the sanguinary conflict. Shortly afterward the Porte launched new offensive preparations, at the same time demanding that Mehemet Ali withdraw his troops to Egypt.[43]

7. THE "SPHINX" SCOUTS FOR EGYPT

Although the battle of Acre represented the principal land engagement of the Turco-Egyptian War, the contingent problem of naval encounters should be mentioned. Hugon in June, 1832, had dispatched the brig "Actéon" to observe the movements of the Turkish and Egyptian squadrons. There were many conflicting reports of naval activity. Fear of the Turkish fleet was expressed by Mehemet Ali until after the return of the French war steamer, the "Sphinx," with its satisfactory report after a scouting trip late in August.

The "Sphinx" was utilized as a scouting ship upon the request of Boghos to Mimaut on August 20. Boghos asked the French government to give Egypt a new evidence of its good will by permitting a war steamer to obtain prompt and correct information on the respective positions of the Turkish and Egyptian squadrons. It was suggested, probably as a smoke screen, that the vessel might be used for the benefit of European commerce at the same time. Boghos specifically requested the "Sphinx," under command of Captain Sarlat, whereupon Mimaut wrote Sarlat that he knew of no reason why the request should not be granted, in view of the benevolent and friendly relations between the governments of France and Egypt. There was natural anxiety when too long a time passed without news, he said, while the conflicting stories also had the effect of making commercial activity more hesitant; hence the "Sphinx" might well make the requested excursion. Boghos had already indicated that coal and other provisions would be provided by the Egyptian government. Sarlat might go to Cyprus also to inform the French subjects of the approach of the Egyptian naval squadron to occupy the island.[44]

The "Sphinx" departed promptly, on August 21, visiting the regions of maritime war. Sarlat learned from the Egyptians that the Turkish and Egyptian squadrons had been in sight of each other on the nineteenth, twentieth, and twenty-first of August but that the Turkish squadron had not offered to fight. The *capitan pasha* having taken the Turkish fleet to Rhodes, Sarlat went there. An officer of the "Sphinx" called on the *capitan pasha*. He learned that the Turks were delighted that Osman Pasha, Egyptian commander, had not engaged them in battle, because they were awaiting the reënforcement of twelve other large Turkish vessels which would give them a superiority over the Egyptian fleet. The English frigate "Alfred" also visited the *capitan pasha,* and its captain's report corroborated that by Sarlat. The "Sphinx" then proceeded to Cyprus as directed. Mehemet Ali was not pleased when he learned that Osman Pasha had missed a good chance to engage the Turkish fleet, but he laughed about the report of the twelve other vessels, knowing that Turkey did not have them.[45] The effect of the almost simultaneous appearance of the "Sphinx" at Rhodes and Cyprus was to provoke ill feeling against France among the Turkish ministers. Shortly afterward, the captain of the "Actéon" was received frigidly by the *capitan pasha.*

The naval campaigns ended early in November without the contestants having engaged in a major battle.

8. Sebastiani Presses for Peace

The maximum limit of the cabinet policy of France throughout the remainder of the Turco-Egyptian War was virtually fixed by Sebastiani in September, 1832. It was essentially a policy of mediation, looking to peace and the Egyptian acquisition of Syria. The policy was outlined in two instructions, the first to Mimaut on the thirteenth, and the second to Varenne on the twentieth. The reasons for the crystallization of French policy at that time were revealed by the dispatches of Mimaut down to July 20 and from Varenne down to August 11, the latest of which had been received in Paris at the time the policy was formulated. As we have seen, Mimaut had reported on June 24 not only the determination of the pasha to retain Syria but also the probability of a reversal of the sultan, while Varenne had sketched the intention of Turkey to continue the war despite her reverses and had suggested the international complications which appeared to be on their way.

The more significant of the two instructions was that to Mimaut. Firm language for the first time was authorized to restrain the pasha in one of the two potentialities, the reversal of the sultan. Nothing would justify Mehemet Ali's support of projects tending to overthrow the sultan, stated Sebastiani. With all her friendship for him, France could not approve such an activity on his part. Such a project would inspire a dangerous reaction in Europe; Egypt would have more to lose than to win by the downfall of the Ottoman Empire. Turkey in her extremity would find European allies, even if she had to purchase their support through new sacrifices. The real interest of Mehemet Ali, more especially now that Russia had shown a hostile attitude toward him, was to come to peace with Turkey. If Mehemet Ali did not do so, he might count on nothing more than friendship from France. As for Syria, Mehemet Ali might now merit further renown by using his success wisely, making his triumph, through prudence and moderation, as solid as it was complete. He should prefer peace on the basis of the conquests to that time rather than a pointless continuation of the struggle. France would aid with her good offices in the negotiations. With such advice, "Mehemet Ali could not doubt the good will and interest France had for him."[46]

Varenne was instructed to propose to Turkey the mediation of France to end the war. The tenor of the language directed was that the Porte should now come to an agreement with Egypt to prevent further losses. Not only the military defeats, but the menace of revolution, the elements of dissolution, the unpopularity of the sultan, and the discontent of the subject peoples all pointed to that conclusion. Above all, the Turkish council must do nothing which might cause the destruction of the Ottoman Empire, an event which would have dangerous consequences for Europe. France offered her mediation because she of all the Great Powers, stated Sebastiani, would have less to win by the fall of the Turkish Empire and because she favored tranquillity between kings and peoples. France advised peace: to Egypt, because she had won her objective; to Turkey, because of the necessity of terminating the perilous situation in which she was then placed. Varenne was to use all his resources to convince Turkey of the urgency for a reconciliation with the pasha. It was suggested by Sebastiani that the offer of French mediation might be less effective at Constantinople than at Alexandria because of the Porte's conviction that France favored Mehemet Ali. Here Varenne was to state to the Turkish ministers that France was sincerely devoted to Turkish interests and was always willing to submit proofs. For example, France had not desired the rupture in the first place. Now the question had become something more than an ordinary revolt of a pasha. The superior military resources of Egypt had been demonstrated. Turkey might solve her problem by abandoning Syria.[47] The consensus of consular opinion at Constantinople, however, was that Mehemet Ali would not now be content with Syria alone.

9. Broglie and French Policy

The offer of the good offices of France to Turkey and Egypt was a step in the direction of a peace. But by the end of October, 1832, it was apparent to Varenne and Mimaut that neither side was yet willing to end the war. The Turkish foreign minister wanted the withdrawal of Egyptian forces from Syria before any agreement; Mehemet Ali wanted to hold all of the territory that he had conquered. Varenne threw out the suggestion late in October that Egypt might make some move of the token type, perhaps the evacuation of Caramania (the district south of Koniah, including Adana and its vilayet). But Mehemet Ali wanted to keep the Adana district especially, because, he said, of its timber resources.[48]

An important change in the direction of French foreign policy occurred during October. Sebastiani, who for several weeks had not been in personal charge of the foreign office, was succeeded on the eighteenth by the Duke of Broglie, who, twelve days later, confirmed the directions of September 20. This meant a renewed insistence at Constantinople upon the urgency, in Turkey's own interest, of coming to an agreement with Egypt. In the instructions to Mimaut on November 12, in which Broglie continued the friendly pressure against Egypt, the problem was analyzed as it then appeared. There had been slightly conflicting reports as to the precise reasons why the Porte had not utilized the "excellent occasion" of the pasha's overture in September for opening negotiations. The question seemed to be how much display of submission was to be made before the negotiation might get under way. Mimaut should therefore continue his efforts to impress upon Mehemet Ali the desirability of coming to an immediate arrangement and should not allow the pasha to forget that general interest in the cause of the sultan was finding free expression throughout Europe, since it was feared that his fall from power would cause disturbances and collisions. The fact that sympathy inclined toward Turkey because of her weakness made it obvious that the prolongation of the conflict would lead to European intervention, "from which Mehemet Ali would probably get less than through direct negotiations with the Divan." The initial refusal of the sultan should not restrain further attempts by the pasha, who, "in his dual role of feudatory and victor over the Sultan, might continue to propose without jeopardizing his dignity." Then, if Turkey persisted in the war, Mehemet Ali would be relieved of the responsibility for subsequent events. "It is much less to acquire," stated Broglie, "than to perfect and repair." Mehemet Ali knew well enough the French disposition favoring him not to appreciate this advice, "dictated by friendship." Pressure would continue to be applied at Constantinople, where soon a new French ambassador would be named.[49]

Broglie in a dispatch to Varenne on November 15 stated that Mehemet Ali had clearly made known his condition for a settlement—the cession of Syria under terms similar to those under which he held Egypt. Not only was it uncertain that the sultan by a second campaign could win back what he had lost but there was also the possibility that his attempt to do so might even result in such great reverses as to ruin the Ottoman Empire. Each day of delay thus placed the future of the sultan in greater jeopardy. The Porte in its own interest should conform to the necessities of the situation. On November 26 notification was made to Varenne of the appointment of Admiral A. R. Roussin as the ambassador. The selection of this moment for the appointment, Turkey was to be told, did not imply that France had abandoned Turkey, nor did it indicate that an attitude of indifference to Turkish problems would be assumed. On the contrary, Roussin would be charged to show the special dangers to be expected from a continuance of the internecine war. The Porte already "had been seriously ill-advised in refusing to accept the proposed conciliation with Mehemet Ali, and by continuing a struggle in which its adversary had enough wisdom to defend what he had conquered." The entrance of Ibrahim into Asia Minor doubtless would demoralize the inhabitants of the Asiatic provinces, and, by dispatching all her available forces to fight in Asia Minor, Turkey would encourage rebellions in the Balkan provinces. The Porte was to be told that the pasha knew he might expect nothing more from France if he now refused to make peace. It seemed, the dispatch continued, that Turkey placed some hope "in the vague promises attributed to Stratford Canning." Turkey might as well know in advance, however, that nothing would come of her expectation of physical aid from England. The announced mission of Namick was "a false démarche." Turkey must understand that the cabinet at London could be no more willing than the French ministry to put its vessels at the disposal of the sultan so that he might attack Mehemet Ali. Broglie could not understand how anyone could have advised the Sublime Porte to so humble itself before a foreign power as to seek support against a rebellious vassal. The circumstance would give the pasha a new and powerful weapon which would react through the religious spirit of the subjects of the sultan. Varenne was to make proper arrangements for the impressive arrival of Roussin, scheduled for January, perhaps by the authorization for the passage of a frigate to bear him through the Dardanelles.[50]

10. Overtures

The Egyptian bases or terms for the eventual mediation, in which France was to play the leading role, were laid in three or four long conversations between Mehemet Ali and Mimaut in November. Meanwhile the pasha ordered a new offensive, the advance to Koniah, key city of Asia Minor, to win better terms. On the sixteenth he received letters from the Turkish grand vizir and Chosrew Pasha, both of which disclosed that Turkey by then had in part appreciated the necessities of the situation. Both letters announced the explicit desire of the Porte to come to terms, providing Mehemet Ali would, as a preliminary gesture, send an agent to Constantinople to request the sultan's pardon. For several days the Porte waited (anxiously and vainly, Varenne believed) while Mehemet Ali thoroughly discussed the possible terms of the pasha with Mimaut.

The replies of the pasha, dated November 26, were not dispatched until after confirmation had arrived (the next day) of the occupation by Ibrahim of the passes to Koniah, opening the route to Constantinople. The contents of the replies, which cleverly took full advantage of the new strategic superiority of Egypt, were detailed to Mimaut, who relayed them with interpretations to Varenne on November 27 and 28. The pasha stated that he did not have a man to whom he would be willing to assign a negotiation of that character, and anyway he preferred to negotiate personally. Hence his *sine qua non* for the negotiation was that it be held in Egypt. He stated that the negotiation would not require many hours, however, and that after the signing of a convention he would send a personal representative to Constantinople to make solemn affirmation of his submission and to request the sultan's pardon.

The bases for the Turco-Egyptian convention were included in a ciphered annex to Mimaut's dispatch to Varenne. Mehemet Ali would agree to order an armistice the moment the Ottoman negotiator arrived, each side holding its respective positions during the negotiations. As a gesture, Mehemet Ali would evacuate all of Caramania except the district of Adana. He would accept the investiture of all of Syria in exchange for an annual tribute, contenting himself with a position analogous to that of the former dey of Algeria in his relations with the Porte.[51] To Broglie Mimaut indicated the necessity for the Porte to act promptly on the pasha's proposals. A curious circumstance may be noted with respect to the replies of Mehemet Ali. They were not received in Constantinople until January 27, 1833. Meanwhile Varenne, on the basis of Mimaut's communications, gave the Porte the Egyptian answer.[52] On December 10 Mimaut reported that Mehemet Ali had repeated again what he had always said. Desiring his pardon and peace, with Syria and its dependencies, he cheerfully accepted France's mediation and intimated that he would do what France asked.[53]

11. Instructions to Roussin

On December 13 Broglie phrased Roussin's lengthy instructions, which sketched the entire problem, emphasizing the developments which had been repeatedly treated in the dispatches to Mimaut and Varenne since August. The latest development predicted the failure of Namick at London, but Broglie here suggested nothing of the possibility of Russia's intervention. The new features in the instruction primarily concerned the attitude of France toward Egypt. Broglie repeated as accepted French interpretation for policy many of the suggestions made by Mehemet Ali to Mimaut in May and called attention to the differences in British and French attitudes toward Egypt. "Mehemet Ali seems to have the dual ambition," stated Broglie, "of making Egypt the center of a new empire and the commercial entrepôt of a part of the world. By an inverse reason, but easy to conceive, this tendency may disquiet England by giving France more the perspective of advantage." The commercial and maritime future of Egypt had already given England some offense, whereas France saw in Egypt, with its three millions of people, its "most beautiful geographical location of two hemispheres," its important markets for French commerce, its sources of excellent cotton for French industry, and its great navy, a state which might some day be allied with France in the Mediterranean. France's intimacy with Egypt, which began with the Drovetti plan, had grown, showing how her policy had been modified since the battle of Navarino. France had refused to sanction the overthrow of the sultan by the pasha but had made no objections to his "organizing his beautiful Syrian conquest." What she now wanted was the restoration and preservation of the tranquillity of the Ottoman Empire. Roussin's principal task would be to get Turkey to come to terms with the pasha. The sultan might be urged to haste by the suggestion that "the loss of a battle could reverse and destroy empires."[54]

12. Turkey Requests Aid

Fearing for the safety of his throne, the sultan now successively appealed for aid to Austria, Great Britain, and Russia, and timidly sought the moral support of France. We have already noted the alleged remarks of Canning at Constantinople, the speculation concerning Russia, and the commissioning of Namick Pasha, whose failure Broglie had foreseen. The refusal of Metternich to accord anything more than diplomatic support no doubt was to be partly attributed to a momentary intensification of Austro-French rivalry in Italy, the result of an unheralded French seizure of Ancona in February, 1832.[55]

The first suggestion of British aid for Turkey was made to Canning before his departure in August. Turkey at that time proposed an Anglo-Turkish defensive alliance and offered additional commercial privileges to the British as a corollary. Namick in London having made the official request, the matter was kept under advisement by Palmerston for several weeks.[56] Meanwhile Namick made a visit to Paris, replying to a question by Broglie that he was authorized to solicit from France only her "moral support and good offices."[57]

There seems no doubt that the ultimate British rejection of the proposal of an Anglo-Turkish alliance was based on the possible hostility of France to a singlehanded intervention of England. This, as well as other important attitudes, is shown in the marginal comments which Palmerston penciled on the requested memorandum prepared by Stratford Canning on December 19, 1832. Canning insisted that England support Turkey, either alone or in concert with any of her allies, not leaving the sultan's independence to chance. He asserted that, if England could find adequate motives for aiding Turkey to put down Egypt and recover Syria, "the presence of a British squadron would suffice to ensure success," since it would act in concert with the Turkish navy. Palmerston did not agree that this was quite certain. Canning's thesis was that to leave the Turkish Empire to itself was to leave it to its enemies; the sultan faced the alternative of abandoning his throne entirely or of turning Egypt, Syria, and the regions to the Persian frontier over to Mehemet Ali, such territorial losses in turn making it more difficult than ever for her "to make head against the encroachments of Russia." Palmerston, in contrast, wondered whether the unwieldy extent of the Turkish Empire was not in itself a great cause of external weakness. Canning argued that commerce would be retarded if the existing war were protracted; Palmerston noted that continual turbulence before had not proved so injurious to commerce. Because Turkey might suppose that England could conceivably take the Egyptian side, Canning pointed out that the sultan would be indisposed to "every kind of foreign interference unaccompanied with moral or physical coöperation in his favor"; he therefore recommended naval support. He urged that support of Turkey would win England "an important influence" in the councils of the Divan, this in turn promoting the progress and reform of Turkey. Palmerston countered that England had rescued Egypt for her once before without such results accruing. On one point only did Palmerston fully concur with Canning: an Anglo-Turkish alliance could be supported if necessary to rescue Turkey from Russia. Since it was a question of Egypt and Turkey, however, the commercial advantages claimed by Canning would in fact not materialize, Palmerston noted, since the gains from Turkey would be balanced by losses in Egypt and Syria. Anyway, Canning had admitted that Turkish commercial concessions were generally applied to all and that the anticipated "reasonable sacrifice" for English aid, falling outside the generality, might be a grant of British steam navigation of the Euphrates for communications with India or a grant of shipbuilding timber from the extensive forests of Turkey. Canning suggested that Turkey would look with preference to

England and that aid from France would be accepted only out of deference to England.

> Many acts of France during the last forty years [wrote Canning], concluding with the occupation of Algiers, have rendered the Porte extremely mistrustful of that Power. The concurrence of France in the supposed case could therefore be desirable to Great Britain only as it might tend to allay jealousy or enable her to operate more effectively on the pasha of Egypt. The motives which at present prevail with the French ministers to cultivate the good will and confidence of England might possibly suffice to reconcile them to her single interference in the affairs of Turkey.

Palmerston's marginal note replied: "Surely it would be very strange if it did—should we be easily reconciled to the 'single' interference of France? Yet France is both by position and ancient connection more directly interested in Turkish affairs than ourselves." Canning suggested further that the nonconcurrence of France "could hardly fail to increase the difficulties already existing, and it is well known that the French cabinet has long regarded the Levant, and Syria and Egypt in particular, with more than common interest." Austria would welcome British interference, whereas Russia would dislike it but would hardly oppose it, thought Canning.[58] Palmerston was convinced that in the end physical strength rather than the power of the Caliphate[59] would determine the outcome of the Turco-Egyptian conflict and expressed the greatest doubt that the success of Mehemet Ali would be favorable to the security of British India, a point made at the time by pro-Egyptian Samuel Briggs.

The result was that Palmerston declined to offer direct aid to Turkey. The reasons were the disunity of cabinet opinion on the problem, preoccupation with Ireland and the still unsettled Belgian question, the assurance given by Tsar Nicholas during the year that Russia desired the maintenance of Turkey, and Palmerston's doubt whether he could count on France.

The Egyptian control of Koniah made the pressure of Ibrahim's armies too insistent for Turkish inaction while the outcome of Namick's mission was awaited. On December 17 Reshid Pasha had left to challenge Ibrahim before Koniah, and Russia had already indicated her willingness to save Constantinople for Turkey; hence the sultan now turned to his traditional enemy and received the promise of naval and military aid.

The Black Sea squadron under command of Admiral Lazarev prepared for an expedition to Constantinople as soon as weather conditions permitted. On December 25 General N. N. Muraviev arrived at the Turkish capital on a war frigate to complete the arrangements. The reason for the Russian démarche, assigned in the circular of notification to the Powers, was the belief that the continued advance of the Egyptian armies would result in placing before Russia a neighbor who would be little disposed to uphold the Treaty of Adrianople.[60] A menacing attitude was deemed necessary to prevent an Arabic establishment on the Turkish Straits.

As reported to Paris by Varenne, Muraviev conveyed the tsar's offer to place his Mediterranean fleet under Ricord at the disposal of the sultan. If that were not enough, he would send his Black Sea fleet, and even a land expedition. If the sultan accepted, Muraviev would go to Egypt to summon Mehemet Ali to submit without condition. Varenne supposed that, if the pasha refused, Ricord would be ordered to act against him at once.[61]

Any consideration of action in the Mediterranean, however, was eclipsed by the new imminence of disaster to Constantinople. News arrived of the annihilation of Reshid's army in a six-hour battle at Koniah on December 21, along with the capture of Reshid. The statement of Muraviev that an army of some thirty to forty thousand Russians awaited the order to move from Sevastopol was now of especial appeal to the sultan and his ministers of war and foreign affairs. On December 31 the foreign consuls were advised of the approaching departure of Muraviev for Alexandria on board the Russian frigate.

Varenne apparently was not able to keep abreast of all the secret negotiations which centered around Butenev and Muraviev, for we read in his dispatches that on December 31 he went to the Turkish foreign minister to advise Turkey not to accept the Russian offer because an arrangement with Mehemet Ali was about to be concluded. He supported his advice by the offer to dispatch to Mehemet Ali a pressing recommendation that the pasha yield in the face of the Russian menace and to write to Ibrahim Pasha advising that the commander withhold any further advances until after he had heard from his father. Varenne's offer was accepted *ad referendum*. It was submitted first to the Turkish council, where no one spoke against it, and then to the sultan. Varenne reported to Paris, however, his belief that the disaster at Koniah would make it expedient for Turkey to accept the aid of Russia and that already, with the promise of support at hand, there was discussion among the Turkish ministers of a renewed campaign against Egypt. He did not doubt that Muraviev would be successful in his negotiation with the pasha, for the general spoke Turkish, was seasoned to military operations in western Asia, and would treat with the authority and approval of the tsar. Several Turkish-speaking officers had accompanied him.[62]

NOTES TO SECTION V

[1] Cf. FO 195 Dardanelles 95; AE Turquie 272.
[2] In contrast to its usual routine, the Russian Black Sea squadron was kept in readiness for the sea as late as December, 1830 (FO 65 R 188).
[3] M. Sabry, *L'Empire égyptien sous Mohamed Ali et la question d'Orient* (Paris, 1930).
[4] G. Douin, *La première guerre de Syrie* (Cairo, 1931). The writer has compared most of Douin's documents with the originals in the French archives and finds them to be faithful reproductions.
[5] AE Egypte 2. Mimaut wrote in April that, if the Syrian expedition were attempted, Ibrahim Pasha would command it.
[6] Mimaut to Sebastiani, May 19, 1831, *ibid.*
[7] *Ibid.*
[8] *Ibid.*
[9] The reaction in Constantinople, after the open break between Turkey and Egypt, was for the sultan to order the cherif replaced (May, 1832).
[10] Canning remained only until August, 1832, however.
[11] AE Egypte 2.
[12] AE Turquie 263.
[13] Sebastiani to Mimaut, March 7, 1832, AE Egypte 2.
[14] AE Turquie 263.
[15] AE Egypte 2.
[16] *Ibid.*
[17] AE Turquie 263.
[18] AE Egypte 2.
[19] Mimaut to Sebastiani, May 29, 1832, AE Egypte 2.
[20] MM, BB⁴, carton 544, quoted by Douin in *La première guerre de Syrie*, I, 208.
[21] AE Egypte 2.
[22] AE Turquie 264.
[23] AE Egypte 2.
[24] *Ibid.*
[25] *Ibid.*
[26] AE Turquie 264.
[27] MM, BB⁴, carton 544, quoted by Douin in *La première guerre de Syrie*, I, 241.
[28] Mimaut to Sebastiani, September 3, 1832, AE Egypte 3.
[29] So Abdullah later detailed it to Boislecomte (AEMD Turquie 72). At that time an English engineer was inspecting the port of Kosseir, the British government still planning some day to reopen the old route to India through Egypt (AE Egypte 2).
[30] *Ibid.*
[31] HHSA Alexandrien, fol. 1. The protest was directed to Mehemet Ali and the problem was referred to their respective governments; signing the protest were the consuls of Sardinia, the United States, France, Austria, Tuscany, and Great Britain.
[32] AE Turquie 264.
[33] *Ibid.*
[34] Quoted by Douin in *La première guerre de Syrie*, I, 265.
[35] AE Egypte 2.
[36] AE Turquie 264.
[37] *Ibid.*
[38] AE Egypte 2.
[39] See pp. 89–93.
[40] AE Egypte 2.
[41] AE Turquie 264.
[42] AE Egypte 3.

[43] *Ibid.*
[44] AE Egypte 2.
[45] *Ibid.*; and MM, BB⁴, carton 544, quoted by Douin in *La première guerre de Syrie*, I, 355, 410–411.
[46] AE Egypte 3.
[47] AE Turquie 264.
[48] *Ibid.*; AE Egypte 3.
[49] AE Egypte 3. Mimaut the same day was directed to favor the cause of Sidi Ali as against the claims of Mohammed Bey in the current rivalry in Tripoli.
[50] AE Turquie 265.
[51] Mimaut to Varenne, November 27–28, 1832, AE Egypte 3.
[52] AE Turquie 265.
[53] AE Egypte 3.
[54] AE Turquie 265.
[55] This step, in answer to the Austrian occupation of Bologna, was taken during the brief tenure of Casimir Perier. Despite protests, the French remained in Ancona until December, 1838.
[56] FO 78 T 472.
[57] AE Turquie 265.
[58] FO 78 T 211, published by C. W. Crawley in *The Question of Greek Independence*, pp. 237–245.
[59] Acerbi reported to Metternich (August 28, November 16, 1832) that all the Muslim populations as well as the partisans of the former janissaries seemed to have great admiration for the aggressive government of Mehemet Ali (HHSA Alexandrien, fol. 1).
[60] AE Turquie 265.
[61] *Ibid.*
[62] *Ibid.*

VI. FRANCE MEDIATES

THE PEACE OF KUTIAH

THE FOREGOING section has presented French policy in the Turco-Egyptian War as that of a Power officially neutral but showing consistent favoritism to Egypt through friendship, advice, and encouragement. It also outlined the motives and the facts of France's offers of mediation to both contestants. The outstanding recorded developments were the admission by France, in advance, of Egypt's right to Syria and the determination of France to prevent, if possible, any European intervention in the contest. By the end of 1832 intervention by Russia had become a foregone conclusion. We now consider the period in which France vigorously pressed her self-appointed role of mediator.

1. VARENNE THE INTERMEDIARY

Early in January, 1833, there appeared to be some amelioration of the pressing problems confronting Turkey. Muraviev had departed for Alexandria to warn Mehemet Ali of the dangers involved if the advance of Ibrahim's armies toward the Turkish capital continued. A Russian officer had been appointed to go to the camp of Ibrahim Pasha, but his departure was delayed while Turkey considered the advisability of accepting Butenev's invitation to have a Turkish agent accompany the Russian. Halil Pasha, ex-*capitan pasha*, had been commissioned to negotiate with Mehemet Ali if Muraviev's mission was successful, the Porte thus making a tardy response to the indispensable requirement of Mehemet Ali's answer to Turkey on November 26. Varenne had suddenly become an important figure in Turkish counsels. The Turkish foreign minister told him that Halil had been appointed as negotiator in deference to his recommendation.

More important, the sultan accepted Varenne's offer of December 31 to write letters to Mehemet Ali and Ibrahim, proving that Turkey was now ready to act upon the opportunity which Mehemet Ali had presented in November. The Turks were not yet ready to announce their concessions in the interest of peace, but Varenne believed they would do much more than cede Syria, including the pashalic of Damas, if necessary.

Varenne drafted three letters, instead of two, phrasing the third for indirect communication through pro-French General Seve, of Ibrahim's staff, to the conquering commander. Those to Mehemet Ali and Ibrahim, bearing the date of January 8, were approved by the Turkish council after additions were made, and then passed under the eyes of the sultan. The Russian officer carried those for Ibrahim and Seve; Halil served as the messenger to Mehemet Ali.[1]

In the three letters the war was termed a "debate," the sultan appearing as the sovereign and Mehemet Ali the vassal, the character and position of each being scrupulously observed; neither the words "war," "negotiation," "armistice," nor any other term which would signify the relations of Power to Power were employed in Varenne's communications. Varenne's letter to Mehemet Ali announced that the Porte had received favorably the overtures addressed through the intermediary, Mimaut, and sincerely hoped to see terminated the "deplorable debate which agitated the empire and attracted the attention of Europe." The letter concluded with an addition introduced by the Porte which stated that the sultan had available large forces on land and sea and the promise of aid from his allies; but, since he wanted to use conciliatory measures instead, the responsibility for the future would now rest upon Mehemet Ali. The letter to Ibrahim stated that Halil was en route to Alexandria with full powers to conclude an accommodation with the pasha, the decision having been taken in response to proposals made by Mehemet Ali through Mimaut. Varenne stated he was being used as the source for this notification because he was the agent of a Power which, although desiring to see the Ottoman Empire prosper, had on numerous occasions shown its confidence in Mehemet Ali. Varenne here confined himself to the attestation of the state of affairs and to the expression of the hope that Ibrahim would deem it proper to halt his advance. He had been assured by the Turkish government that, if Ibrahim adopted that attitude, the forces of Turkey likewise would remain inactive during the negotiations. Such inaction on both sides would conform with Mehemet Ali's own original proposal. The letter to Seve solicited that officer's aid for the success of the proposal made to Ibrahim. Seve was requested to impress upon Ibrahim the facts that the intervention of the Russian armies was imminent and that

---

[1] For notes to section vi, see pp. 211–213.

collective mediation was being talked by the diplomats. If either Russian or collective intervention occurred, the position of Mehemet Ali would suffer. At least Seve might show Ibrahim the desirability of halting his march until after he had heard again from Mehemet Ali.[2]

Varenne's comment on the possibility of collective intervention was fully substantiated in two important dispatches which Broglie addressed to Egypt and Turkey about a week later. Basing his new comments on the reports of Ibrahim's advances down to the end of November and upon the reactions which had reached Paris from other capitals, Broglie again directed Mimaut to speak sharply to Mehemet Ali. Great Britain, he said, probably would take some resolution to guarantee the Porte effectively against the dangers which Mehemet Ali's ambitions presented; Austria was not less alert, especially to prevent the complications for Europe which would inevitably follow a revolution at Constantinople. As for France, the previously announced policy was repeated. If Mehemet Ali was not content with the government of Syria, if he "consulted neither his own nor the interests of Europe" to extend his ambitions, "if he carried his conquests into Asia Minor at the risk of shaking the empire to its foundation, he must cease to count on France." Moreover, he must expect France in that event to take a front rank among those who would oppose his ambition. "France wished, as did England and Austria, that the Ottoman Empire remain intact; that nothing occur to compromise the general peace." Broglie criticized the conduct of Ibrahim in the same dispatch, both for crossing the Taurus and for the tone of his bulletins to the populations, which had indicated that Mehemet Ali acted as a sovereign equal with the sultan. Mehemet Ali was criticized for not having sent a negotiator to Constantinople.[3]

A copy of this dispatch was sent to Varenne, with instructions to show it to the Turkish foreign minister in order to "convince him of the benevolent and impartial mediation offered to him" by France and as evidence "of the lively interest France still held for the Ottoman Empire." Broglie suggested that the tone which Mimaut would use in the representation could not fail to impress the pasha. Clarifying his reference to the attitude of Great Britain, Broglie stated that England was considering some sort of aid to Turkey but that he had spoken against any direct intervention.

With respect to the peace terms he thought that Turkey should award Syria to Egypt but disapproved of the pasha's further claims to Adana and a relationship with the Porte as detached as that of the former dey of Algeria. Mehemet Ali should be content with the four pashalics of Syria, under grants like those under which he held Egypt and Crete. The Porte was to be cautioned against the illusions still noted about the ultimate results of the war; even the loss of a battle by Ibrahim would not terminate the war nor return Syria to the sultan. Varenne was to exploit all circumstances, such as the Egyptian menace to Constantinople and the inconveniences of foreign intervention, to advance the cause of French mediation.

Varenne was also directed to inquire of the Turks whether their rule of closure of the Straits was now to be changed in favor of Russia. If so, the other maritime Powers would claim the same right and the Porte would find itself in the position of being unable to refuse. News of Koniah and of the arrival of Muraviev at Constantinople reached Paris on January 21. Broglie at once sent another instruction to Varenne. France was surprised that Turkey was ready "to become the voluntary vassal of Russia, the natural enemy of the Ottoman power." The other Powers, especially France and England, would not remain indifferent to such an abdication of sovereignty by Turkey. A concert would likely be formed with England to hasten, "with means as efficacious as the circumstances may require," the end of the war. But support of Turkey would be accorded only on condition that she did not alienate herself in favor of Russia. Roussin was at last leaving Toulon and similar instructions were being sent to him. Mimaut was given the same suggestions, with new directions to redouble his efforts, using "peremptory language," to end the war. France wanted Mehemet Ali to negotiate directly with the Turkish council.[4]

2. Muraviev and Halil at Alexandria

The conversations between Muraviev and Mehemet Ali took place in mid-January. The pasha had been prepared for a language of intimidation and menace, but Muraviev used conciliatory phrases instead. It was shown to be agreeable to Russia for Egypt and Turkey to make their own terms, perhaps through the intermediary of a common friend like France; what Russia wanted was peace. Apparently, suggested Mimaut later, Muraviev depended upon appearances and the belligerent language of Acerbi to make his implied threat effective. Acerbi reported that he had seconded Muraviev; Mimaut, that Acerbi did so in conformity with the instructions from Ottenfels. Austria clearly showed, through Acerbi's language and his impatience with Mehemet Ali, said Mimaut, that she was the enemy of the Egyptian revolt and the friend of the sultan. Upon winning the object of his mission—the pasha's agreement to suspend hostilities during further negotiations—Muraviev suddenly departed. During his stay courtesy calls were exchanged with Mimaut, but in these nothing was said about the object of Muraviev's visit to Egypt. The details of the discussions were revealed by Boghos to Mimaut, with the explanation that the order for Ibrahim to halt his advance had been signed in conformity with the French request.[5]

The attitude of Muraviev indicated that Russia would confine her action, if any was taken, to the defense of Constantinople and the Straits, conforming with the new Russian policy effective since 1829. Certainly the reported comments of Muraviev, approved by the subsequent Russian attitude, could only have been interpreted by the pasha as a distinct disinclination for Russia to regain Syria for the sultan.

Although Halil Pasha was at Alexandria at the same time, Muraviev did not talk with him or attempt to concert with him. Varenne's letter was transmitted to Mehemet Ali. It at once became evident that there was a contradiction between the terms of the letter and the terms brought by Halil. Halil conveyed only the sultan's willingness to pardon Mehemet Ali and to concede Acre and its dependencies. Evidently the pasha at least convinced Halil of the Egyptian point of view, for at the end of the month Halil decided to write to Constantinople to see whether the terms could not be modified.

Meanwhile, word reached Alexandria that Ibrahim was continuing his advance. The pasha hoped the restraining order would be delivered to his son at least in time to stop him at Brusa, which was envisaged as a good winter headquarters. In order to expedite the reference to Constantinople, Mehemet Ali asked Mimaut to place the "Sphinx" at the disposal of Halil, which Mimaut declined to do. The pasha then made ready one of the best Egyptian frigates (February 4). Halil took back with him the proposals of Mehemet

Ali, which, briefly, called for the cession, under tribute, of Syria and the district of Adana. After his departure, upon the insistent advice of Mimaut, the order for Ibrahim to halt was repeated by Mehemet Ali.[6]

3. RUSSIAN ARMY SUMMONED

The rapid advance of Ibrahim toward Constantinople brought a new crisis at the end of January. Heedless of Varenne's letter, Ibrahim continued his march. He had answered on January 17, saying he would not be justified in stopping until after he had learned the intentions of his father. Through Seve's reply it was learned also that Ibrahim intended to winter at Brusa. Both letters were communicated to Akif Effendi, the Turkish foreign minister, as a matter of course. Akif suggested that Ibrahim's letter was perhaps the work of a European. His opinion being solicited, Varenne replied that the coming of Ibrahim to Brusa would be unfortunate and that the Porte should neglect nothing that would turn him from that intention. "But," he added, "if Ibrahim insists, it would be better to consent than to force the issue."[7]

The real effect of Ibrahim's letter was to force Turkey into the hands of Russia. The sultan asked Butenev to hold the Russian armies of the Crimea and the Danube in readiness because, if Ibrahim actually advanced as Seve had indicated, the summons for prompt aid would be issued. Varenne at once interposed objections to this Turkish attitude, adding the gloomy prophecy that the appearance of the Russians on the Bosporus would mean the end of the Ottoman Empire. Mandeville, the British chargé, supported this view with his opinion that it would be dangerous to call the Russians.[8] Varenne counseled negotiation with Mehemet Ali, believing that only at Alexandria could a definite solution be reached. Akif nevertheless requested Varenne to write again to Ibrahim. Varenne made the counterrequest for Turkey to suspend her summons to Russia for ten days, to await the reply. This was taken *ad referendum*. Varenne assured Akif that France and England would not leave Turkey in the lurch and suggested that "it was even possible that those two Powers would be disposed to provoke some diplomatic stipulations to guarantee the integrity of Turkey's territory or to hasten the needed ameliorations."[9]

Varenne's second letter to the Egyptian commander was dated

January 30. It informed Ibrahim of the "serious complication" which his proposed march to Brusa had produced in Constantinople. Although Varenne in no sense wished to intimidate the commander, he thought it his duty to suggest that bravery did not exclude prudence. The appearance of Russia would be a certainty if he came on; then the whole Egyptian success up to that point would be compromised. Since Halil was carrying on negotiations at Alexandria and since Mehemet Ali had originally proposed to halt all movements upon the first appearance of a Turkish negotiator, Ibrahim was advised to defer his advance until the result of that negotiation was known. To Seve also Varenne wrote again, repeating the same points but suggesting that similar advice from this responsible officer in Ibrahim's camp would probably restrain Ibrahim from further advances. Not only was it essential for Ibrahim to halt, Varenne stated, but it was also necessary for him to revise his language; some phrases of deference to the Porte were in order. The same day Varenne wrote again to Mehemet Ali. Here he confined himself to the problem of the imminent danger of Russian intervention, making "conciliation an imperious necessity."[10]

On February 2 the sultan sent Akif to Butenev to accept formally the Russian support "on land and sea, to force the submission of the rebel Mehemet Ali and his son Ibrahim." Varenne at once requested that the invitation to Russia be countermanded. Thereupon Akif countered with the request that France and England undertake to stop Ibrahim's advance beforehand.[11] Of course neither Varenne nor Mandeville had any authority even to discuss that speculative probability.

4. IBRAHIM HALTS AT KUTIAH

Ibrahim reached Kutiah early in February. Varenne was on the point of making a third démarche by letter when the answers to the second letters were received (February 10). Ibrahim explained that he had continued to Kutiah in the interest of winter provisions for his army but that he would remain there, in conformity with the new directions of Mehemet Ali. Seve also gave assurances that Ibrahim would not go beyond Kutiah.[12]

Encouragement for the harassed Varenne also came from Alexandria. Muraviev, who had taken a slow return trip, calling at Greece, arrived on February 12 with the information (which

Varenne said was not news, as he had been saying the same thing for three months), that the pasha would be able to come to terms with the sultan in short order. But Turkey refused to countermand the invitation of February 2 to Russia. Mimaut from Alexandria wrote Broglie on February 13 that the war was over in fact, according to interpretations in Egypt. No one thought that Turkey would reject the proposal transmitted to Constantinople by Halil. It was believed, moreover, that, if any European Power made a "suspect demonstration," Russia would occupy the Dardanelles. Hatred of Russia was quite in evidence in Egypt at the moment.[13] Events soon proved that the Egyptian optimism was unwarranted.

5. Egyptian Policy of France Opposed

None of the Powers had been ready for the suddenness with which affairs in Asia Minor had reached a climax. Only Russia had prepared to interpose physical aid. Indicative of the lack of preparation for the problem as it was posed early in February, 1833, was the fact that Roussin, long since appointed, had not yet arrived at Constantinople. Nor had England had an ambassador at the Porte since the departure of Canning.

Great Britain became active with news of the defeat of Reshid at Koniah and the acceptance of Russian support by Turkey. The departure of the new ambassador, Ponsonby, was hastened, and Patrick Campbell, a new consul general with the augmented title of "agent consul general," was sent to replace Barker. The instructions to Campbell reflected the great disparity in British and French views on the cession of Syria.

As transmitted to Broglie, Campbell's instructions were based on two hypotheses. If the negotiations had produced the desired result by the time of his arrival, he would assume the routine duties of his office; if not, he would do everything possible to lead Mehemet Ali to conclude peace, using a language analogous to Mimaut's. The British government instructed Campbell to disapprove formally of the conduct of Mehemet Ali and to assess against him the responsibility for the original break with Turkey. The British cabinet was also concerned about the possibility of the extension of the pasha's power to the Persian Gulf, an idea which Broglie had sought to discourage.[14] Nothing was said about Syria, but Campbell was also to state to the pasha, as shown by the British records, that the British government attached great importance to the maintenance of the Ottoman Empire and considered Turkey a material element in the European balance of power. Any lessening of the sultan's Asiatic resources would reduce his ability to defend his Balkan possessions. The British government deemed it "of importance to prevent not only a dissolution, but even a partial dismemberment of the Turkish Empire."[15] We shall see later that Campbell's secret and contingent instructions related also to the fleet as a factor for the repression of Egypt, but nothing was said in them about a concert with France in that particular. The documents clearly reveal the dissimilar views of the two Powers on Egypt. We have also seen that the same dissimilarity was true, at least in the methods, of both the Russian and the French policies with respect to Egypt.

Austria also became active, and in an anti-French sense, about the same time. Prokesch-Osten was commissioned by Metternich for a special mission to Egypt (on February 23). The secret instructions for Prokesch, supplementary to his more general and ostensible instructions (which were communicated to Russia and England), showed that Metternich shared Palmerston's, and opposed Broglie's, views on Egypt. Prokesch's special and ostensible object was to make a formal demand of the pasha for the evacuation of Asia Minor. In this he was to coöperate with Campbell and to preserve a unity of views at least with Russia and Great Britain.[16] In addition, as revealed by his secret instructions, the Austrian envoy was to advance two policies. The first was to condemn the pasha's revolt, and the second, to make it clear that Austria would in no sense act as a mediator between sovereign and vassal. It was stated by the chancellor that the Powers were in agreement on the first point, whereas France had indicated that she would not conform to the second. Notwithstanding these stern assertions, Metternich further instructed Prokesch to admit to the pasha that the latter's acquisition of Syria was possible, if won by legal means. The area known as Syria, however, Metternich pointed out, was capable of various delimitations. Metternich thought that the sultan intended to grant only the pashalic of Acre; Mehemet Ali would want much more. Austria would not oppose the inclusion of the pashalic of Damas but would not agree to the inclusion of Caramania, which would menace the heart of Ottoman power. Perhaps the Porte would ask in exchange a limitation of the Egyptian fleet, in which event a European understanding might be necessary.[17]

6. Roussin Guarantees Peace

Varenne for weeks had known of the disparity between French views and those of Russia and Austria and had also remarked on the relative lack of coöperation of England. With the Russian intervention about to become a fact, the essence of the tenability of the now almost isolated French position on Syria had become a question of speed in the reëstablishment of peace between Turkey and Egypt.

The arrival of Roussin on February 17 was the signal for some interesting developments. Guided throughout by Varenne, Roussin at once became a principal party in the negotiations at Constantinople. Within four days he had assumed the role of guarantor of the signature of peace on Turkey's terms, thus going far beyond the policy of mediation which was the official policy of France at the time. The reason for his aggressiveness was not so much the attitude of Turkey or Egypt as it was the new preponderance of Russia at the Turkish capital. His initial diplomatic effort was to repeat Varenne's attempt to have Turkey countermand the invitation for Russian aid. But his effort came too late; the first contingent of the Russian fleet, comprising ten vessels, anchored in the Bosporus (almost under the windows of the French ambassador's palace, he said) on February 20. Hence Roussin had two principal tasks: (1), to get the peace signed and (2), to try to get the Russian forces withdrawn from the Bosporus.

Two days before the Russians arrived, Roussin had used his best arguments to have their coming stopped. He even threatened that, if they came by the Bosporus, it might be expected that the French would come by the Dardanelles; in support of this thesis he permitted the Turkish foreign minister to misinterpret his title of admiral in the French marine as one currently designating his command of the French naval station in the Levant. Akif on February 18 promised to support the French demand for a counterorder to Russia and to hasten the understanding with Egypt.[18]

On February 21 the first of Roussin's principal objectives was virtually accomplished, he thought. On that day he signed with Turkey a convention by which in the name of France he guaranteed

that Egypt would accept the terms for peace which he had found
Turkey willing to accept, in exchange for the Turkish promise to
request the Russians to leave Turkey. The negotiation of the convention had followed his vain attempt on the day of the Russians'
arrival to bluff Turkey into the belief that he was going to depart at
once. He had declared that the arrival of the Russian squadron had
deprived Turkey of her independence, hence he saw no need for a
French ambassador. Upon Akif's assurance that Turkey would do
something about the Russian problem—specifically, that she
would withdraw the invitation to Russia upon satisfactory guarantees that peace with Egypt would be signed—he claimed he had
won his point and launched the immediate negotiation which put
the Turkish and his own promises into writing. The terms on which
peace was guaranteed were those originally taken to Egypt by
Halil Pasha. This meant that Egypt would win only part of Syria,
without Damas and without Adana, the additional territory claimed
by Mehemet Ali in his counterproposals returned on February 4.

In accepting the Turkish limits of the four pashalics of Syria
which centered in Acre, Roussin recognized that he was in fact
opposing the known desires of the Chamber of Commerce of Marseille and of the fourteen southern *départements* of France. But, he
inquired in his report to Broglie, "What consideration can balance
the immense fact of a Russian squadron anchored under the walls
of Constantinople?" In his convention with Turkey he had acted
alone. There was no Egyptian on hand of whom he might inquire
whether the terms were satisfactory to the pasha, considering the
conditions; in Mandeville he found an attitude which he described
as approaching "stupor" but which nevertheless was willing to encourage anything which would relieve the Russian intervention.
Among the other diplomats he found absolute reserve, except for
the Austrian and Prussian representatives who were anti-French.
It had seemed to him mandatory, he said, to seize the occasion "to
conserve the integrity of the independence of Turkey by withdrawing the Russian squadron from Constantinople as the essential object."[19]

Such was Roussin's decision. In the convention he signed with
Turkey, however, he said nothing about how he would guarantee
the signature of peace, nor did he say how the Russians were to be
made agreeable to the transaction which involved them. He did not

promise to employ force (nor might he, under his instructions from Broglie). To the Turks the contrast between an undefined promise and the presence of the physical power of Russia already at hand must have appeared striking. Several technical problems were discussed but left unanswered when the convention was signed. Among these was the question whether the Russians were to be forced out, if they declined to leave when requested, the Egyptian army still being at Kutiah; and also whether, if found agreeable, they were to be permitted to await favorable winds (presumably, those blowing with adequate force in the direction of Russia). Another important doubtful point was which part of the convention would be applicable first, the peace or the withdrawal of Russia. Roussin seems to have taken for granted that Mehemet Ali would accept his recommendation of the best available terms for peace. Events proved this supposition to be unsound. And Roussin's particular role of mediator was soon to be found injurious to the French position both in Constantinople and in Alexandria.

7. BROGLIE DISAPPROVES

In London the reduced area to be assigned to Mehemet Ali under Roussin's convention found approval. Palmerston wrote:

The terms to be imposed on the pasha are good, inasmuch as he does not get Damascus or Aleppo, and so has not the avenues of Mesopotamia; and, moreover, he is to hold his pashalics from year to year, as he is supposed to hold that of Egypt.... Besides, Turkey is as good an occupier of the road to India as an active Arabian sovereign would be. We must try to help the Sultan in organizing his army, navy, and finances; and if he can get these three departments into good order he may still hold his ground.[20]

The reactions in Paris to Roussin's opposition to Russia were favorable, but the reactions to his limiting of Egypt's territorial gains were unfavorable. The public discussion centered about Russia and more especially about an article, presumably inspired by the French ministry, which appeared in the *Journal des débats*, opposing the Russian support of Turkey. Broglie refused to disavow the implications of the article.

The official ministerial response to Roussin's activity took two courses, neither of which had anything to do with making good Roussin's guarantee of peace. One was the order of the French marine which reënforced the French squadron in the Levant and directed Hugon to follow the instructions of Roussin except in the employment of force (which was not to be used "without the positive and direct order of the government"). If peace were signed, the supplemental ships might be used to complete the long-delayed evacuation of the Morea. The other course taken by the cabinet was the order for Broglie to send Roussin a comprehensive new instruction directing the ambassador to return to the official French policy of mediation and to favor the cession of all of Syria to the pasha.[21]

Broglie's instruction was contained in a lengthy confidential communication. Its principal points may be summarized. (1) Despite Russia's protests about Roussin's conduct, every support would be given the ambassador as far as his attitude toward the Russian intervention was concerned. Yet even here France was exercising care to keep out of the official correspondence anything reflecting a passioned approach or anything attacking the person, character, or loyalty of intentions of Tsar Nicholas. (2) The French government would have preferred a less specific pronouncement of the terms for the peace between Turkey and Egypt than those provided by the ambassador's convention of February 21. The evacuation of Asia Minor might be proper. But it was easy to see that Mehemet Ali would not be content with less than all of Syria. In any event, France did not favor the use of force against Egypt. The precise territorial delimitation of Syria was of secondary interest for France; her first concern was not to jeopardize her interests in Egypt, and still less to abandon them without real necessity. Moreover, the terms borne by Halil had not represented the maximum areas Turkey was willing to cede, as Akif had told Varenne. (3) Roussin thereafter was to work for the evacuation of Asia Minor and to let Egypt have all of Syria. Although in his correspondence with Mimaut Broglie stated he was supporting the ambassador, Roussin was nevertheless to have the terms changed if possible. (4) Roussin might well return to the policy of vigorous mediation. The cession of all Syria would represent a compromise between the two extremes sought by Turkey and Egypt.[22]

Thus Broglie was willing that Egypt take less than what Mehemet Ali had claimed (all of Syria plus Adana in Caramania), but he was unwilling that Turkey should make no additional concessions besides the already proffered four central pashalics of Syria.

8. The Egyptian Ultimatum

Despite the halting of Ibrahim at Kutiah and the cajolings of Roussin, it was obvious that Turkey would not be likely to renounce the support of Russia until the Egyptian forces had retreated from their menacing position on the way to Constantinople.[23] Nor would the Russians be likely to withdraw until that event occurred.[24] The withdrawal, however, would be carried out only after Mehemet Ali had ordered it. The negotiations for the moment shifted to Alexandria. From February 22 to March 24 Roussin impatiently awaited the answer of the pasha to his convention, well surmising that the prestige of France in the Levant depended upon it. During the period Roussin (on March 1) brusquely addressed Ibrahim in Turkey's behalf to help restore the authority of Turkey in Smyrna.[25]

In order to make doubly sure that Mehemet Ali would give prompt and careful consideration to the guarantee of peace in the Franco-Turkish convention, Roussin had instructed Mimaut to use striking language to win the pasha over to Roussin's views. Conforming to the instructions must have seemed strange to Mimaut after his constantly friendly communications to the pasha for four years, and the word conveyed by him must have sounded still more strange to Mehemet Ali after the four years of protestations of French friendship for him. The authorized language included verbal threats for the appearance of the French and British fleets off the coast of Egypt and the preparation for the withdrawal of the French officers from the service of the pasha.

Mimaut's communication of the ambassador's guarantee of peace with terms short of the cession of Damas and Adana brought an ironical laugh from Mehemet Ali. The pasha stated that he had been abandoned by the Powers most interested in Egypt and that, although his refusal was his decree of death, he would "die with sword in hand." In vain Mimaut sought to convince the pasha of the continued good will of France. But he followed his instructions and emphasized that "the urgency for acceptance was such as to admit of no modifications of the fixed bases" for peace. Mimaut's communication was weakened by several factors, aside from the strategic position the Egyptian army occupied in Asia Minor. The implied British flattery in the designated new title for Campbell permitted Mehemet Ali to feel his power in Europe,[26] and the pasha had positive information that the squadrons of which Roussin spoke were composed of only a few frigates and light ships. Mehemet Ali astutely observed, moreover, that the alleged urgency in the situation was the presence of Russian forces in Turkey, hence, since that was annoying the French and British, the appearance of the Anglo-French fleets off Alexandria would be an ineffective way to meet the challenge of Russia at Constantinople. He understood also that there was the constant menace of revolution at Constantinople. The threat to withdraw the French officers was answered by the elevation of Cerisy to the rank of Egyptian general. Mehemet Ali said his position was misunderstood in Europe; that independence was not his goal. In any event, he would resume his advance in Asia Minor rather than have his victory sacrificed.[27]

Mehemet Ali had ready both his answer to Roussin and his new plans of action on March 8. His letter to Roussin reviewed the communications he had received and asked the question, "How could the ambassador thus sacrifice Mehemet Ali?" Confining his gains to a small province, "which the ambassador called pashalics," would in fact decree his political death. He was certain, however, that France and England would not refuse him justice. He hoped the ambassador would advise the acceptance of his last propositions, those made through the intermediary, Halil Pasha.[28] Thus did the pasha decline to submit to the injunctions of the French ambassador; thus had Roussin failed to attain the peace he had guaranteed.

Mehemet Ali commissioned a special envoy, Reshid Bey, to go to Constantinople to bear an ultimatum. This forbade a diminution of his terms for peace and gave Turkey five days for its answer. Equally important, Mehemet Ali took alternate decisions with respect to his subsequent procedure, based on the outcome of his ultimatum. Authority was sent to Ibrahim Pasha to treat for the definitive peace if Turkey accepted, and the commander was further authorized to begin his retreat if the Turkish acceptance were properly authenticated. If Turkey declined, however, the pasha planned to renew the struggle.[29]

One concrete result had appeared from Roussin's effort, the renewed promise of Ibrahim (March 1) that he would not advance farther without orders from Mehemet Ali. Meanwhile, at Constantinople Roussin had already pronounced his convention a dead letter, owing to the failure of Turkey to send the Russians away. Not only had the squadron not departed, but news was at hand on March 7 of the approaching embarkation (which took place March 23) of a land army of 14,000 Russians at Odessa.[30]

Mehemet Ali's ultimatum was received on March 24, giving Turkey until the twenty-ninth for its consideration. Those five days were busy ones for Roussin, although his personal intervention had been rendered powerless by the Egyptian refusal.

Roussin's attitude was frankly pessimistic when he phrased his report to Broglie on March 24. Aside from his untenable charge that Turkey had killed his ill-advised convention of February 21 by nonfulfillment[31] and by the summoning of the Russian reënforcements, there were other more pressing matters for the future. Roussin presented his private opinion that Mehemet Ali should be stopped, "even at the price of a war against him." The Porte must at once decide, he said, whether to accede to Egypt in order to escape immediate collapse or to pass under Russian tutelage. The second alternative Roussin thought more probable. Turkey now knew, he reported, that French interest had been withdrawn; it was for the government at Paris to decide what to do next. Apparently not quite sure whether French policy really favored the maintenance of Turkey, Roussin added the words, "under the supposition of the system of conservation of the Turkish state," to the foregoing sentence. Roussin then exaggerated the effect of the Egyptian answer. Correctly stating Egypt's terms (Egypt wanting all of Syria, including Aleppo and Damas, as well as Adana), Roussin interpreted that these required "the dissolution of the Ottoman Empire and the inevitable fall of the Sultan."[32]

Far from turning Turkey over to Russia, Roussin two days later in a two-hour conference with the Turkish foreign minister advised Turkey to accede to the demands of Mehemet Ali rather than to permit the continued intervention of Russia. Still later he threatened to withdraw from the negotiation if Turkey did not yield. In his report Roussin asked Broglie to decide which representative was fulfilling the instructions of the French government: Mimaut, whom the Turks charged had encouraged Mehemet Ali to overthrow the Ottoman Empire, or himself, who sought to preserve the Ottoman Empire. In writing Mimaut that he was trying to get the Turks to accept the Egyptian terms, he made a significant statement, which also had been true of French policy for twenty-five years: "I have found in my instructions (which are stated to be common) the positive and express wish to conserve (if possible) an [not 'the'] Ottoman Empire." Mimaut replied that the confusion suggested by Roussin was the natural result of the distances involved, the divergence in the correspondence between Alexandria, Paris, and Constantinople, and the rapidity of events.[33]

9. THE PEACE SIGNED

On the one hand the ultimatum of Egypt and on the other the knowledge that Ibrahim now had full powers to negotiate for peace resulted in the formulation by Turkey of compromise terms for Ibrahim. Turkey agreed to conclude peace on the fundamental basis of according all of Syria to the pasha, leaving the question of Adana undecided. Reshid Bey agreed to accompany Varenne, commissioned by Turkey and by Roussin to bear the new proposals to Ibrahim's camp at Kutiah.[34]

A few days later almost the same type of compromise was worked out at Alexandria. Despite Campbell's and Mimaut's arguments, Mehemet Ali seemed to insist upon holding to the full terms of his ultimatum. Then Prokesch-Osten arrived, adding his voice to the persuasive talents now available in Egypt. The pasha was worn down. The discussions evoked Egypt's reduced *sine qua non* for peace—namely Mehemet Ali's possession of all of Syria under tribute, which, if granted, would be followed by the retirement of his forces from beyond the Taurus.[35] Hence both at Constantinople and Alexandria the terms had reached an approximate unity.

Significant as another illustration of the simultaneous emergence of a compromise solution was the dispatch phrased by Broglie at Paris on November 6. Its tenor was to instruct Roussin to see that Egypt got more than originally offered, but, in any event, to obtain as the principal French object the retirement of Russia from Turkey. The instruction that Roussin work with England represented the beginnings of the Anglo-French entente against Russia. According to these new instructions the apparent isolation of the French embassy at Constantinople was to be terminated, and no overt hostility was to be shown Butenev. Boislecomte, a special negotiator ordered to Alexandria, was to advise Egypt to accept all of

Syria, including Damas but excluding Adana. Roussin was placed on his own responsibility with respect to the type of language to be employed to Turkey; he might speak energetically or in a conciliatory tone.[36] By this date Roussin, in speculating on the coming of the French fleet, advised the French foreign minister that the fleet would do more harm than good, since Russia was already master of the situation at Constantinople.

It is not surprising, considering the developments, that a peace was signed at Kutiah on April 9, embodied in a convention of the type of an armistice (without, however, bearing that designation). Varenne presented the Turkish offer and watched the exchange of signatures. Syria was ceded, Adana being left to the future disposition of the sultan. Mehemet Ali had always spoken of the timber resources of the Adana district as his objective, but all the other comments on it during the days which preceded the peace had emphasized its strategic importance.[37] Although Ibrahim still insisted upon the inclusion of Adana, which controlled the passes of the Taurus, he expressed enough confidence in the existing dispositions of Turkey to agree to withdraw his army into the territories of Syria proper, and on the tenth his retreat began. This withdrawal was made a part of the convention, along with the promise of the sultan to grant full amnesty to the participants in the rebellion. Varenne had influenced Ibrahim's decision by the statement that it was unlikely that either France or England would agree to the inclusion of Adana.[38] Roussin regarded the convention as restoring the French position in the Levant.

The reactions to the Convention of Kutiah were varied. With first news of the tenor of the discussions, Roussin already had written Ibrahim that the cession of Adana was impossible. After Varenne's return the ambassador pointedly wrote the same to Mehemet Ali (on April 18); the latter regarded the status in which Adana was left as the Porte's way of preparing for the later transference of the region to Egypt. Ibrahim wrote to Roussin on April 20 that he was counting upon the later cession of Adana and that he had agreed to retreat on that basis. The Porte exercised its prerogative of the convention when on April 18 the new designation of the administration of Syria did not mention Adana.[39]

Thus, although peace had been signed, the question of Adana was still open. The presence of the Russians, whose embarkations continued, had served, and might still serve, to stiffen the Turkish resistance anew.

10. BOISLECOMTE'S NEGOTIATIONS

The solution of the remaining two problems of the Turco-Egyptian settlement, the question of Adana and the completion of the Egyptian evacuation of Asia Minor, was effected early in May. The final settlements were associated, as far as the negotiations at Alexandria were concerned, with the mission of Baron Boislecomte to Egypt at that time. We have already encountered Boislecomte, who, as director of political affairs at the French foreign office in 1829, had collaborated with Polignac in the Polignac and Drovetti plans. Since the July Revolution he had been in retirement but now he was called into service by Broglie.

Boislecomte's instructions, dated April 8—just one day before the Convention of Kutiah was signed—reveal French policy at Paris immediately before the peace. Broglie reviewed the details of the discussions of terms for peace which we have seen repeated so many times preceding the convention. The Turco-Egyptian question, added Broglie, had been made European with the advance of Ibrahim into Asia Minor and the intervention of Russia. Since it was important that the question promptly lose that serious character, France must now act more strongly than ever to secure the evacuation of Asia Minor by Egypt. Hence Boislecomte was to go to Egypt and state to Mehemet Ali that he would lose the good will which every Frenchman, following the lead of the government, bore him if he did not now come to terms with Turkey. The French government did not state whether Egypt should give up its claim to Adana, but presumably this sacrifice was considered in order, to facilitate the signing of peace. Boislecomte's object was to get results. Since Broglie recognized that the rapidity of events might already have intervened to effect a settlement, he instructed Boiselecomte in that event to make a general survey of the Levant with particular reference to the possibility of expanding French commerce.[40]

As reported by Broglie in a subsequent dispatch, the British cabinet, almost simultaneously with the departure of Boislecomte, ordered a more emphatic stand than theretofore in opposition to the seemingly adamant position of Mehemet Ali. It directed a large

squadron to proceed toward Alexandria,[41] to be at the disposition
of Campbell. The British order, modeled on that given the three
allied commanders before the battle of Navarino in 1827, directed
that, if peace had not yet been signed, the fleet might be employed
by Campbell to intercept all troops, munitions, and provisions destined for Ibrahim's army. In receiving Palmerston's communication from Granville, Broglie observed that the British instruction
provided for action only in the contingency of Turco-Egyptian
relations, whereas the greater danger of Russia at Constantinople
was not provided for. Broglie also termed the instruction "singu-
lar," since it gave Campbell broad powers without stipulating the
conditions to which Mehemet Ali might be expected to submit to
prevent the application of the contingent order for British interference. He explained to Granville that the French squadron had
been placed at the disposition of Roussin at Constantinople, not of
Mimaut at Alexandria—an indication of the divergence of the English and French objectives—for the purpose of a simple demonstration and that anything beyond that would have to wait for further
instructions from Paris. Campbell had been directed to concert
with Mimaut and Prokesch, indicating less of a disparity in Anglo-
French objectives than seemed evident from the fleet order alone.
At the same conference Broglie clarified the objects of the mission
of Boislecomte, who was authorized to use his own discretion as to
whether he made any use of the information about the British fleet.[42]
It seems that Boislecomte was in possession of the information (on
May 4) in advance of Campbell, permitting him to use it to advantage in his important conference with Mehemet Ali on May 5.

This new development in London was of great concern to Broglie,
who analyzed the problem to Roussin. British policy was his preoccupation. Adding to his dissatisfaction with Russian intervention, news had already reached him through Vienna—and was
seemingly confirmed by Mimaut's reports from Egypt—which indicated that England and France tended to go in opposite directions since it now appeared that England had shifted to a policy of
hostility to Mehemet Ali. Broglie thought that England's dis-
quietude concerning the Egyptian mastery of Syria came because
of Mehemet Ali's holding the routes of commercial communication
between the eastern Mediterranean and the Persian Gulf. Although
Broglie admitted that England clearly was not indifferent to the

presence of the Russians, it was also clear that England assigned their presence almost exclusively to Egypt. The differences in policy were obvious from the contrasting objectives of the western fleets, the British alone being contingently able, upon consular orders, to repress Egypt. Broglie stated he had suggested to England that the seeming divergence in western policies would give Mehemet Ali a reason for delaying his settlement with the sultan.[43]

Boislecomte was received in formal audience by Mehemet Ali on May 1,[44] the private audience for official discussions being held four days later. The discussions turned on whether the pasha should accept Syria, without Adana, Boislecomte advising him to do so. Mehemet Ali stated that he wanted Adana for strategic defense against Constantinople; Boislecomte reminded him that Adana was strategically offensive against Constantinople and added that France gave him no encouragement for starting a new war. The problem of Asia Minor was discussed fully. Mehemet Ali maintained that his troops had passed the Taurus only to fight the approaching Turks better; he had never had for his object the complete subversion of the Ottoman power. The pasha, at first taking lightly Boislecomte's injunction to move out of Anatolia, said that, if England and France wanted him out, they had the means to force Turkey to cede him Adana. The information about the British fleet order was used for additional pressure. Boislecomte let Mehemet Ali understand that he fully understood the idea of the strategic advantage which the pasha sought in his quest for Adana. Then Mehemet Ali made a significant observation: "It can be useful for you [France] to let me have Adana; it can be a power for you as well as for me." This Boislecomte interpreted as nothing less than a proposal for the eventual reversal of the sultan in alliance with France. Boislecomte did not want to make a direct reply, so he spoke in general terms of the desirability of the pasha's "abandoning projects and illusions which presented a real danger." He judged that the encouragement of the pasha in this line of reasoning would, as he wrote Broglie, be "more dangerous than advantageous." He emphasized to Broglie, however, that the suggestion of the pasha indicated the evident willingness of Mehemet Ali to concert with France on general policy. Boislecomte recommended consideration of the obvious advantages which the aid of the powerful Egyptian army and navy could render in the event of a general war involving France. To the pasha Boislecomte refuted the idea that Turkey should be eliminated eventually. He stated:

The Powers are united in the objective of ending your struggle with the Porte and of conserving the Ottoman Empire; they have differed only in the method to be employed. The Russians believed armed force necessary; we have thought that moral influence would suffice.

As long as the Egyptian troops were in Anatolia, the crisis would continue.

The insistence of Boislecomte and his utilization of the fleet orders had its effect. The following day Mehemet Ali announced his consent to recall his troops at once, "without regard to the chances of the negotiation with the Porte which he had opened relative to Adana," Boislecomte requesting that the decision be put into writing. The order to Ibrahim was drawn up. The pasha gave directions that it be postdated to May 3, so that it would not appear that he was acquiescing to the news of the British fleet order. He still expected a favorable reply about Adana and had offered the Porte a relatively large indemnity to get the concession. But he announced that he would submit to whatever decision was taken on the matter at Constantinople and called Boislecomte's attention to the benefit of his rule for the Christians who visited the Holy Places of Palestine. In showing his willingness to surrender his claims to the key to Anatolia, he asked that the Powers now accord him their protection against the sultan.[45]

The Boislecomte–Mehemet Ali discussions had reached just this favorable point when there arrived letters from Roussin, Mandeville, and Stürmer which ordered their respective consuls to oppose the acquisition of Adana by Egypt, even if the Porte consented. Campbell already had eased the tension created by the announcement of the coming of the British fleet by arranging for Admiral Malcolm to pay a friendly call on the pasha. Even though the intervention of the ambassadors at the Porte now seemed to him to be too severe, Boislecomte joined the others in communicating the letters to the pasha (on May 12). Not wishing it to appear that there was a disparity between the language at Constantinople and at Alexandria, Boislecomte, in a separate conversation with Boghos, softened the effect of the communication as far as Roussin's letter was concerned. The difference in the attitudes came from the addition to the communication by Prokesch and Campbell of menacing

Puryear: France and the Levant 203

language, which Boislecomte and Mimaut thought should be resorted to only when really needed.

The question of Adana was soon adjusted by a curious device. Announcement was made at Alexandria on May 16 that the sultan had decided to grant Adana to Ibrahim, thus not directly granting it to Mehemet Ali. None of the foreign agents at Alexandria interposed an objection to this arrangement.[46]

The reports of Boislecomte down to May 16 were answered on June 26 by Broglie, who approved the negotiator's labors.

Besides some important results in the question of peace between the Porte and Egypt [wrote Broglie], your mission will have had the effect of rendering to our relations with Mehemet Ali the friendly character which causes independent of our wishes had temporarily suspended. These relations are following their natural course, and if there still remain in the thoughts of the pasha some impressions on the less benevolent attitude that the force of circumstances had dictated in his regard, we hope to dissipate them and to convince him that at basis our friendship for him has never diminished.[47]

The aftermath of Boislecomte's political mission in Egypt was a lengthy series of comprehensive reports on the Levant by that careful observer.[48] During the last weeks of his stay in Egypt Boislecomte prepared full reports on the status of Egypt at the time, basing them on his conversations with the pasha and on his own observations, which detailed the economic, political, and cultural organization of Egypt. Boislecomte took leave of Mehemet Ali on July 3, after which he went to Syria for similar studies. Finally he went to Constantinople, more than six months in all being used exclusively for his various reports, an analysis of which with critical annotations would require a substantial monograph.

11. Failure of the Western Fleet Objective

The intervention of Russia in Turkey in 1833 had the paradoxical effect of bringing Austria and Russia closer together, ending over six years of antagonism in the application of their policies in the Levant. This may have been the result of the assurances given Austria when the Russian forces moved to the Bosporus. Nicholas at that time, so Lamb reported, took "a solemn engagement, if the Turkish empire should fall to pieces, not to appropriate a single village." This satisfied Metternich.[49] Indeed, the ground was cleared for the alliance of Russia and Austria at Münchengrätz in

September, which stipulated their coöperation in all subsequent Turkish problems. Palmerston ostensibly accepted the Russian assurances that nothing would be done by Russia to disturb the equilibrium provided in the Levant by Turkey.[50] But we shall see from the subsequent British orders that the fleet was not intended to be kept entirely aloof from the Russian intervention. France already had envisaged the Russian problem as the principal Levant concern. Together with the liberality of French policy toward Egypt and the known dislike of Nicholas for Louis Philippe, circumstances precluded any close concert between the two Powers. On the other hand, in the problem of the Russian intervention, unlike the Syrian question, France and Great Britain in reality held similar objectives.

Palmerston notified Ponsonby, the new British ambassador en route to Constantinople, on May 10 that Pulteney Malcolm was assuming command of the British fleet. Directions at the same time were given to the admiralty for Malcolm to keep the fleet at Alexandria only until peace was concluded. Then he was to go to Besika Bay and wait, pending conditions and further orders. This last phase brought the British orders into substantial agreement with the French fleet orders. The British admiral was to communicate with Ponsonby; he was to try to prevent a collision between the French and Russians; quite significantly, he was to treat the French admiral as his ally and to coöperate with him. But under no circumstances was Malcolm to make a hostile step without further orders from London; in particular, he was directed to refrain from taking the squadron into the Dardanelles without new orders from the cabinet. This, however, was not to preclude his sending in single ships if they were in the service of communications with the embassy.[51]

Now that the British and French fleets had been placed with the common objective of a display of strength before the Dardanelles for whatever moral persuasion they might provide to encourage the withdrawal of Russia, France was found ready to go further than England in providing for the contingency of Russia's failure to withdraw. On May 26 Broglie instructed Talleyrand to suggest to the British the desirability of advance orders to meet that contingency, but more especially the contingency of the Russian occupation of the Dardanelles. To Broglie it seemed wise to provide the two ambassadors with orders to cover two contingencies (1), if the Russians by their movements gave reason to fear that the seizure of the Dardanelles was a possibility, and (2), if reënforcements arrived from Odessa or Bucharest, "such reënforcements having no other objective than to assure to Russia an impregnable position." In either event Broglie thought that the western fleets should pass the Dardanelles, "after which they would stop, not approaching Constantinople, avoiding all aggression, and contenting themselves in case of necessity with the repulsion of force by force." Also England was notified that the French council had decided to indicate to Russia the expectation that from the moment of peace in the Levant "Russia would not seek any pretext for remaining at Constantinople."[52] Palmerston reserved his answer until the reports of Ponsonby arrived.

Stürmer learned of the arrival of the French squadron in the Near East on May 11. Guilleminot told the internuncio that the ships were destined for service against Mehemet Ali if necessary, but Stürmer (quite correctly) did not believe him. Stürmer was inclined to think that the ships were destined to pass the Straits to balance the Russian naval forces. The British chargé at that time was showing reserve in his communications with Stürmer and had assumed a passive attitude toward Orlov.[53]

Ponsonby arrived at Constantinople in mid-May. He may be said to have been given an official welcome by a squadron of some ten Russian war vessels, anchored just off the Russian legation. Ponsonby's first care, discharged en route, was to inquire of Vice-Consul Lander at the Dardanelles whether the Russians were directing any increased fortifications on the Dardanelles. To this Lander replied on May 18 that no new works of any kind were under way but that he had observed some Russian agents, including engineers, visiting the towns and places on the Gallipoli peninsula.[54]

Count Orlov, one of the signatories of the Peace of Adrianople, was now in Constantinople. Both Ponsonby and Roussin disliked the too close presence of the Russian war vessels. The Russian army was encamped on the plains of Unkiar-Iskelessi, on the Asiatic shores of the Bosporus. The Russian vessels moved about, attracting constant attention. On June 6 Roussin reported the arrival of four vessels under Ricord from the Mediterranean. He said it seemed that they came by advance arrangement and might conceivably be utilized for troop transports. Another item of interest reported that day was that the Turkish foreign minister had succeeded in excusing himself from an invited visit to the Ricord squadron by pretexting an indisposition. "You can see," Roussin observed, "that here they are becoming more and more civilized." Orlov excused himself for not having invited Ponsonby and Guilleminot to join in a welcome of the squadron to the sultan, justifying himself by the uncertainty in which the matter had been held until the morning of the visit and by the appearance of inclement weather that day. "We were very easy to console," reported Roussin. To make his polite explanation more cordial, Orlov suggested that, if the sultan should also visit the Russian troops before their departure, the ambassadors would be invited in advance to attend. Roussin observed that the reason for the suggestion was not alone the good will of Orlov; it also came from a remark attributed to the sultan.[55]

According to Ponsonby's first reports to London, the general impression was current in Constantinople that the Russians were making ready to withdraw their forces from the Bosporus. Orlov assured Ponsonby that the withdrawal would follow the retreat of Ibrahim's army. "Such an assurance having been given on all sides," reported Talleyrand to Broglie, "it is impossible not to regard it as well founded." Appearances indicated, concluded Talleyrand, that the partition of Turkey was a remote possibility but that the Russian advantage lay in accustoming the Turks to the presence of Russian soldiers. Ponsonby had reported also that a proposal of Roussin to Turkey to admit the French squadron to the Bosporus had been made just at the moment of the Russian announcement of intention to withdraw. Talleyrand regretted Roussin's step, "because," he said, "in any case it would have been too early or too late." Ponsonby had advised Roussin to withdraw his request.[56]

Ponsonby gave his reaction to Palmerston's restriction against the passage of the Dardanelles in his dispatch of June 7, at which time he also suggested a reason why the British officers were soon to check up on Russian activities at the Dardanelles. "It might be a dangerous thing," he wrote, "for the British squadron to attempt to enter the Dardanelles by force," especially if Russia were improving the fortifications. The fleet was being held for its moral effect alone until it should be large enough to assure its success. "If the Russians are about to retire," he added, "it would be prudent to avoid raising any question."[57]

Malcolm's squadron of seven ships of the line, one frigate, and one cutter, arrived at Tenedos on June 22. Shortly thereafter the French squadron arrived also. Several days previously two British officers, Copeland and Graves, undertook a minute study of the channel of the Dardanelles. The French squadron included three ships of the line, a frigate, a corvette, and a brig. By July 14, with British reënforcements, the combined Anglo-French squadron in Besika Bay included fourteen ships of the line.[58]

Malcolm used his authorization to send war vessels through the Dardanelles in messenger service. On June 24 Lander had some difficulty, however, in securing the Turkish firman for the passage of the cutter "Hind," although that vessel had passed repeatedly theretofore. The Turkish governor showed a new imperial order from Constantinople which required every ship of war, of whatever kind, to have an advance authorization for its passage. The "Hind" was delayed until a special firman was sent out from Constantinople to cover its passage. Meanwhile, however, Russian brigs were passing with dispatches.[59]

The departure of the Russian forces was now delayed by the secret negotiations with Turkey of Orlov and Butenev; Roussin's first report of their object was sent to Paris on May 23. His impressions of the reasons for the negotiations, which he thought were aimed at an offensive and defensive Russo-Turkish alliance, were sent to Broglie only on July 2.

Russia [he said] embarrassed by conditions in Eastern Europe, jealous of the political importance acquired by France at Antwerp and at Ancona, concerned over Anglo-French coöperation, and founding her hope on internal preoccupations in England, wishes to profit by present conditions to make the advance which she has awaited so long.

Roussin and Ponsonby, having conferred with respect to the procedure they should adopt in view of the now disclosed negotiations, decided to adopt an attitude of observation and to abstain from all direct opposition. They were persuaded that their first interest was to avoid anything which might prevent the evacuation of the Bosporus by Russia. The question was whether the actual presence of the Russian troops at that time, or an alliance for the future, was the lesser evil. Anyway, Roussin reported, both agreed that any attempt to pass the Dardanelles (which was not authorized by their instructions) would probably fail. Roussin considered that any sort of demonstration by the western naval forces would be "more detrimental than useful."[60] This may explain why Orlov and Butenev were able to proceed without interference in their negotiation of the famous Treaty of Unkiar-Iskelessi, signed on July 8 and followed two days later by the departure of the Russian forces from Turkey. The western fleets through inaction had failed to counterbalance Russia.

The Treaty of Unkiar-Iskelessi confirmed all other treaties then in effect between Russia and Turkey and for a period of eight years stipulated their "peace, amity, and alliance" for "the common defense of their dominions against attack," under mutual obligations of substantial aid. In a separate article, however, Turkey was relieved, if Russia were attacked, of the obligation of military and naval aid in exchange for "closing the Strait of the Dardanelles; that is to say, in not allowing any foreign vessels of war to enter therein under any pretext whatever."[61]

The treaty gave the Russian answer to any development that might make ineffective her own policy of supporting Turkey, specifically meeting the potential danger of any further compression of the sultan's territories by Egypt and answering the challenge of the western squadrons. Roussin and Ponsonby, almost at once divining its secret terms, conferred anxiously, holding their fleets at Besika Bay until the reactions at Paris and London were known. An account of the reactions has been published elsewhere by the writer: France and England protested both to Turkey and Russia—being rebuffed at St. Petersburg—and took steps to confine Egypt and thus to prevent the necessity of Turkey's calling upon Russia under the alliance; great antagonisms were engendered, forcing Russia to seek the support of Austria at the conference of Münchengrätz in September of 1833.[62]

12. Status Quo

French policy with respect to Turco-Egyptian relations from 1833 to 1841 encouraged the maintenance of the status quo of the Peace of Kutiah. This policy, the basis for which was expediency, was first formally pronounced by Broglie on June 26, 1833, in his dis-

patch to Boislecomte which answered Mehemet Ali's suggestion of
May 5 for some kind of alliance with France. Broglie stated:

> Now that peace . . . has ceased to be a question, now that the concessions of
> the Porte to Mehemet Ali must have satisfied his ambition, we believe we
> are again acting in conformity with his real interests by giving him a new
> proof of friendship through our advice to him to use wisely his position which,
> because it may be a subject of inquietude and watchfulness for Europe, thus
> imposing upon him additional prudence and circumspection, inclines us to the
> belief that he will put aside every new enterprise on his part against the Porte,
> every new plan of aggrandizement beyond the Taurus, which would put the
> Powers, and France first, under the necessity of opposing him with energy.

Mimaut had been directed, further stated Broglie, to caution Mehemet Ali "against certain illusions which those around him were showing themselves to be quite disposed to entertain regarding him, and in which he would be considered as called to regenerate the Ottoman Empire and serve as a barrier against Russian encroachments." Doubtless the position to which Mehemet Ali had been raised might contribute, because of the weakness and dependence of the Ottoman Empire, a salutary counterpoise in certain circumstances against the preponderant action of Russia over the Porte; Broglie was "far from denying the part which it would be proper for him to take" in that event. That factor might even form a part of the contingent French policy in the Levant, said Broglie, and was to be kept in mind. But "France thought that, for the time being, it would be premature, and, until the time came for a new order, prudence dictated the duty of avoidance of everything which might indicate a system of entente between France and the pasha as against Russia." Mimaut would place these ideas before Mehemet Ali in his own way and try to dissipate the pasha's projects, "or rather illusions."[63]

By the time Mimaut received this instruction he was busy trying to counteract the effects of some attempts to lead Mehemet Ali away from his preference for France and into a pro-British policy.[64] The intervention of the Treaty of Unkiar-Iskelessi made Broglie limit more specifically than ever the prospective further advances of Mehemet Ali. If Mehemet Ali attacked Turkey again, the Russians would be now legally obligated to return to help the sultan. Broglie wrote on September 16:

> It is important that Mehemet Ali remain with care within the limits of his
> duties toward the Porte; that in his attitudes and in his language he pru-

dently avoid giving the Sultan any inquietude or wounding of pride.... Such must be constantly, I repeat, the conduct of Mehemet Ali and of his; and I insist more especially on this point because of reports from Syria that Ibrahim Pasha, less circumspect than his father, has not put aside the intention to utilize the first occasion for renewing the war with the Porte to reverse the empire and overthrow the Sultan.[65]

Such in general was the inception of what we have termed the expedient French policy of maintenance of the status quo of Kutiah, under which the Muslim world for the time being had been split into two parts. Officially France said much about status quo during the next few years. At first the policy was a restraint against Egypt; by 1839 it was regarded by France as a restraint against Turkey, after the sultan announced his intention to force the pasha again under his control.

NOTES TO SECTION VI

1 Reports by Varenne, January 1–12, 1833, AE Turquie 265.
2 *Ibid.*
3 AE Egypte 3.
4 AE Turquie 265; AE Egypte 3.
5 Mimaut to Broglie, January 26, 1833, AE Egypte 3; Acerbi to Metternich, January 17, 1833, HHSA Alexandrien, fol. 1.
6 AE Egypte 3.
7 AE Turquie 265. Ibrahim's army at Koniah numbered some 33,000 men.
8 *Ibid.* It is to be noted that Austria was not mentioned in the concerted opinion. Ottenfels professed to believe that the offer of Russia had been one of moral and not physical support for Turkey, reported Varenne.
9 Varenne to Broglie, January 29, 1833, *ibid.* In Broglie's dispatch to Varenne on February 8, mention was made of the prosperity, but not the territorial integrity, of the Ottoman Empire.
10 AE Turquie 265.
11 Varenne to Broglie, February 4, 1833, *ibid.* Reshid (then the prisoner of the Egyptians) was replaced by Raouf Pasha as grand vizir early in February.
12 AE Turquie 265.
13 *Ibid.*; AE Egypte 3.
14 Broglie to Mimaut, February 7, 1833, AE Egypte 3.
15 Palmerston to Campbell, February 4, 1833, FO 78 T 226.
16 Cf. Metternich, *Mémoires*, Doc. No. 1093.
17 HHSA Türkei 42.
18 AE Turquie 265.
19 *Ibid.*
20 H. L. Bulwer, *Life of Palmerston*, II, 145.
21 AE Turquie 265.
22 *Ibid.*
23 This they notified to Roussin on March 23 (*ibid.*). Ibrahim's army was within five days' march of the Bosporus.
24 Conferences with Butenev convinced Roussin of this; by March 23 Roussin was convinced that the intervention of France and England would be necessary to balance the intervention of Russia and so suggested to Broglie (*ibid.*).
25 Roussin's object here was to forestall the use of the overturned government of Smyrna as a pretext by Russia for remaining in Turkey, and in this he was later supported by Broglie (*ibid.*).
26 Campbell on board a British corvette went directly to Alexandria from Plymouth in one month, arriving March 22 (AE Egypte 3).
27 *Ibid.*
28 AE Turquie 265.
29 AE Egypte 3.
30 AE Turquie 265.
31 Roussin's interpretation, both to Turkey and in his report to Broglie, that the Turks were bound to have the Russians withdraw immediately is not in conformity with the agreement of February 21. This reads, "The Sublime Porte on its side engages to countermand immediately all foreign support which might have been previously invoked." The Porte had done this by its immediate notification to the Russian legation that it had told the French ambassador that the Russian war vessels would retire at the first favorable winds.
32 AE Turquie 265. Roussin's language here seems intended to force the cabinet to support him in having signed the convention with Turkey; nothing in his communications to Turkey at the moment supports his view, whereas the fact that Egypt eventually won the points claimed shows that "the fall of the Sultan" was pure speculation.

[33] *Ibid.*
[34] *Ibid.* The second division of the Russian squadron arrived on April 6. The Russian troops landed at once, and some of them manned the Turkish forts on the Bosporus.
[35] AE Egypte 3. Prokesch's policy was on a line intermediary between the attitudes of Mimaut and Campbell (see his instructions on pp. 189–190).
[36] AE Turquie 266.
[37] AE Egypte 3.
[38] Roussin to Broglie, April 16, 1833, AE Turquie 266.
[39] Turkey's list, incidentally, still included Algeria, Tunisia, and Tripoli, but it did not designate a governor for any of those provinces.
[40] AEMD Turquie 72.
[41] Broglie assigned the date of April 10 for the fleet order. This probably was rather the date for the directions to Campbell, since PRO Admiralty Secret Orders 1695 notes that the squadron was ordered to sail from Malta to Alexandria on April 3.
[42] AEMD Turquie 72.
[43] Broglie to Roussin, April 16, 1833, AE Turquie 266.
[44] As a tribute to the "protecting influence" of France for Egypt under the pasha Boislecomte insisted upon the observance of formalities equal or superior to those accorded Muraviev in January.
[45] AEMD Turquie 72.
[46] *Ibid.*
[47] *Ibid.*
[48] AEMD Turquie 73–78. Some of these reports have been reproduced by G. Douin in *La mission du baron de Boislecomte*. Copies are found in other series in the archives, for example, AE Constantinople 74.
[49] Lamb to Palmerston, March 8, 1833, FO 97 T 404.
[50] FO 65 R 211.
[51] FO 195 T 109.
[52] Duc de Broglie, ed., *Mémoires du prince de Talleyrand*, V, 177.
[53] HHSA Constantinopel 41.
[54] FO 195 Dardanelles 95.
[55] AE Turquie 266.
[56] Talleyrand to Broglie, June 11, 1833, AE Angleterre 641. At the moment, it appears from the London-Paris correspondence, there was no exchange of the respective confidential information of Orlov's secret negotiations with Turkey.
[57] Ponsonby to Palmerston, June 7, 1833, FO 146 F 143. Doubtless Ponsonby had in mind the ill-fated Duckworth exploit of 1807, in which the Turks alone almost "bottled up" the British squadron within the Sea of Marmora. The moral effect of the presence of British battleships within the Straits, or near the entrance of the Straits, appears as a frequently emphasized point in the correspondence of all the British ambassadors who served at Constantinople in times of crisis. Here was an instance in which the moral effect did not suffice, owing to the fact that the Russians were already in their entrenched position. But the recent attempt of a British writer to explain away the validity of the point in instances in which Turkey was in coöperation with England and France is tenable only if we ignore the clear implications of the dispatch above and the more emphatic statements of the same principle by Gordon in 1829 and by Canning in 1849 and 1853. Any correct appraisal of the backgrounds of the Crimean War must include the British-fleet question as a prime factor. The documents for each epoch shout for themselves the appearance of the problem to responsible contemporaries.
[58] Reports by Lander, FO 195 Dardanelles 95.
[59] *Ibid.* In the period of several months before the Crimean War the British agents arranged for blank or substitute firmans to expedite the admission of their then more numerous messenger vessels.

[60] Roussin to Broglie, July 8, 1833, AE Turquie 267.
[61] Text is in E. Hertslet, *Map of Europe by Treaty*, II, 925.
[62] See Vernon J. Puryear, "L'opposition de l'Angleterre et de la France au traité d'Unkiar-Iskelessi," *Revue historique*, CLXXXII (1938), 283–310. One immediate reaction may be noted here. Malcolm, sailing to Constantinople in a 74-gun ship of the line on July 20 under pretext of delivering some guns as a gift to the Ottoman ruler, not only was refused an audience by the sultan but had his unauthorized passage of the Straits protested (FO 146 F 144).
[63] AEMD Turquie 72.
[64] Mimaut to Broglie, July 29, 1833, AE Egypte 3.
[65] Broglie to Mimaut, September 16, 1833, *ibid.*

VII. INFERENCE

FRANCE AND THE LEVANT

MANY FACTORS contributed between 1814 and 1833 to the restoration of the Near East to something of its former relative importance for western Europe. Among these were eight years of military activity in, and naval activity about, Greece, with attendant difficult diplomatic and commercial problems; the Russo-Turkish War; the establishment of the Greek national state; the dissolution of the English Levant Company; the British quest for a shorter route to India; the acceleration of agricultural production in southern Russia; and the continued strong leadership of Mehemet Ali in Egypt and his winning of Syria, to be held until 1840. France contributed to the recovery by her commerce and utilized Egypt as a steppingstone to imperialism in northern Africa.

The foregoing account has placed French policy in the Levant in new perspective for a period which, from the documentary standpoint, has been heretofore too much ignored. Sharp contrasts emerge from this study of twenty years. French policy was hesitant at the beginning, reflecting the defeat of 1814 and the end of a great epoch and a great empire. But success came after two decades, whether from the beginnings of the new empire in Algeria or through the less tangible indirect penetration through Egypt.

French policy in the Near East was inevitably connected with the recovery of the French position of equality in the European states' system. Her return to the Near East restored France to her traditional role in the Mediterranean, while making Egypt the pivot of her policy returned her to the concept, but not the method, of Bonaparte in 1798. This time, France went with diplomacy, not with armies.

Economic recovery, a fundamental part of the program of the Restoration, made the Levant one of its chief avenues. The historically preponderant position of Marseille in the French trade of the Levant and the thesis of the Marseille Chamber of Commerce which advocated restoration of its monopoly led to hopes for a revival both of trade and of the privileged position of Marseille, to which the great prosperity of southern France had been attributed before the Revolution. The new insistence upon equal opportunities for all France precluded the complete restoration of the privileged position of Marseille; trade nevertheless was on the way to recovery when new obstacles were found—the competition of other Powers and the restrictive laws at home. Commerce languished especially when the disturbance of the Greek War discouraged new advances. France joined with the other Powers in keeping open the avenues of trade and in reaffirming the traditional and liberal trading prerogatives in Turkey. French policy had, however, been definitely reoriented to the Levant; so much so that by 1828 France could send an expeditionary army to the Morea with the blessing of Russia and Great Britain, although it proved a thankless task.

French political policy, directed at first toward equality with the other Powers, did not become aggressive until after 1821. Her policy was well on the way to a new focus in the Levant when the Spanish question dramatically interposed itself; so it was not until 1824 that a more vigorous French policy was opened up in the Near East. It was then that France began to turn again to Egypt, reversing the historical policy centering in Turkey.

Egypt had always been kept in mind, whether by the project of Bonaparte or by the earlier schemes for an isthmian canal and penetration to India. Primary among the individuals who influenced the new attention to Egypt was Consul General Drovetti. It was he who laid the foundations for a close French concert with the founder of modern Egypt. His successor, Mimaut, completed the task. The steady growth of French influence in Egypt was a tribute to the ceaseless work of Drovetti and Mimaut, before a succession of foreign ministers at Paris and before the rise of the astute Mehemet Ali. The first evidences of the political penetration of France into Egypt as recorded for 1824 were the sending of a pretentious military mission to instruct the pasha's armies and the plan to construct certain naval vessels for him in the shipyards of Marseille. The increased production of desirable Egyptian cotton added an economic incentive to the political speculation which envisaged Egypt as the powerful lieutenant of France in the eastern Mediterranean. A French engineer laid the foundations for rebuilding the Egyptian navy after the battle of Navarino.

The French policy of favoritism for Egypt was not continuous throughout the decade in which it was oriented there (1824–1833). A sharp interruption came in 1827, when humanitarian reasons and the great objective of further rebuilding her position in Europe led France to join with England and Russia at Navarino. But when Polignac took the helm in August, 1829, French policy in the Levant was vigorously pressed, it then taking a pro-Russian as well as a pro-Egyptian position. When France returned to Egypt, it was Russia to whom Polignac turned for close friendship. The policy of concerting with Russia against England continued until the July Revolution of 1830. In 1833, as the reaction to the Russo-Turkish Treaty of Unkiar-Iskelessi, France entered an entente with Great Britain against Russia. It was the opposition of Great Britain which caused the failure of the Drovetti plan in 1829 for using Egypt in the conquest of the Barbary regencies.

But friendship with Egypt had been cemented anew, despite the failure of Egypt to participate in the conquest of Algeria. French policy and diplomacy aided and encouraged Egypt, even at the threat of near isolation in 1832 and 1833; and Egypt won Syria.

There has been much discussion of the precise policy of France in the first Turco-Egyptian war over Syria. Some writers charge Mimaut with having consistently encouraged Mehemet Ali in his claims to the whole of Syria and in the pasha's reported ambition to succeed to the throne of the sultan. The documents do not show that Mimaut inspired the acts of the pasha. They do show that he, as well as the French foreign ministers (Sebastiani especially), had consistently flattered the pasha and supported his claims to Syria. They do not show that the French friendship and encouragement were unconditional or that they gave Mehemet Ali *carte blanche* to wreck the Ottoman Empire. Although France supported the pasha in his winning of Syria (Broglie's prime policy), she sharply opposed him when he sought to go further, either territorially or governmentally. Besides Egypt's military and naval successes, it was the powerful French mediation, at one stage misdirected by Ambassador Roussin, which paved the way for the transfer of Syria to the administrative cares of Mehemet Ali. Russia's going to Constantinople only hastened the end of the Turco-Egyptian conflict; it did not change the terms originally outlined for the peace. The evidence has shown that among the four Great Powers active in the Levant France was the only one which really mediated between Turkey and Egypt. Because of the comprehensive military successes of Ibrahim Pasha, the mediation concerned only the question of whether to assign Egypt less than all of Syria or all of Syria and a part of Asia Minor. The French compromise favored all of Syria, and this policy was ultimately adopted. The other Powers either displayed force against Egypt—illustrated by the intervention of Russia to protect Constantinople and by the contingent British orders for the fleet to restrict Mehemet Ali—or employed diplomatic pressure, illustrated by the menacing language attributed to Acerbi of Austria. France used persuasion, no better evidence having been recorded than in the letters of Varenne and the reports from the special mission of Boislecomte. Persuasion was also consistently applied at Constantinople.

The potential reward to France for her benevolence to Egypt was never tabulated. Whatever conjectures were drawn on both sides concerning the future of Franco-Egyptian relations—and there were many—were purely from the sum of the attitudes of the successive French cabinets and the often-repeated promises of the pasha, not from specific commitments. The nearest approach to a specific commitment was in the drafted Franco-Egyptian convention of 1830, which failed because of the abrupt shift of French policy with respect to Algeria. Indeed, Mehemet Ali often employed the device of playing off London against Paris whenever Paris evidenced the slightest deviation from the policy of encouragement to him; but French policy continued its ascendancy because England gave the pasha less encouragement.

The complex history of the policies of the Powers in relation to Turkey from 1829 to 1833 is a study in paradoxes, relating in general to Turkey's ability to survive. Twice during the period Turkey appeared to be on the brink of ruin—when the armies of Diebitsch were at Adrianople in 1829, and when the armies of Egypt were in the heart of Asia Minor early in 1833. All four Powers admitted that Turkey was a misfit in Europe, but all for different reasons reached the decision to uphold her. Yet none of them included in their policy the maintenance intact of all of the Ottoman Empire. This accounts for their willingness to see Turkey surrender Greece in 1829 and Syria in 1833. The new policy of Russia in 1829 presented the most striking paradox of all: even with her conquering armies at Adrianople she secretly decided to favor the contingent maintenance of Turkey. Having made such a decision, it was Russia, the traditional enemy of Turkey, who accorded the efficacious physical support deemed necessary in 1833 to save at least the heart of Turkey. Then Russia proceeded to give that same policy of support a treaty basis for the future. Here appeared another paradox. Although both England and France had adopted the policy of maintenance of Turkey, they vigorously opposed any subsequent Russian leadership in attaining that objective.

Still other paradoxes must be noted. French policy in 1829 was pro-Turkish at Constantinople and pro-Russian at Paris even though Turkey and Russia were at war. At Paris Polignac planned to align with Russia to connect the fortunes of eastern Europe with the revision of European frontiers in the west, an idea which became important again with the French threat to invade Belgium in March, 1853. At Constantinople, meanwhile, the French ambassador coöperated with the British ambassador in doing what he thought should be done to save Turkey from Russia and from internal anarchy. French policy during the Turco-Egyptian war was pro-Egyptian and anti-Russian; British policy at the same time was pro-Turkish and anti-Russian. Fortunately for French policy, the Turco-Egyptian phase of the two immediate problems of the Levant was adjusted with the Peace of Kutiah (April 9, 1833), three months before the Russian phase became insistent following the conclusion of the Treaty of Unkiar-Iskelessi (July 8, 1833). The paradox appeared quite striking in February, 1833, when the Russian forces landed on the Bosporus. Neither France nor England desired to encourage the too close friendship of Russia and Turkey, but both the western Powers followed divergent policies toward the two Levant factions which threatened to split the Muslim world into two parts. Another paradox of the moment appeared in Austria's support of Russia after her previous opposition.

The account projected for this volume closes with Egyptian success and the beginning of the experiment with a modern Egyptian empire. That empire collapsed in 1840, as is well known, when Syria was restored to Turkey. The Sphinx, emblem of silence and mystery, holds the key to just what France had won or lost in the twenty years of her new policies in the Levant. Certainly nothing as yet had foretold the post-World War French mandate over Syria.

APPENDIX

Note on the British Fleet Episodes at the Dardanelles in 1849 and 1853

SINCE THE FOREGOING ESSAY discusses the moral and possible physical effects of the presence of the British and French naval squadrons at the Dardanelles in 1829 and 1833 (pp. 86–88, 203–208), a postscript may here be added to the writer's documented initial study that similarly treats the period of the Crimean War in Volume XX of this series (*England, Russia, and the Straits Question, 1844–1856* [1931]). This supplementary analysis, differing slightly in detail, will include additional findings from a later and wider search of the archives to support his essential conclusions respecting the British fleet episodes of 1849 and 1853 (*ibid.*, pp. 153–188, 278–280, 290–294, 304). Important as were these episodes in the preliminaries of the Crimean War, the resulting controversy over their details and their interpretation—mentioned by M. Hauser in the introduction (p. v)—has perhaps overemphasized this aspect of British relations at the Dardanelles.

The general problem needing further clarification seems primarily to concern the sultan's—and, after 1840, Europe's—exclusion of foreign warships from the Dardanelles and the Bosporus during Turkish peace. Also in question are the sizes of the foreign light vessels of war which, through precedents established in the aftermath of the first Turco-Egyptian war over Syria, became exceptions to the rule in being permitted to carry the correspondence of the embassies and legations at Constantinople.

Under the European Straits conventions of 1840 and 1841, Turkey was required to admit "light vessels" when in diplomatic service, in accordance with her antecedent practice, but the Straits were closed during peacetime to all other foreign vessels of war. Turkey's practice respecting the permitted sizes of foreign vessels admitted to the Straits, whether of commerce or of war, had fluctuated, though she well knew what constituted a light vessel. Down to the Peace of Adrianople in 1829 she preferred to exclude all foreign warships at all times except when in alliance with herself during war. Even these were rarely admitted, Britain failing to win their admission in 1809. Turkey likewise excluded, under the capitulations, commercial vessels over 600 tons. (See above, pp. 35–36, the case of the "Thalia" in 1823, an armed merchantman carrying nine guns, which was excluded.) During and after the critical times of the war over Syria, Turkey—suffering duress or seeking further aid against Mehemet Ali—did not apply such a severe restriction to dispatch carriers, but admitted Russian brigs (carrying twelve to eighteen guns) as dispatch boats. Despite this basically reciprocal favor to Russia, however, brigs were not generally approved—witness the refusal to pass a French brig in 1834 (FO 195 Dardanelles 120). Jealousy among the Great Powers thereafter kept Turkey from special concessions except in critical times, unless she was willing to face protests and demands.

Always vexing, therefore, was the question respecting the size of "light" ships carrying dispatches, whether before or after the Straits convention. The treaty of 1856 specified (as insisted upon by Palmerston, FO 27 F 1167) that the "light vessels of war" kept by Russia and Turkey in the Black Sea should not exceed 800 tons and fifty meters in length; and this size Turkey applied in 1859 to all dispatch carriers, after, she said, mistakes had occurred. (Parliamentary Papers, Turkey No. 16 [1878].) Although dispatch boats stood in 1840 without such precise definition, Turkish practice up to that time certainly did not authorize frigates (up to sixty guns) for messenger service. A peremptory British demand for the firman was needed in 1835 to win the passage of a British war vessel bearing Ambassador Durham to Constantinople en route to Russia, the British squadron meanwhile standing by at Vourla until he got through. His passage of the Bosporus en route to Odessa on a frigate was refused; the voyage was made instead on a ten-gunner, the "Pluto." This war steamer won passage disguised as a "steam yacht," though Slade boasted that it could have impressed a Russian brig. (A. Slade, *Turkey, Greece, and Malta* [London, 1837], II, 54, 317, 319, 535; HHSA Odessa 38.) Russia protested when the "Gannet," carrying thirteen guns, transported Ambassador Bulwer to Constantinople in 1862.

Quite another matter was the convention's absolute and undebatable exclusion of all other foreign war vessels during Turkish peace, an exclusion that Great Britain, as one of the signatories, agreed to respect. When in 1904 the British steam yacht "Nemesis" was halted at the Dardanelles until its two cannons were landed (under the rules unchanged since 1840), Lansdowne not only did not protest, but cited the case as an admission of Turkey's duty to observe the Straits convention. (*British Documents on the Origins of the War* [London, 1926–1938], IV, 51.) The same had been true before 1840, under the unilateral Turkish rules. A French war schooner was barred from passing the Bosporus on a "scientific" mission in 1836; and an English corvette, ready to follow, did not even make the application. (FO 195 T 122; AE Turquie 272.) Any methods of gaining admission, fictitious or otherwise, concerned other Powers besides Turkey after the Europeanization of the rule of closure in 1840, and the exceptions thereafter were few indeed except as the preliminary to war.

All this has pertinence in view of the British violations of the convention in 1849 and 1853, a phase of the writer's previous documentary findings that has been criticized: Professor Temperley, armed with new but inadequate evidence, once contended that the instances cited were "evasions," not violations; or that all the boats in 1853 were dispatch carriers; or that in 1849—when an entire fleet entered the Dardanelles—bad weather justified the British conduct; or that frigates up to thirty guns were perhaps authorized dispatch carriers. Though he frankly charged the British cabinet with violating the convention, Dr. Temperley gave Stratford Canning a clear bill until in 1938 he admitted that the unpublished documents did not look so good for that ambassador. New studies based on archival material reaffirm, however, that any foreign war vessel, no matter how small or in what weather, was from 1841 to October 24, 1853—times of Turkish peace—excluded from the Straits unless in actual messenger service.

Puryear: France and the Levant 221

The chief offender against the Straits convention during the preliminaries of the Crimean War remains Stratford Canning. He frequently held dispatch boats at Constantinople beyond any reasonable time (once continuously for fourteen months) for taking on or delivering messages, as in April, 1853, he admitted having done "without necessity or propriety" and without the support of Admiral Dundas. (S. Lane-Poole, *Life of Stratford Canning* [London, 1888], II, 260.) He permitted the full British squadron to enter and remain inside the Dardanelles for eleven days in November, 1849, for an unnecessary strategic advantage over Russia and in an unsuccessful attempt to win an alliance with Turkey. (FO 78 T 781 and 783.) This, the most sensational violation of the convention before the Crimean War, was freely admitted as such by contemporaries, including the London *Times* of December 26, 1849.

According to a letter not heretofore utilized, the British ambassador as early as October 15, 1849, arranged secretly with Turkey to have the fleet pass all the way to Constantinople. This he did while yet unaware (in the absence of telegraphic communications) either of his cabinet's decision to place the fleet at his disposal or of the adjustment at St. Petersburg of the pending diplomatic dispute. In his own words, he acted "to promote our [British] interests and to confirm our influence here, irrespective of whatever turn the state of things may ultimately take." (FO 352 Stratford Canning Papers 32.) Already in September, upon Canning's urgent call to the admiral for support "without bringing attention to the real object" (*ibid.*), Parker had sent to Constantinople suitable naval officers, the "Odin" (of twelve guns), and the more impressive "Tartarus," one of the best war steamers, "for the conveyance of a dispatch, or any other service for which the 'Tartarus' is calculated." (FO 195 T 309.)

Because of Canning's secret direction to a British vice-consul (October 25, 1849, after cabinet authority was in his hands for use if imminent danger to Turkey should come), an embarrassed Turkish governor of the Dardanelles castles was induced to admit the entire fleet (FO 352 Canning Papers 32) despite the absence of dangerous developments from the Russian side, the settlement having in fact been reached on October 14. Since the fleet went up only to the central passages of the Dardanelles—the "trouble" being over (FO 195 T 309)—Turkey introduced the pretext of inclement weather, saying there had been no time to solicit official permission (FO 78 T 783); this claim was necessary to placate Russia, who threatened to move her fleet a similar distance inside the Bosporus, thus placing it before Constantinople. The pretext was much exaggerated in the subsequent explanations to Russia, by whom it was refuted and ridiculed. (FO 65 R 385.) Austria likewise protested the action as "a serious violation" of the treaty. (FO 78 T 783.) None of the private letters of the British officials concerned claimed actual bad weather; one British officer in the fleet, indeed, said the squadron had to wait for favorable winds to take it inside (E. J. Parry, ed., *The Correspondence of Lord Aberdeen and Princess Lieven* [London, 1939], II, 365). Canning had Parker move away as soon as Russia's countermove was hinted, unless the fleet "were to be really and seriously endangered" outside the Dardanelles. In any event the Straits convention made no exception for inclement weather; and Palmerston said, if there really had been such weather, the fleet should have gone the other way. It was difficult to argue, he added, that entering the Dardanelles did not violate the treaty. (A. Ashley, *Life of Palmerston* [London, 1876], I, 164–165.)

For purely political purposes Canning held the steam frigate "Retribution" (of 1641 tons, carrying twenty-eight guns, the largest steamer in Dundas' squadron) within the Straits from June 15, 1853, to the coming of war on October 24. Along with the thirteen-gun British brig "Niger" and two French warboats it surveyed the defenses of the Bosporus and lent Turkey moral support against Russia. (FO 352 Canning Papers 36; FO 195 T 309; FO 195 Dardanelles 391; AE Turquie 213.) When Canning called two additional war steamers to Constantinople on September 11, 1853 (to reënforce the "Retribution," the French boats, and the three and six-gun messenger boats already there—altogether, ten western war vessels), his admitted object was not messenger service but rather, as he himself stated in seeming rejoinder to Temperley's thesis, "to protect us from any immediate attack and to enable us to assist the [Turkish] government in case of an outbreak threatening its existence." Coming when he momentarily feared warparty violence if Russia should send a pacific reply to the Turkish modifications of the Vienna Note, the steamers were meant for emergency service when the reply arrived. Canning secretly arranged the move with pro-British Reshid Pasha "under cover of the steam communications continually plying between the fleets and the capital." (FO 78 T 938.) (Reshid had been reinstated as foreign minister at Canning's insistence on July 9, Lane-Poole, *op. cit.*, II, 282.) Later, when Austria demanded written evidence of a Turkish request for these ships, Clarendon could deliver none. (FO 96 Drafts 23.) Neither Canning nor Clarendon, nor the French (who also called two extra steamers, upon Canning's proposal) claimed officially or privately that these war vessels were dispatch carriers. Any foreign vessel of war, no matter of what size, sent in peacetime with such objects did violate the treaty; else we belie the facts. Clarendon did not dispute the immediate Russian charge of treaty violation. Indeed on September 27, 1853, he admitted to Brunnow at London that Canning "had called up a portion of that [British] squadron to Constantinople." (FO 65 R 438.)

BIBLIOGRAPHY

THIS LIST is limited to the periods discussed in the foregoing work. A projected volume, *Napoleon and Eastern Europe*, will, if completed, include those items for the background periods which might otherwise be found here. Economy of space makes it necessary to exclude most of the items which already appear in the annotated bibliography of the writer's companion volume, *International Economics and Diplomacy in the Near East* (Stanford University Press, 1935), pp. 230–266, and those which have been treated in the notes of the present study. The explanation of abbreviations for the archive collections appears above, p. xvi.

A. THE LEVANT AND COMMERCE, 1815–1821

1. France and Her Markets in the Near East

a) Documents

Archives du ministère des affaires étrangères, mémoires et documents (AEMD).
AEMD Turquie 14, 31 (1808–1819).
Archives du ministère des affaires étrangères (AE).
AE Constantinople 78–80.

b) Printed Materials

S. CHARLÉTY. *La restauration, 1815–1830* (Paris, 1921).
 Includes a chapter on the economic policy of France in reference to the objectives of French political parties.
M. AMÉ. *Etude sur les tarifs de douanes et sur les traités de commerce* (2 vols., Paris, 1876).
 Volume I has a chapter on the grain laws of France to 1821, a problem which is also treated in the following reference.
O. NOËL. *Histoire du commerce extérieur de la France depuis la révolution* (Paris, 1879).
CÉSAR MOREAU. *Examen comparatif du commerce de la France avec tous les pays du monde* (London, 1828).
 A brochure of statistical tables.
E. JURIEN DE LA GRAVIÈRE. *La station du Levant* (2 vols., Paris, 1876).
 A vice-admiral's record for 1816-1830, based on the Marine archives, sees a connection between the regeneration of Greece and the rebirth of the French navy.

2. The Monopoly of Marseille

a) Documents

AEMD Turquie 9, 19 (1816–1835).
AE Constantinople 81.
Archives modernes de la chambre de commerce de Marseille (CCM).
 CCM, dossier, Commerce du Levant, 1802–1855.

b) Printed Materials

P. MASSON. *Histoire du commerce français dans le Levant au XVIIIe siècle* (Paris, 1911).
The chief background for the subject.

P. MASSON. *Marseille depuis 1789* (Vol. I, Paris, 1921).
The leading work on the commerce of Marseille in general for the period 1789–1814, although it is not intended to cover trade with the Levant as such. The statistics for trade with Turkey are not adequate but are quite helpful.

P. MASSON. *Le mouvement économique*, Vol. IX of *Les bouches du Rhône* (Paris, 1922).
This summarizes and extends to 1828 the preceding study.

JULES JULLIANY. *Essai sur le commerce de Marseille* (2 vols., Marseille, 1842).
Statistics on commerce down to 1834 are given, including a chapter on the trade of the Black Sea.

O. TEISSIER. *Inventaire des archives modernes de la chambre de commerce de Marseille* (Marseille, 1882).
Quite incomplete, there being no adequate work on the subject.

3. Barbary Piracy

a) Documents

AEMD Turquie 31.
AE Constantinople 78-80.

b) Printed Materials

E. PLANTET. *Correspondance des deys d'Alger avec la cour de France, 1579–1833* (2 vols., Paris, 1889).
Based on the French ministerial archives and those of the Chamber of Commerce of Marseille.

A. DEBIDOUR. *Histoire diplomatique de l'Europe depuis l'ouverture du congrès de Vienne jusqu'à la clôture du congrès de Berlin* (1814–1878) (2 vols., Paris, 1891).
Largely superseded but still useful for its bibliographies.

4. Russo-Turkish Relations, 1816–1821

G. YAKSHICH. "La Russie et la porte ottomane de 1812 à 1826" (Part 1, for 1816–1821), *Revue historique*, XCI (1906), 281–306.
Reproduces a document which summarizes the negotiations of Stroganov at Constantinople.

Cambridge History of British Foreign Policy. Volume II.
W. A. Phillips suggests the attitudes of Castlereagh.

Correspondance diplomatique de Pozzo di Borgo et Nesselrode, 1814–1818 (2 vols., Paris, 1890).
This correspondence is useful for Russian policy in general.

B. THE PERIOD FROM 1821 TO 1830

1. The Greek War of Independence

E. DRIAULT and M. LHÉRITER. *Histoire diplomatique de la Grèce de 1821 à nos jours* (5 vols., Paris, 1925–1926). Vol. I, 1821–1830, Vol. II, 1830–1862.
  Based primarily on the English, French, and Greek archives. Excellent bibliographies are included.

G. ROSEN. *Geschichte der Türkei, 1826–1856* (Leipzig, 1866).

E. A. BETANT, ed. *Correspondance du comte J. Capodistrias* (4 vols., Paris, 1836–1837).
  Letters from April 20, 1827, to October 9, 1831.

J. C. FILIOTTI. *Rôle diplomatique des phanariotes de 1700 à 1821* (Paris, 1901).
  Features French relations with Moldavia and Wallachia.

N. YPSILANTI. *Mémoires* (Paris, n.d.).
  Gossipy comments on the Ypsilantis, 1860–1820.

G. ISAMBERT. *L'Indépendance grecque et l'Europe* (Paris, 1900).
  A doctoral thesis.

C. W. CRAWLEY. *The Question of Greek Independence* (London, 1930).
  Stresses British policy.

W. ALLISON PHILLIPS. *The War of Greek Independence* (London, 1877).
  An early account, based on the standard secondary sources, extends the treatment to 1833, as does the preceding work.

L. J. GORDON. *American Relations with Turkey, 1830–1930* (Philadelphia, 1932).
  Illustrates the attitudes of states less directly concerned with the affairs of Turkey.

2. The Levant Policy of France, 1821–1827

a) Documents

AE Turquie 235 (instructions to, and reports of, Latour-Maubourg in 1822); 237 (reports of Beaurepaire, 1823); 238–243, 246–249 (reports of Guilleminot, 1824–1827).
AE Constantinople 82, 83 (1823–1829).
AE Athènes 3, 4.
AE Egypte 1, 2, 3.
AE Alexandrie, 21, 22, 23 (1821–1829).
AE La Canée 24 (1824–1833).
AEMD Turquie 19.
CCM, dossier, Commerce du Levant, 1802–1855.
CCM, Lettres pour Paris, 13 (1826–1829).
Archives du ministère de la marine (MM).
  MM, BB[4], cartons 426, 445, 455, 475 (the Levant squadron, 1822–1826).

b) Printed Materials

Georges Teissier. *Canning et Chateaubriand* (Paris, 1934).
  Reproduces one important document (March, 1822) for French policy in the Levant.

G. Douin. *Une mission militaire française auprès de Mohamed Aly** (Cairo, 1923).
  The most important of the preserved letters exchanged between General Belliard at Paris and General Boyer in Egypt, 1824–1826, are reproduced here as extracts from the Archives du ministère de la guerre, "Egypte."

G. Douin. *Les premières frégates de Mohamed Aly, 1824–1827** (Cairo, 1926).
  This monograph, based principally on the archives of the French ministry of marine, includes a chapter on the official support France gave Mehemet Ali in the construction of naval vessels.

3. Policy of Great Britain

a) Documents

Archives of the British Foreign Office (FO).
  FO 78 T 40, 183, 192, 195 (negotiations and problems at Constantinople).
  FO 78 T 112, 119, 136 (the Levant Company).
  FO 65 R 130, 150, 167, 174, 182, and FO Trade Papers 1 (relations with Russia).
  FO 65 R 144 and FO 78 T 119 (negotiations of Stratford Canning in 1825).

b) Printed Materials

S. Lane-Poole. *The Life of Stratford Canning* (2 vols., London, 1888).

Proceedings of the Levant Company (London, 1825).
  A pamphlet covering the surrender of the charters.

E. J. Stapleton, ed. *Some Official Correspondence of George Canning, 1821-1827* (2 vols., London, 1887).

———. *The Political Life of George Canning* [1822–1827] (3 vols., London, 1831).
  Discusses domestic affairs.

C. K. Webster. *Foreign Policy of Castlereagh, 1815–1822* (London, 1925).
  This chronologically and topically precedes the following reference.

Harold Temperley. *The Foreign Policy of Canning, 1822-1827* (London, 1927).

———. *The Crimea* (London, 1936).
  Professor Temperley's *Crimea*, in excellent literary style, covers British policy in the Levant during the first half of the nineteenth century in a general way; here, however, the point of view is often nationalistic and hence a great many of the author's new theses, such as his exaggeration of the pacificism of Stratford Canning, are subject to revision on the basis of a more careful reference to the British documents.

---

* An asterisk denotes a publication of the Société Royale de Géographie d'Egypte.

4. Policy of Russia

T. SCHIEMANN. *Geschichte Russlands unter Kaiser Nikolaus I* (4 vols., Berlin, 1904–1911).

This is the standard authority on Russian policy.

G. YAKSHICH. "La Russie et la porte ottomane de 1812 à 1826" (Part 2, for 1821–1826), *Revue historique*, XCIII (1907), 74–89, 283–310.

G. D. BIBESCU. *Règne de Bibesco* (2 vols., Paris, 1893–1894).

The historical sketch in the preface is of value for certain aspects of the Convention of Ackerman.

A. NESSELRODE, ed. *Lettres et papiers du comte de Nesselrode* (11 vols., Paris, 1904–1912). Vol. VI, 1819–1827, Vol. VII, 1828–1839.

The letters are usually of a personal nature.

A. MAGGIOLO. *Pozzo di Borgo* (Paris, 1890).

A biography.

A. BALLEYDIER. *Histoire de l'empereur Nicolas* (2 vols., Paris, 1857).

A general work.

VERNON J. PURYEAR. "Odessa: Its Rise and International Importance, 1815–1850," *Pacific Historical Review*, III (1934), 192–215.

Commercial development.

J. DE HEGEMEISTER. *Mémoire sur le commerce des ports de la nouvelle Russie, de la Moldavie, et de la Valachie* (Odessa, 1835).

Includes statistical tables for 1824–1835.

K. A. SKALKOVSKII. *Les ministres des finances de la Russie, 1809–1890* (Paris, 1891).

Treats Kankrin's protective system.

M. TUGAN-BARANOVSKII. *Geschichte der russischen Fabrik* (Berlin, 1900).

Presents a view of early Russian manufacturing.

5. Policy of Austria

C. L. W. VON METTERNICH. *Mémoires, documents et écrits divers* (10 vols., Paris, 1880).

H. SRBIK. *Metternich; der Staatsmann und der Mensch* (2 vols., Munich, 1925).

A scientific biography.

E. FORÇADE. "L'Autriche et la politique du cabinet de Vienne dans la question d'Orient," *Revue des deux mondes*, XXII (1854), 849–893.

PROKESCH-OSTEN, ed. *Dépêches inédites du chevalier de Gentz aux hospodars de Valachie pour servir à l'histoire de la politique européene 1813 à 1828* (3 vols., Paris, 1877).

Interesting dispatches which follow the principal events and reflect Austrian policy in a general way.

ADOLF BEER. *Die orientalische Politik Oesterreichs seit 1774* (Leipzig, 1883).

A general history with a documentary appendix.

———. *Oesterreichische Handelspolitik im neunzehnten Jahrhundert* (Vienna, 1891).

Has a chapter on Austrian commercial relations with Turkey.

———. "Die Zollpolitik und die Schaffung eines einheitlichen Zollgebeites unter Maria Theresa," *Mitteilungen des Instituts für österreichische Geschichtsforschung*, XIV (1893), 237–326.

Shows the basic principles of Austria's customs policy.

C. J. BAICOÏANU. *Geschichte der rumanischen Zollpolitik* (Stuttgart, 1896).

Includes comments about early steam shipping on the Danube.

A. HEIDERICH. *Die Donau als Verkehrstrasse* (Leipzig, 1916).

Emphasizes the commercial importance of the Danube.

6. Battle of Navarino

a) Documents

FO 78 T 187 and 191.

MM, BB⁴, cartons 488, 489, 1016.

b) Printed Materials

E. DRIAULT. *L'Expédition de Crète et de Morée, 1823–1828** (Cairo, 1930).

Documents on Egypt.

G. DOUIN. *Navarin (6 juillet–20 octobre 1827)** (Cairo, 1927).

A scholarly study.

E. BOGDANOVICH. *La bataille de Navarin*, translated from the Russian (Paris, 1887).

Until the appearance of the preceding work by Douin, this was perhaps the most satisfactory monographic account in spite of its tendency to eulogize. It includes biographical sketches of Heyden, Lazarev, and Greigh.

B. J. BOURCHIER. *Memoir of the Life of Admiral Sir Edward Codrington* (2 vols., London, 1873).

The final chapters of Volume I and all of Volume II are pertinent.

W. JAMES. *Naval History of Great Britain* (6 vols., London, 1886).

Volume VI is useful.

EDWARD CODRINGTON. *Piracy in the Levant* (London, 1934).

For the period after Navarino. Supplementary to Bourchier, this deals with the operations of the pirates and the steps taken to suppress them.

G. DOUIN. *L'Egypte de 1828 à 1830** (Rome, 1935).

The problems of Egypt after the withdrawal from Greece are presented from French consular reports.

7. The French Expedition to the Morea

AE Turquie 251–255.

AE Athènes 6–10.

AE Autriche 412.

MM, BB⁴, cartons 500, 502, 510 (Levant squadron, 1828–1829).

Archives du ministère de la guerre (MG).

MG, D², cartons 1–5 (general correspondence 1828–1833).

MG, D², cartons 6 and 7 (the expeditionary corps, 1828–1833).

CCM, dossier (in process of classification), Evénements politiques en Turquie, 1828–1829.

8. The Russo-Turkish War of 1828–1829 and the Peace of Adrianople

a) Documents

AE Turquie 251–255.
AE Constantinople 83.
FO 65 R 178 (Aberdeen's instructions to Heytesbury).
FO 65 R 227.
FO T 178–181, 184–187 (the reports of Gordon).
FO 27 F 389, 390, 395.
FO 64 Prussia 158–159.
FO 78 A 211.
Haus-, Hof-, und Staatsarchiv (HHSA).
HHSA Preussen 132.
HHSA Russland varia 18.
Akten des auswärtigen Amtes (AA).
AA, Rep. I, Russland 79.

b) Printed Materials

T. SCHIEMANN. *Geschichte Russlands unter Kaiser Nikolaus I* (4 vols., Berlin, 1904–1911).

This is the comprehensive reference authority. Especially useful are the documents in the appendix of the volume which relate to negotiations for the Peace of Adrianople.

9. Russia's New Policy in 1829

ROBERT J. KERNER. "Russia's New Policy in the Near East After the Peace of Adrianople: Including the Text of the Protocol of 16 September 1829," *Cambridge Historical Journal*, VI (1937), 280–290.

This is the first publication of the protocol of the special committee which laid down the fundamental bases of the new policy of supporting Turkey. The protocol is accompanied by a penetrating analysis, which for the first time fully clarifies the many-sided ramifications of the new policy. The protocol is reproduced from a photostatic copy in the possession of Professor Kerner.

F. F. MARTENS. "Etude historique sur la politique russe dans la question d'Orient," *Revue de droit international et de législation comparée*, IX (1877), 69–72.

This is an early sketch without source references.

N. K. SHILDER. *Imperator Nikolai Pervyi* (2 vols., St. Petersburg, 1903).

The appendix includes two documents showing the immediate application of the new policy.

10. The Polignac Project
a) Documents
FO 27 F 1140 (the papers on the problem communicated to England in 1856).
FO 27 F 396.
AE Turquie 255.
AE Russie 178 (memoranda on the plan).
AE Autriche 411.
AE Prusse 272 (correspondence on the alleged Austrian project of the same time).
HHSA Frankreich 388, 389.

b) Printed Materials
ALFRED NETTEMENT. *Histoire de la restauration* (8 vols., Paris, 1860–1872).
Volume VIII has documents on the subject.
T. SCHIEMANN. *Geschichte Russlands unter Kaiser Nikolaus I* (4 vols., Berlin, 1904–1911). Vol. II.

11. Reactions to the Peace of Adrianople
a) Documents
AE Angleterre 627, 629, 639.
AE Russie 178.
AE Turquie 255, 259, 260.
AE Constantinople 83.
AEMD Turquie 14, 34.
AA, Rep. I, Russland 77, carton IX.
FO 27 F 390, 396, 405, 407.
FO 78 T 179, 181, 188–192, 194–196.
FO 78 T 403 (consular).
FO 195 T 265.
FO 65 R 123, 140, 174, 184, 188, 209, 227.
FO 359 Trade Papers 1.
FO 7 A 211.
FO 64 Prussia 158–159.
HHSA Russland varia, cartons 17, 18.
HHSA Türkei, cartons 21, 31.
HHSA Preussen, carton 132.
HHSA Frankreich, carton 388.
HHSA Constantinopel, carton 37.
HHSA Alexandrien, fol. 1.

b) Printed Materials
DUKE OF WELLINGTON. *Correspondence on the Eastern Question* (London, 1877).
A. M. ZAÏONCHKOVSKII. *Vostochnaia Voina 1853–1856g. v Sviazi s sovremennoi ei Politicheskoi Obstanovkoi* (2 vols., St. Petersburg, 1908–1913).
  The comprehensive documentary appendix of this account of the Crimean War and the contemporary political situation sketches Russo-Turkish relations from the Peace of Adrianople.

12. The Cruise of the "Blonde" in 1829

a) Documents

FO 27 F 396, 405–406.
FO 78 T 188–189, 195.
Public Record Office (London).
PRO Admiralty Secret Orders 1694.
AE Autriche 411.
AE Turquie 255.
HHSA Türkei 21, 31, 33.
AA, Rep. I, Autriche 115.

b) Printed Materials

S. M. EARDLEY-WILMOT. *The Life of Vice-Admiral Edmund Lyons* (London, 1898).

13. The Drovetti Plan

a) Documents

AE Egypte 1, 2.
AE Alexandrie 23, 24.
AE Turquie 255, 260 (dispatches to and from Guilleminot).
AE Russie 178, 180.
AE Autriche 411, 412.
AE Angleterre 629.
AE Prusse 273.
FO 78 T 181, 184, 188, 190, 192, 196.
FO 27 F 390, 396, 405.
AA, Rep. I, Autriche 115, ii.
HHSA Alexandrien, fol. 1.
HHSA Türkei 31.

b) Printed Materials

G. DOUIN. *Mohamed Aly et l'expédition d'Alger, 1829–1830** (Cairo, 1930).
    This important published collection reproduces selections from the Archives du ministère des affaires étrangères noted above.

M. SABRY. *L'Empire égyptien sous Mohamed Ali et la question d'Orient, 1811–1849* (Paris, 1930).
    Utilizes many of the French and Egyptian documents on the problem.

J. TRAVERS. *Journal d'un ministre, comte de Gueron-Ranville* (Caen, 1873).
    Includes some reactions coming from the sessions of the French ministry in 1830.

BARON CHARLES D'HAUSSEZ. *Mémoires du baron [Charles] d'Haussez, dernier ministre de la marine sous la restauration* (Paris, 1897).
    Has comments which are critical of the Drovetti scheme.

14. France Enters Algeria, 1830

a) Documents

AE Turquie 261–264 (dispatches to and from Varenne).
AE Angleterre 630.
AE Alger 47 (1824–1829).
AE Alexandrie 24 (1830–1831).
MG, D⁴, Algérie (several hundred cartons, specially catalogued, beginning in 1830). Cartons 1–5 are for 1830.
MM, BB⁴, cartons 520–524.
FO 27 F 406.
HHSA Alexandrien, fol. 1.

b) Printed Materials

E. PLANTET. *Correspondance des deys d'Alger avec la cour de France, 1579–1833* (2 vols., Paris, 1889).
[Ministry of Foreign Affairs.] *Correspondance des beys de Tunis et des consuls de France avec la cour, 1577–1830* (3 vols., Paris, 1893–1899).
G. PALLAIN, ed. *Correspondance diplomatique de Talleyrand: ambassade de Talleyrand à Londres, 1830–1834* (Paris, 1891).
   Weak because no dispatches to Talleyrand are included.
H. I. PRIESTLEY. *France Overseas* (New York, 1938).
   Has an excellent account of France's entrance into Algeria.

15. Contemporary Public Opinion in France

F.-R. DE CHATEAUBRIAND. *Mémoires d'outre tombe* (12 vols., Paris, 1849).
F. P. G. GUIZOT. *Mémoires pour servir à l'histoire de mon temps* (8 vols., Paris, 1865).
   A well-known work.
A. JULIEN. "La question d'Alger devant les chambres sous la restauration," *Revue africaine,* 1922.
A. NETTEMENT. *Histoire de la conquête d'Alger* (Paris, 1856).
   This volume sketches the history of Franco-Algerian relations and tells of the military campaigns.
C. GAUTHEROT. *La conquête d'Alger, 1830* (Paris, 1929).
   Primarily a military account based on the papers of Bourmont, commander of the expedition.
G. ESQUER. *La prise d'Alger, 1830* (Algiers, 1923).
   Includes an excellent chapter on public opinion in France.
CAMILLE ROUSSET. *La conquête de l'Algérie, 1841–1857* (2 vols., Paris, 1889).
   The story of the conquest is continued for a later period.

16. The British View of a Near Eastern Route to India
   a) *Documents*

FO 67 T 184, 186, 191–195, 252, 267 (1835).
FO 195 T 116, 122.
AE Alexandrie 23.
AE Turquie 262.

b) *Printed Materials*

JOHN MCNEILL. *Memoir* (London), 1910.
   On Persia.
F. R. CHESNEY. *Narrative of the Euphrates Expedition, 1835–1837* (London, 1868).
   Has an appendix of letters and reports.
H. L. HOSKINS. *British Routes to India* (New York, 1928).
F. CHARLES-ROUX. *L'Isthme et le canal de Suez* (2 vols., Paris, 1901).
   The history and status of the region in 1900.
C. W. HALLBERG. *The Suez Canal, Its History and Diplomatic Importance* (New York, 1931).
A. T. WILSON. *The Suez Canal* (London, 1933).

C. THE PERIOD OF THE TURCO-EGYPTIAN WAR, 1831–1833

1. The Rise of Mehemet Ali

P. MOURIEZ. *Histoire de Méhémet-Ali* (3 vols., Paris, 1855).
   An early general history.
M. SABRY. *L'Empire égyptien sous Mohamed Ali et la question d'Orient, 1811–1849* (Paris, 1930).
   The first work to utilize the archives at Cairo, this has now supplanted the preceding reference.
F. MENGIN. *Histoire sommaire de l'Egypte sous le gouvernement de Mohamed-Aly* [1823–1838] (Paris, 1839).
   The first part has statistical resources for Egypt; the last part gives geographical and historical studies of Arabia by M. Jomard.
E. DRIAULT. *Mohamed-Aly et Ibrahim* (Cairo, 1933).
   Part of Volume III of *Précis de l'histoire d'Egypte*.
H. DODWELL. *The Founder of Modern Egypt* (Cambridge, 1931).
   Summarizes the early rise of the pasha and analyzes his administrative system.
L. BRÉHIER. *L'Egypte de 1798 à 1900* (Paris, 1903).
A. HASENCLEVER. *Geschichte Ägyptiens im 19. Jahrhundert* (Halle, 1917).
   Still useful as an outline. It parallels the preceding work.

2. The Egyptian Conquest of Syria

a) Documents

AE Turquie 263-266, 272.
AE Egypte 2, 3.
AE Alexandrie 25 (1832-1834).
FO 65 R 188.
FO 195 Dardanelles 95.

b) Printed Materials

G. DOUIN. *La première guerre de Syrie** (2 vols., Cairo, 1931).

The principal publication of documents to date. These are French documents relating to the history of Egypt, 1831-1833. The first volume carries the problem down to the acceptance of the Russian offer of intervention at the time of the battle of Koniah and includes commercial correspondence; the second volume especially features the activity of Roussin at Constantinople.

A. PROKESCH-OSTEN. *Aus den Tagbüchern des Grafen Prokesch-Osten* [1830-1834] (Vienna, 1909).

DUC DE BROGLIE. *Souvenirs, 1785-1870* (4 vols., Paris, 1886).

R. CATTAUI. *Le règne de Mohamed Aly d'après les archives russes en Egypte** (3 vols., Cairo, 1931-1936).

Consular reports giving sidelights.

A. J. RUSTUM. *The Royal Archives of Egypt and the Origins of the Egyptian Expedition to Syria, 1831-1841* (Beirut, 1936).

This contrasts the ostensible and real causes of the expedition. A previous publication by the same author treats the campaigns of Ibrahim in Syria and Asia Minor.

E. MOLDEN. *Die Orientpolitik des Fürsten Metternich, 1829-1833* (Vienna, 1913).

Adds interesting comments about the reactions to Roussin's negotiations early in 1833.

S. GORIAINOV. *Le Bosphore et les Dardanelles* (Paris, 1910).

This documented study summarizes the Muraviev mission to Egypt in 1833.

3. Mission of Boislecomte, 1833

a) Documents

AEMD Turquie 72-78 (the official reports).
AE Turquie 267 (duplicating some of the reports).

b) Printed Materials

G. DOUIN. *La mission du baron de Boislecomte* and *L'Egypte et la Syrie en 1833* (1 vol., Cairo, 1927*).

Extracts from AEMD 72 and 73. The first part includes some of the papers relating to the problem of Adana; the second sketches the general situation after the Peace of Kutiah. The published work does not include Boislecomte's subsequent long reports on Turkey and his analysis of French commerce in Turkey.

4. The Russo-Turkish Treaty of Unkiar-Iskelessi, 1833

a) Documents

AE Angleterre 641–642.
AE Turquie 267–268 (Roussin).
AE Russie 187.
AE Constantinople 85.
FO 27 F 220, 224, 466.
FO 65 R 208, 209, 211.
FO 195 T 95, 109.
FO 146 F 143, 144.
PRO Admiralty Secret Orders 1695.
HHSA Alexandrien, fol. 1.
HHSA Türkei, cartons 41, 42.
HHSA Varia de Russie, carton 32.
HHSA England, carton 265.
HHSA Constantinopel, carton 41.

b) Printed Materials

DUC DE BROGLIE, ed. *Mémoires du prince de Talleyrand* (Paris, 1892). Vol. V.
  Contains material on Anglo-French relations.
R. E. MOWAT. "The Near East and France," *Cambridge History of British Foreign Policy*, II, 161–198.
P. E. MOSELY. *Russian Diplomacy and the Opening of the Eastern Question in 1838 and 1839* (Cambridge, 1934).
  Russian documents interpretative of the treaty are reproduced in the appendix.
H. L. BULWER. *The Life of Palmerston* (2 vols., London, 1871).
  Volume I gives extracts from pertinent documents.
H. C. F. BELL. *Lord Palmerston* (2 vols., London, 1936).
  A biography which features Palmerston's reactions to issues rather than the way he handled them officially.
VERNON J. PURYEAR. *England, Russia, and the Straits Question,1844–1856* (Berkeley, 1931). Chapter I.
———. "L'opposition de l'Angleterre et de la France au traité d'Unkiar-Iskelessi en 1833," *Revue historique*, CLXXXII (1938), 283–310.

INDEX

Abbreviations for the archive sources, xvi

Abdullah Pasha of Acre: aggressiveness of, in 1831, 148; reports of projects credited to, 149; Egyptian expedition to chastise, 150; resistance of, at Acre, 153

Aberdeen, Lord, British foreign secretary: seeks to separate Greek and Russo-Turkish questions, 54; threatens break of relations with Russia, 60; thinks Ottoman Empire might disintegrate, 70, 102–104; favors opening of the Straits to commerce, 75; reactions of, to the Peace of Adrianople, 100–101; remarkable state paper by, 102; agreement of, with Tsar Nicholas in 1844, 103; replies to Metternich's complaints, 103; objects to the Drovetti plan, 128–129; views of, on the proposed new mail route to India, 140

Ackerman, Convention of (1826): between Russia and Turkey, 49–50; infractions of, 53

Acre: detached practices of pashas of, 2; no active French commerce at, 7; Egypt's punitive expedition against, 150; siege of, and strong resistance at, 152; results of fall of, 162–166; pashalic of, mentioned by Metternich, 189

Adana: occupied by Egypt, 173; cession of, to Egypt demanded, 186; not ceded in Peace of Kutiah, 198; strategically important, 201; assigned to Ibrahim Pasha, 203

Adrianople: occupied by General Diebitsch, 71–72; peace of (*see* Peace of Adrianople)

Agoult, Hector d', French minister at Berlin, thinks Powers must arrange for the succession to Turkey, 76

Akif Effendi, Turkish foreign minister, views of, 186

Aleppo, government of, sought by Mehemet Ali, 165

Alexander I of Russia (*see* Tsar Alexander I)

Alexandria: new war vessels arrive at, 48; port of, 52; blockade of, threatened, 55; blockade of, by England, 58; Huder of France negotiates at, 132; market operations of, 137–138; plague at, 138; opinions at, 152; Muraviev visits, 182, 184–186; peace negotiations shift to, 194

Algeria: Hussein, dey of, 9; war of, with France, 49; mission to, 113; French move against, approved, 130–131; active preparations against, 132; French conquest of, 135

Algiers: bombardment of, in 1816, 8; French blockade of, 125

Anglo-French entente: not effective in 1830, 105; cemented, 204, 216

Anglo-Turkish Treaty of the Dardanelles (1809), 5

Appendix, 219–222

Apponyi, Austrian ambassador in Paris, discusses alleged Austrian plan to partition Turkey, 82

Arabian Caliphate, revival of, considered by Mehemet Ali, 149, 154

Archives: sources employed, vi; abbreviations for, xvi

Argout, C. d', French minister of commerce, turns down Egypt's request for a loan, 159

Asia Minor: Egyptians penetrate, 172, withdraw from, 198; *see also* Adana, Caramania, Taurus Mountains

Index

Asiatic littoral of Black Sea held by Russia, 15, 89

Austria: profits of, from war trade, 12; trade of, at Constantinople, 30; proposed acquisitions of, under Polignac plan, 77–79; alleged plan of, to partition Turkey, 79–83; circumstantial character of plan of, 81; natural ally of England, 120; notified of Drovetti plan, 126; reactions of, to Drovetti plan, 127; impatient with Mehemet Ali, 185; opposes pro-Egyptian policy of France, 189; Convention of Münchengrätz between Russia and, 203-204; see also Metternich

Barbary piracy: a common problem, 8; most efficient protection against, 8; Turkey exposed to danger by, 9; enslavement of Christians under, 49; a reason for the Drovetti plan, 105; desirability of purging, 118

Barker, British consul general in Egypt: warns Mehemet Ali, 129; analyzes various routes to India, 141

Battle of Koniah (1832), 177

Battle of Navarino (1827), 49–51

Beaujour, inspector general of French commerce in the Levant, 9

Beaurepaire, Count, French chargé at Constantinople: opposes Marseille monopoly, 13; makes recommendations for improving trade, 30

Belliard, General: recruits military mission for Egypt, 43; writes on French objects in Egypt, 44

Bernstorff of Prussia: at the Congress of Aachen, 8; and the alleged Austrian plan, 81–82

Besika Bay, western fleets appear at, 204

Bessarabia, Russian troops assembled in, 166

Bibliography, 223–235

Black Sea: trading in, 4; opened to England, 5; new appeal of, for the British, 6; Asiatic littoral of, held by Russia, 15, 89; British right to free trade in, 28

Black Sea trade: Compagnie de la Mer Noire for, 5; restrictions to, 25; complaints of British subjects engaged in, 75; and Peace of Adrianople, 93–96

Blockades: must be effective, 24, 161; George Canning and, 39; during Greek war, 39, 58; problems of, in the Levant, 59–63; of Egypt by Turkey, 159

"Blonde," British frigate: arrives at Constantinople, 62; held by Gordon despite closure of Straits, 96–98

Boghos, Egyptian minister: negotiates on the Drovetti plan, 120; chief of commercial administration, 137; requests a French scouting vessel, 167; negotiates with Boislecomte, 202

Boislecomte, Baron: memorandum by, 77; mission of, to Egypt, 199–203; reports of, respecting the Levant, 203

Bosporus (see Straits)

Bourmont, French minister, 124: advocates direct expedition to Algeria, 124; commander of French expedition against Algeria, 132

Boyer, Pierre: and French military mission to Egypt, 43; rivalry of, with Gaudin, 48

Bretonnière mission to Algeria, 113

Bribes for Ottoman officials, 18

Index 239

Briggs, Samuel, English merchant in Egypt: and the cotton trade, 137; and proposed new mail route to India, 141
British (*see* Great Britain)
Broglie, Duke of, French foreign minister: succeeds Sebastiani, 170; instructions of, to Roussin, 173–174; directs sharp language to Mehemet Ali, 183; disapproves Roussin's convention with Turkey, 192–193; special instructions of, to Roussin, 193; instructions of, to Boislecomte, 199; wants western fleets to pass the Dardanelles, 204–205; favors the status quo of the Peace of Kutiah, 208–210
Brusa, threatened by Egypt in 1832, 185–187
Butenev, Russian minister to Turkey: visits Alexandria, 166; assists in negotiating Treaty of Unkiar-Iskelessi, 207

Campbell, Patrick, British agent consul general in Egypt: special instructions to, 188–189; contingent instructions of, respecting the fleet, 200
Canning, George, British foreign secretary: at the Congress of Verona, 26; warns Turkey, 29; fears coalition against England, 39; sends Stratford to Russia, 40
Canning, Stratford, British ambassador to Turkey: mentioned by M. Hauser, v; appointed, 18; special envoy to Russia in 1825, 40; failure of negotiations of, with Nesselrode, 41–42; opposes lifting Cretan blockade, 58; dismissed by Aberdeen, 59; earns Nesselrode's ill will, 42, 65; return of, to Turkish capital, 154; expedites news of Turkish firman against Mehemet Ali, 165; insists that England support Turkey against Egypt, 175–176; offender against Straits convention before the Crimean War, 221–222
Capitulations: 3-per cent duty at all Turkish ports, 3; violation of, by Egypt in Syria, 163; sizes of vessels under, 219
Capodistrias: at the Congress of Aachen, 8; as provisional president of Greece, favors French expedition to the Morea, 55–56; project of, for a partition of Turkey, 91–92
Caramania: Austria opposes cession of, to Egypt, 189; occupied by Egypt, 173
Cartwright, John, British consul general at Constantinople, influences British commerce, 6
Castagne, Louis: analytical memorandum by, 30; views of, on the Peace of Adrianople, 94–95
Castlereagh, British foreign secretary: at the Congress of Aachen, 8: follows a "hands-off" policy, 21
Cerisy, French marine engineer: directs construction of naval vessels for Egypt, 45; becomes creator of Egyptian navy, 53, 156, Egyptian general, 195
Chabrol, Count, French minister of marine, and naval construction for Egypt at Marseille, 45, 124
Chamber of Commerce of Marseille: compares tariffs, 6; seeks reëstablishment of its monopoly, 10, 30; directing agency for unified and monopolistic control, 11; more successful than the English Levant Company, 11; renews request for heavy duty on Levant shipping, 11, 13; advances new arguments (1820), 12; objections of, raised, 13; protests of, against Turkish in-

240 *Index*

ternal duties, 28; hostile to Greek pirates, 51; studies Levant commerce after Peace of Adrianople, 99; Roussin opposes views of, 191

Charles X, King of France: ascends throne, 31; accepts Polignac plan for a partition of Turkey, 77; and Algeria, 113; approves French counterproposal to Egypt, 124

Chateaubriand, French foreign minister, 23; ambassador at London, 24

Chesney, F. R., surveys by, in Asia Minor, 141–142

Closure of Straits to foreign warships, 219–222

Codrington, British admiral: arrives at Navarino, 50; concludes a convention with Mehemet Ali, 57; *see also* Battle of Navarino

Coehorn, Baron, of French foreign ministry, analysis by, 116–117

Collective intervention threatened in Turco-Egyptian war, 183

Commerce in the Levant: after the Peace of Adrianople, 99; and the rediscovery of the eastern Mediterranean, 128; French, in Egypt, 135–139; and Mehemet Ali, 136; halted by plague in Egypt, 151; new regulations for, in Syria, 163; *see also* Capitulations, various Powers

Compagnie de la Mer Noire, 5

Conference at St. Petersburg (1825), failure of, 42

Congress of Aachen (Aix-la-Chapelle, 1818), 8

Congress of Verona, 27

Constantinople: negotiations at, on the Drovetti plan, 122–123; route to, opened by Ibrahim Pasha, 172, 177

Continental blockade ineffective in the Levant, 16

Convention of Ackerman (1826), 49–50, 53

Convention of Münchengrätz (1833), 203–204

Corsairs, Barbary: active during Turco-Egyptian war, 162; *see also* Barbary piracy

Cotton: of Egypt, 46, 47; Samuel Briggs and, 137; offered as guarantee for French loan to Egypt, 159; *see also* Commerce in the Levant

Courvoisier, J. J. A., French minister, 124

Crete: Greek forces occupy a part of, 51; raising blockades of, 58; Heyden at, 59; Russian blockade of, illegal, 61

Crimean War, naval preliminaries of, 221–222

Cyprus visited by Captain Sarlat, 168

Damas, Baron: French foreign minister, 23; and French military mission to Egypt, 44; orders consul general to return to Egypt, 52

Damas (Damascus), pashalic of: Varenne believes Turks will cede, 181; Austria willing to transfer, to Egypt, 189; *see also* Syria, Turco-Egyptian war

Danube, the: territorial delimitation along, 15; and Peace of Adrianople, 93–96

Dardanelles (*see* Straits)

Deval, French consul at Algiers, insulted by Hussein of Algeria, 49

Diebitsch, General, Russian commander: occupies Adrianople, 71–72; replies to Turkish memorandum, 72; willingness to negotiate, 79; negotiates with Turkey, 83–85; receives plea by western ambassadors, 85

Index 241

Disraeli, Benjamin, mentioned, 134
Drovetti, French consul general in Egypt: returns to Egypt, 12; instructions to, in 1827, 52; confidence of, in Mehemet Ali, 114; outlines details for a concert with Mehemet Ali, 115–116
Drovetti plan, the, for a Franco-Egyptian conquest of the Barbary regencies: Russian support solicited for, 100; the initial project, 113–114; considered by French council, 114–117; alternate to Polignac plan, 115; subsidies for, 115; negotiations on, 115–134; premature publicity compromises, 131; disruption of negotiations under, 134

East India Company (English): ships of, explore Red Sea ports, 140; four trips by steamer of, 142
Egypt: monopolies of, 7, 46–47, 71, 137–138; gives the foreign merchant protection, 8; war profits of, during Napoleonic period, 16; coercion against, planned, 50; increase of trade of, with France, 53; and French policy, 112–113; rupture of French negotiations with, 132; French commerce in, 135; cholera in, 151; war of, with Turkey, 156–198; monopolies of, extended to Syria, 163; peace ultimatum of, 194–197; terms of, for peace, 196; *see also* Mehemet Ali
Egyptian (*see* Egypt)
England (*see* Great Britain)
English Levant Company (*see* Levant Company)
Enslavement of Christians by Barbary pirates, 49
Erzurum falls to Russia, 63

Fictitious manifests: Turkish restrictions evaded by means of, 17; British merchants issue, 18
Firmans (formal authorizations) for passage of the Straits, necessity for, 4, 207
France: to regain her prestige and influence, 1; established legal bases for the Levant trade of, 3; original capitulatory grants to, 3; applies all newer and lower specific duties, 7; encourages revival of Levant commerce, 7; unsuccessful efforts of, to end Barbary piracy, 8; favorable to views of Russia, 21; takes a more active part in European politics, 21; steps of, to prevent a Russo-Turkish war in 1821, 22; policy of, interpreted, 24; trade outlook of, gloomy, 29; trade of, at Constantinople, 30; and Egypt, 42–49, 112–134; conflict of, with Algeria, 49; joins with Great Britain and Russia in the Treaty of London, 50; withdraws ambassador from Constantinople, 51; coöperates with Egypt after Navarino, 52; dispatches expeditionary force to the Morea, 54; displeased with Mehemet Ali, 55; policy of, in September, 1829, 74–75; policy of, oriented to favor Russia, 76; proposed acquisitions for, under Polignac plan, 77–79; partially evacuates the Morea, 98–99; entente of, with England, 105, 204, 216; alternatives facing, after the Peace of Adrianople, 112; counterproposal of, to Egypt, 124; to support Egypt, 125; Mediterranean fleet of, inferior to British, 125; objectives of, in the Drovetti plan, 125; notifies Powers of the Drovetti plan, 126; to protect Mehemet Ali against Turkey, 127; policy of, abruptly shifts to

France (*Continued*)—
   conquest of Algeria, 130–131; and Egyptian cotton, 136–137; gives Algerian vessels to Mehemet Ali, 138–139; applies steam to the Mediterranean, 142–143; approves Egypt's campaign against Syria, 154; policy of strong favoritism of Egypt on the part of, modified to official neutrality, 158; refuses to recognize Turkey's blockade of Egypt, 160, 162; favorable reaction of, to Egypt's victory at Acre, 164–165; negotiates for peace in Turco-Egyptian war, 169–170, *passim*; Varenne the mediating agent of, 181–184, 194–199; wishes to preserve the Ottoman Empire, 183, 196–197; favors award of Syria to Egypt, 184; approves Roussin's opposition to Russia, 192; policy of, in March, 1833, 199; policy of (1833–1839), 208–210; summary of policy of, in the Levant (1814–1833), 214–218

Franco-Turkish convention of 1833: negotiated by Roussin, 191–193; disapproved by Broglie, 192–193; nullified, 196

Franco-Turkish tariffs of 1802 and 1816: restrictions in, 6; Sebastiani's views of, 136

French (*see* France)

French commerce in the Levant, inspector general of, 10; studied, 53; *see also* France

French military mission in Egypt, decreased authority of, 48; *see also* Egypt

French ministry of war: note by, 23; considers possibilities, 52

French trade in the Levant: substantial recovery of, 9; handicaps to, 9; though weak from 1826 to 1828, increases in Egypt, 47; *see also* France

French war with Algeria: causes of, 49; blockade of Algiers and debates on, 113

Gaudin, Colonel, and the French military mission to Egypt, 43

Georgia: held by Russia, 14; *see also* Asiatic littoral of Black Sea

Gordon, Robert, British ambassador to Turkey: appointed, 59; opposes extension of Russian blockade, 61; returns to Constantinople, 62; advises Turkey to submit to Russia, 72; sends letter to Diebitsch, 72; believes Constantinople menaced, 72; views of, 73–74; appeals to Russian commander to make peace with Turkey, 85; willing to call fleet to Constantinople, 86; more aggressive than Guilleminot, 87; reactions of, to Peace of Adrianople, 94; friendly with Turkey, 95; holds British frigate "Blonde" at Constantinople despite closure of Straits, 96–98; views of, on Turkey's ability to survive, 103; plans of, to transport Ottoman envoy to Russia on warship, 106

Grain trade in Egypt, 137

Great Britain: new economic era for, 5; Ionian protectorate of, 5; consular expansion of, in the Near East, 5–6; fears Russia in the Mediterranean, 8; sympathizes with Turkey in the Russian phase of her problem, 21; protests to Turkey, 29; trade of, at Constantinople, 30; policy of, favors Greeks, 39; joins with France and Russia in the Treaty of London, 50; withdraws ambassador from Constantinople, 51; does not participate in expedition to Morea, 57; to hold Ionian protectorate, 75; proposed acquisitions for, under Polignac plan, 77–79; ambassadors of, rely on fleet, 87–88; notification of the Drovetti plan to, 126; objects to Drovetti plan, 128–129; responsible for

Index 243

shift of French policy to Algeria, 130; establishment by, of a route through the eastern Mediterranean, 140; new interest of, in Turkey, 188–189; contingent orders for fleet of, to repress Mehemet Ali, 200; contraventions of Straits convention by, 221–222

Great Powers: diplomatic opposition of, to Turkish preëmption order, 17; notifications to, of the Drovetti plan, and reactions by, 126–130; aware of menace of Mehemet Ali, 147; paradoxical policies of, in the Near East, 217–218; jealousies of, 219

Greece: to become self-governing, 49; French military instructors sent to, 52; proposed customs rates in, 58; negotiations respecting, 63; Turkey accepts principle of independence of, 73; problem of, nearing solution, 74; independence of, won, 89; French evacuation of, 98–99; hostile to England, 125

Greek pirates, depredations by, 47

Greek rebellion: reasons for, 16; opposed by Metternich, 21; *see also* Greek War for Independence

Greek slaves to be freed, 57

Greek War for Independence: might interfere with French trade, 12; reasons for, 16; opposed by Metternich, 21; internationalization of, 37–68; blockades during, 58; *see also* Greeks, the Morea, Russo-Turkish war

Greeks: threaten revolt, 12; commerce of, prepares for national independence, 16; Napoleonic war profits of, 16; most active merchants in Levantine waters, 16; disposed to piracy, 39; enslavement of, 55; blockade Attica, Negropont, and Gulf of Volo, 61; independence presaged, 64, won, 89

Greigh, Russian admiral, occupies Midia, 84

Gueron-Ranville, French minister, 124

Guilleminot, French ambassador at Constantinople: letter by, 28; returns to Constantinople, 62; advises Turkey to submit to Russia, 72; sends letter to Diebitsch, 72; views of, 73–74; appeals to Russian commander to make peace with Turkey, 85; willing to call fleet to Constantinople, 86; commended for advising Turks to yield to Russia, 100; views of, on Turkey's ability to survive, 103; directed to solicit a firman placing Tripoli, Tunis, and Algeria under the authority of Mehemet Ali, 117; negotiates with Turkey on the Drovetti plan, 122–123; leaves Turkish capital, 152

Gulf of Saros, Russia's blockade of, 60

Halil Pasha, Turkish negotiator, and Mehemet Ali, 181, 184–186

Hardenberg at the Congress of Aachen, 8

Hauser, Henri, Introduction by, v-ix

Haussez, French minister, opposes Drovetti plan, 124

Heyden, Russian admiral: and battle of Navarino, 50; naval commander in the Mediterranean, 59

Holy Places of Palestine, levies against the Christian pilgrims to, abolished, 154

Houssart, French commander of Egyptian war vessel, 152

Huder, Captain, aide-de-camp of Guilleminot: negotiates at Alexandria, 121–122; supplemental instructions to, by Polignac, 124–125; transformed negotiations of, 130; fails in modified Drovetti plan, 132–134

Index

Hugon, Admiral, commander of French naval station in the Levant: transmits Mimaut's report regarding Syria, 151; to conform with instructions from Varenne, 162; precluded from using force in naval demonstration at the Dardanelles, 193; Malcolm to concert with, 204

Hussein, dey of Algeria: refuses to give up piracy despite warning, 9; French grievances against, 49; insults French consul, 49

Ibrahim Pasha, Egyptian military commander: ravages the Morea, 43; under blockade at Navarino, 50; ultimatum to, 50; defies the allies, 52; alternatives confronting, 56; proposed to command expedition under Drovetti plan, 124; negotiates with Huder, 132–134; Syria won by, 148, 198; occupies passes to Koniah, opening route to Constantinople, 172; halts at Kutiah, 187–188; authorized to treat for peace, 195; withdrawal of, from Asia Minor, 198, 202, 206; Adana assigned to, 203

India: acquires a new importance for England, 5; Board of Control of, studying feasibility of steam communications with India by way of the Red Sea, 139; expeditious transport of mail to, considered, 140

Introduction by M. Henri Hauser, v-ix

Janissaries, revolt of, and their dissolution, 50, 103
Jerusalem occupied by Ibrahim Pasha, 153
Jurien de La Gravière, E., French rear-admiral, warns Hussein of Algeria, 9

Kochubei, Count, and Russia's new policy for Turkey, 90–93
Koniah: Egyptian army advances to, 172; battle of, 177
Kosseir, land transport from, 141
Kutiah, peace of (*see* Peace of Kutiah)

La Ferronays, French foreign minister, 52, 53; satisfied with the tsar's moderation, 54
Langsdorff, special French agent to Egypt, 131
Latour-Maubourg, French ambassador at Constantinople: succeeds Riviera, 12; friendly to the Chamber of Commerce of Marseille, 12, 13; instructions to, 12, 22; memorandum by, 23; letter by, 31
Laval, French ambassador at London, negotiates on the Drovetti plan, 129–131
Lazarev, Russian admiral, prepares expedition for Constantinople, 177
Lesseps, F. de, French vice-consul at Alexandria, 138
Levant Company (English): politically influential, 5; arguments of, 7; critical relations of, with Turkey, 25; handicaps to trade of, 28; reasons for dissolution of, 37–38; steps in dissolution of, 39
Liban, the, a pashalic of Syria, 47
Liston, Robert, British ambassador to Turkey, 7
Livron, Marshal: and French military mission to Egypt, 43; solicits French officers for Egyptian service, 44; and the warship orders placed by Mehemet Ali, 45
Louis, Baron, French minister of finance, denies Egypt's request for loan, 159

Index   245

Louis Philippe, King of France, tsar's dislike of, 204
Lyons, Edmund, commander of British frigate "Blonde," maps the Straits, 98

Maison, Lieutenant General: commands French expedition to the Morea, 57; instructions for, 57
Malcolm, Pulteney, British admiral: lifts blockade of Crete, 59; sends units of his squadron to the Dardanelles, 72; stationed before Algiers, 129; takes British fleet to the Dardanelles, 204, 207
Mandeville, British chargé at Constantinople, opposes coming of Russians to the Bosporus, 187
Marseille: urges France to regain her position in the Levant, vii; population of, 10; Restoration government acts with favoritism to, 10; inspection of merchandise by, 10; favors prohibitory surtax, 11; favors Egyptians against Greeks, 47; *see also* Chamber of Commerce of Marseille
Marseille Chamber of Commerce (*see* Chamber of Commerce of Marseille)
Marseille monopoly, the, 10; question of, permanently adjourned, 14; *see also* Chamber of Commerce of Marseille
Martignac, premier of France, 52
Mediterranean grain prices, 18
Mehemet Ali, pasha of Egypt (1805–1849): increasing importance of, 7; monopolies of commerce of, 7, 46–47, 71, 137–138; strong government of, 8; request of, for French instructors, 47; plans of, to move into Syria, 47; distrusts France, 48; suggests an alliance with Great Britain, 48; solicits French engineers, 52; evacuates the Morea, 57; concludes a convention with Admiral Codrington, 57; pleased with Turkey's defeat by Russia, 96; and the Drovetti plan, 113–134; demands subsidies from France, 121–122; wins France's "good offices" against England, 124, protection against Turkey, 127; treated as virtually independent, 125; master of Arabia, 147; rebuilds his navy, 148; opinions of, in reference to Egypt and European policy, 149; decides to chastise Abdullah Pasha of Acre, 150; not to take sultan's throne, 151; Ottoman commissioners confer with, 153; flattered by Sebastiani, 155; termed a rebel by Sultan Mahmud, 156; prophecies of, for the future of Franco-Egyptian relations, 157; disregards sultan's firman against him, 158; refuses a commercial loan in France, 159–161; abolishes levies against Christian pilgrims to the Holy Places of Palestine, 154; advised by France to seek peace, 168–170; terms of, for peace with Turkey, 171; accepts French mediation, 173; negotiates with Muraviev and Halil Pasha, 184–186; agrees to suspend hostilities with Turkey, 185; refuses Roussin's terms for peace, 194–195; wins Syria, 198; British fleet to repress, 200, 202; negotiates with Boislecomte, 201–203; prospective further advances of, limited, 209
Metternich, chancellor of Austria: at the Congress of Aachen, 8; opposes Greek revolt, 21; and failure of Stratford Canning at Vienna, 41; opinions of, 54; frankly pessimistic, 76; alleged plan of, to partition Turkey, 79–83; shares Aberdeen's views on the Drovetti plan, 131; sends Prokesch-Osten to Egypt, 189; *see also* Austria

Milosh, prince of Serbia, restive, 84

Mimaut, Jean-François, French consul general in Egypt: appointed, 59; first conferences of, with Mehemet Ali, 59; instructions to, respecting the Drovetti plan, 119–120; negotiates at Alexandria, 120–122; new instructions to, 124–125; transformed negotiations of, 130; seconds Huder's negotiations, 132–134; Mehemet Ali confers with, 153; intimate with Egyptian pasha, 156; Sebastiani's instructions to, 168–169; *see also* Mehemet Ali, Turco-Egyptian war

Minciakii, Russian envoy, negotiates for withdrawal of Turkey from Moldavia and Wallachia, 29

Moldavia: revolt in, 16; withdrawal of Turkish forces from, 20, 29; autonomy of, 89

Monopolies, Egyptian commercial (*see* Egypt)

Montmorency, French foreign minister, 23; opinion of, 24

Morea, the: its evacuation by Egypt required, 50, 56; French expedition to, in 1828, 52, 54–58; protocol authorizes armed French intervention in, 57; French objectives in, 57; French army in, 58; *see also* Greek War for Independence

Mortemart, Duke of, French ambassador at St. Petersburg: and Polignac project, 78; reports of, 90; approves Peace of Adrianople, 105

Müffling, special Prussian agent: neutral negotiator, 69; advises Turkey, 71; views of, 73–74

Muraviev, General N. N.: arrival of, at Constantinople, 177; peace mission of, to Alexandria, 177–178, 182, 184–186; visits Greece, 187

Namick Pasha, mission of, to London, mentioned, 171, 174, 176

Navarino: arrival of Egyptian reënforcements at, 50; battle of, 49–51; Turkey's anger after, 51

Nesselrode, Count, Russian vice-chancellor: at the Congress of Aachen, 8; confers with Stratford Canning, 41–42; coöperates with Great Britain for a self-governing Greek state, 49; considers alliance with France, 54; and Russia's new policy for Turkey, 90–93; reports of, to the tsar, 97

New bases of Russia's policy (1829), 89–93

Nicholas I, tsar of Russia (*see* Tsar Nicholas I)

Odessa: grain ships at, 4; Turkey depresses wheat prices at, 18; embarkation of Russian army at, 196

Orlov, Count: Russian negotiator of Peace of Adrianople, 83; at Constantinople, 98; negotiates Treaty of Unkiar-Iskelessi, 205–208

Osman Pasha, Egyptian naval commander, avoids direct test with Ottoman navy, 167–168

Ottenfels, Austrian internuncio at Constantinople: jealousy of, 95; views of, on origins of the Drovetti plan, 130

Ottoman Empire, the: ultimate dissolution of, 2; capitulatory right of, to preëmpt grain, 4; under disadvantage of low specific duties, 6; insists on a new tariff with Great Britain, 7; failure to repress piracy, 8; survival of, the question in 1815, 14; hostility of Russia to, 14; insists upon restitution of the Asiatic littoral of Black Sea, 15; fears an Austro-Russian coalition in 1817, 15; refuses guarantees, 15; adopts liberal policy toward Greek merchants, 16; preëmpts foreign produce within the Straits, 17; lifts embargo on wheat, 18; inspects all foreign vessels, 19; declines or evades Russian demands, 20; new zeal of, in searches of Russian vessels, 26; preëmpts Russian grain, 27; promulgates new regulations, 27; evacuates the Principalities, 29; commercial restrictions of, against England, 35; nonintervention a valuable support for, 42; fortifies Danube delta islands, 53; commerce of, with France, 53; war of, with Russia, 1828, 53, *passim*; Russian blockade of, 58; handicaps trade, 60; evades Russia's blockade, 60, 61; threatened with dissolution, 63, 76; urged to accept moderation of Russia, 63; dangers threatening, 69; faces collapse, 71–73; proposed concessions of, favoring Russia, 71; negotiates for the Peace of Adrianople, 83–89; grants request for western fleets to enter Straits, 86; right of, to preëmpt foreign produce ended, 93–94; pessimism respecting, 76, 102–104; declines Drovetti plan, 123; between rival imperialisms, 128–129; tariffs of, not enforced in Egypt, 135; weakness of, 147, 152; anarchy throughout, 149; abandons Syria, 163; requests aid of foreign Powers, 174–176; forces of, beaten at Koniah, 177; France wishes to preserve, 183, 196–197; influence of British warships on, 219–222

Pahlen, Count, Russian negotiator of Peace of Adrianople, 83
Palmerston, Lord, British foreign secretary: marginal notes giving views of, on Anglo-Turkish relations, 175–176; willing to support Turkey against Russia, 175; declines direct aid to Turkey, 176; approves Roussin's convention with Turkey, 192; ostensibly accepts Russian assurances, 204
Parliament, committee of, studies a Near Eastern route to India, 142
Paskevich, Russian commander, wins Erzurum, 72
Pasquier, French foreign minister: admits the preponderance of Mehemet Ali, 12; instructions of, to Latour-Maubourg, 13, 22
Peace of Adrianople (1829): terms of, 89, 93–94; approved by France, 99–100; 118; *see also* Russo-Turkish war
Peace of Kutiah (1833): negotiated, 197; terms of, 198; France favors status quo under, 208–210
Peraldi, French expedition disembarks at, 58
Piracy: protection against, 7; problem of, 25; factor in Franco-Algerian war, 49; and the Drovetti plan, 125; *see also* Greek pirates, Barbary piracy
Pirate vessels, under Greek flag, 51; *see also* piracy, Barbary piracy
Polignac: French ambassador to England, 55; appointed French foreign minister, 70; satisfied with Russia's promises, 71; instructions of, to Ambassador Guilleminot, 74; secret proposal of, for a partition of the Ottoman Empire, 74, 76–79; places fleet under direction of Guilleminot, 75; instructions of, to Mortemart, 78–79; accepts Peace of Adrianople, 100; foresees Turkey's collapse, 104; pro-Russian policy of, 105; favors the Drovetti plan, 116; weighs roles of Russia, Great Britain, and Austria, 120; counters Mehemet Ali's demand for the cession of French war vessels, 123–126; treats Mehemet Ali as virtually independent, 125; supplemental instruc-

Polignac (*Continued*)—
tions by, to Huder, 125; policy of, abruptly shifts to conquest of Algeria, 130–131; authorizes subsidy for Egypt, 131

Polignac's memorandum of 1829, proposing a partition of Turkey, text communicated to England in 1856, 108

Polignac plan, the, outline of, 77

Ponsonby, Lord, British ambassador to Turkey: to concert with Admiral Malcolm, 204; inquiries by, at the Dardanelles, 205

Portalis: satisfaction of, at tsar's moderation, 54; appointed French foreign minister, 59

Porte, the (*see* Ottoman Empire)

Pozzo di Borgo, Russian ambassador at Paris: confident Great Britain would be the principal Russian opponent, 21; opposes western fleets at the Dardanelles, 116; shares Polignac's confidence, 118

Prokesch-Osten, Austrian agent, commissioned for mission to Egypt, 189

Prussia: accepts Austrian commercial schedule with Turkey, 7; no direct interest in the Levant, 21; proposed acquisitions for, under Polignac plan, 77–79; and the alleged Austrian plan, 80–81; notification of the Drovetti plan to, 126; reactions of, to the Drovetti plan, 128

Rayneval: gives objects of expedition to Greece, 58; French ambassador at Vienna, 117; instructions to, 120

Red Sea route to India considered by the British, 141

Reshid Bey, Egyptian negotiator at Constantinople, 195

Reshid Pasha, Ottoman military commander, challenges Ibrahim Pasha before Koniah and is beaten, 176–177

Ribeaupierre: Russian minister at Constantinople, 59; returns to Turkey, 98

Richelieu, premier of France: at the Congress of Aachen, 8; opposes Marseille's monopoly, 11; favors a concert with Russia and armed neutrality in Greek war, 22; continues French policy of neutrality, 23

Ricord, Admiral, commands the Russian war fleet in the Aegean and extends the blockade westward, 61

Rigny, French vice-admiral: instructions to, 24, 73; and battle of Navarino, 50; views of, on French naval policy, 105

Riviera, French ambassador at Constantinople: instructions to, in 1814, 23; tariff negotiated by, in 1816, 6–7

Rosamel, French naval commander, concerts with Admiral Malcolm, 72–73

Rostand, of Marseille Chamber of Commerce, and the Levant trade, 31

Rothesay, Stuart de, British ambassador at Paris, negotiates on Drovetti plan, 129, 131

Roussin, Admiral A. R., French ambassador to Turkey: appointed, 171; Broglie's instructions to, 173–174; delayed arrival of, at Constantinople, 190; signs with Turkey a convention by which Egypt would win only part of Syria, 191–193; reverses French policy for Egypt, 194–195; hints a Russo-Turkish alliance, 207

Royer, Prussian minister at Constantinople, and Peace of Adrianople, 84–85, 89

Index 249

Russia: exceptional resources of southern provinces of, 4; offers to sign a new tariff with Turkey, 7; seeks to check Barbary piracy, 8; sympathy of, for Greeks, 17; protection of commerce of, through the Straits, 17; produce of, 18; demands of, respecting the Greeks, 20; submits claims to Europe, 20; diminution of exports of, 26; and the Congress of Verona, 26; claims of, against Turkey, 28; trade of, at Constantinople, 30; calls conference on Greece, 40; ultimatum of, to Turkey, 49; joins with France and Great Britain in the Treaty of London, 50; withdraws minister from Constantinople, 51; bases of, for action against Turkey, 53; suddenly declares war on Turkey, 53; blockades the Dardanelles and the Gulf of Saros, 60; new policy of, in 1829, to uphold Turkey, 89–93, 185; decisions of secret imperial committee of, in 1829, 92; blockade of Dardanelles by, lifted, 96; protests to Turkey, 97; confirms Austrian plan for a partition of Turkey, 104; support of, sought in Drovetti plan, 106; notification of the Drovetti plan to, 126; reactions of, to the Drovetti plan, 127; reportedly hostile to Mehemet Ali, 166; promises military and naval aid to Turkey, 176, 177; to defend Constantinople and the Straits, 185; army of, summoned to Bosporus, 186–187, embarks at Odessa, 196; fleet of, anchors in the Bosporus, 190; Convention of Münchengrätz with Austria, 203–204; *see also* Tsar Alexander I, Tsar Nicholas I, Russo-Turkish war

Russian commerce, emancipation of, from Turkish restrictions, 94

Russo-Turkish commercial convention of 1783, applies to Great Britain, 25, 36

Russo-Turkish negotiations in 1823, Strangford the intermediary for, 27–29

Russo-Turkish war (1828–1829), 53; neutrals suffer little during, 60; military phases of, 63; *see also* Russia, Ottoman Empire, Tsar Nicholas I

Saint Denys, Juchereau, seeks appointment as French commercial inspector in the Levant, 108

Sarlat, French naval captain, commands the "Sphinx," 167

Scutari, revolt of, 150

Sebastiani, French foreign minister: views of, on commerce with Egypt, 136; opposes Mehemet Ali's commercial system in Crete, 139; letter of, to Mimaut flatters Mehemet Ali, 154–155; refuses Egypt a loan, 160; suggests possible European intervention in Turco-Egyptian war, 165; presses for peace in Turco-Egyptian war, 168–170, *passim*

Serbia, autonomy of, 89

Sevastopol, Russian armaments arrive at, 166

Seve, pro-French Egyptian general with Ibrahim Pasha, letter to, 182

Silistria, fall of, 63

Simulation: practice approved by the French, 5, 18; methods of, 19; major Powers take recourse to, 26

Smyrna, sequestration of property at, 26; settlement of claims at, 28; general stagnation of, 61

Social Science Research Council, grant from, xi

Société Royale de Géographie d'Egypte, documentary publications of, 148, 226–235

Spain commands attention, 1

"Sphinx," the, French war steamer, scouts for Egypt, 167–168

Straits, the: Turkey's control of, 4; transshipment of grains forbidden within, 4; firmans necessary for passage of, 4, 207; Russian commerce through, 17; prohibited cargoes pass, 18; restrictions again placed against Russian commerce in, 18; inspection of all foreign vessels that passed, 19; precautions for passage of, 23; and Russian vessels, 26, 27; lessening of handicaps to shipping in, 27; navigation of, 27; closed to neutral shipping as reprisal for the battle of Navarino, 51; closure of, 53; Russian blockade of (Dardanelles), 60; large British warships held out of, 62; British frigate held within, 62; Polignac does not assign, to Russia, 77; Russia's method for guaranteeing freedom of commerce in, 84; problem of passage of, by foreign warships, 87–88, 219–222; western fleets concentrated near, 88; and Peace of Adrianople, 93–96; French fleet leaves entrance of, 96; mapped by British, 98; policy of England and France at, 105–107; British squadron expected to pass, 106; Russia able to dominate, during Turco-Egyptian war, 166; Admiral Roussin to pass (Dardanelles), on a frigate, 172; maritime Powers claim right to pass, 184; to be defended by Russia, 185; Russian army summoned to (Bosporus), 186–187, anchors in, 190; western fleet not to enter, 204; entrance of, by force considered dangerous, 206, 208; Russian brigs pass, in diplomatic service, 207; foreign warships excluded from, 219–220; note on the British fleet episodes at, 219–222

Strangford, British ambassador at Constantinople, intermediary for Russo-Turkish negotiations in 1823, 27–29

Stratford (see Canning, Stratford)

Stroganov, Baron, Russian minister at Constantinople: somewhat bellicose, 14; negotiations of, slow and difficult, 15; confirmatory commercial agreements claimed by, 15; protests preëmption, 17; protests inspection, 19; breaks off relations with Turkey, 20

Stürmer, Baron, Austrian internuncio at Constantinople, 205

Suez Canal mentioned, 2, 134

Suez, Isthmus of, explorations by the British at, 140

Sultan Mahmud II (1808–1839): summons Mehemet Ali to aid him, 43; holder of important maritime keys, 117; plan to depose, 149; decision of, to punish Mehemet Ali, 154; accepts Russian military and naval aid, 176, 187; *see also* Ottoman Empire

Syria: won by Egypt in 1833, 148, 198; reports of projects for, credited to Abdullah Pasha, 149; Mehemet Ali considers time ripe for advance into, 149; goal of ambitions of Mehemet Ali, 150; internal troubles in, 152; occupied by Ibrahim Pasha, 152; refusal of Mehemet Ali to withdraw from, 153; war over, 156–198; Egyptian position consolidated in, 163; cession of, sought by Mehemet Ali, 170; capable of various delimitations, 189

Taurus Mountains crossed by Ibrahim Pasha's army, 183

Temperley, H. W. V.: mentioned by M. Hauser, v; brief criticism of writings of, on Stratford Canning and the fleet episodes at the Straits, 87–88, 219–222

Index 251

Tariffs: difficult to win Turkey's enforcement of, 6; Franco-Turkish (of 1802, 1816), 6; French do not permit the immediate application of, 6; automatic continuance of, 7; Austro-Turkish, 7; variable rates of, in Egypt, 135; *see also* Capitulations

"Thalia," armed British merchant ship, case of, 27, 35–36

Tsar Alexander I: proposes a maritime league, 8; unfinished business of, with Turkey, 14; does not promise Greeks support, 16; difficult position of, in 1821, 17; and the conference on Greece, 40; death of, 49; *see also* Russia, Greek War for Independence

Tsar Nicholas I: accession of, 49; first terms of, for peace with Turkey, 54; dissatisfied with Great Britain, 75; accepts new policy for Turkey, 92–93; dislikes Louis Philippe, 204; *see also* Russia, Russo-Turkish war

Treaty of Adrianople (1829) (*see* Peace of Adrianople)

Treaty of Bucharest (1812): nonfulfillment of, by Turkey and Russia, 14; interpretations of, 14, 20; explanations of, 15

Treaty of the Dardanelles, Anglo-Turkish (1809), 5

Treaty of Gulistan (1813), 14

Treaty of London (1827), terms of, 50

Treaty of Unkiar-Iskelessi (1833): negotiated, 207; terms of, 98, 208; western opposition to, 208

Tripoli mentioned, 8, 117; *see also* Drovetti plan

Tunisia mentioned, 8, 117; *see also* Drovetti plan

Turco-Egyptian war over Syria (1832–1833): French policy in, 148–213; France seeks to prevent, 155; first encounters in, 155; no major naval battles during, 168; peace negotiations to end, 181–199; *see also* Egypt, Mehemet Ali, Ottoman Empire

Turkey (*see* Ottoman Empire)

Turkish Empire (*see* Ottoman Empire)

Unkiar-Iskelessi: Russian army encamped at, 205; treaty of, (1833), closes Dardanelles to enemies of Russia, 98, 208

Varenne, Baron J. E., French chargé d'affaires at Constantinople: to promote calm at Constantinople, 154; notification by, 156; proposes French mediation, 169–170; negotiates for peace, 173–177, *passim*; intermediary for Turco-Egyptian peace in 1833, 181–184; letters of, to Mehemet Ali, Ibrahim Pasha, and General Seve, 182–183, 187; negotiates Peace of Kutiah, 197–198

Vaublanc, French minister of the interior, letter by, 7

Villèle, Count, premier of France: replaces Richelieu, 23; instructions of, to Boyer, 44

Wallachia: revolt in, 16; withdrawal of Turkish forces from, 20, 29; autonomy of, 89

War ministry of France, note by, 23; *see also* France

Wellington, Duke of: at the Congress of Aachen, 8; at the Congress of Verona, 27; trip of, to St. Petersburg, 49; opposes Russo-Turkish war, 55; letter of, 75; agrees with Russia on Greek independence, 75; resents economic provisions of the Peace of Adrianople, 101; objects to Drovetti plan, 128–129

Wheat: Egypt expands export of, 53, 137; *see also* Commerce in the Levant, Black Sea trade, Straits, Ottoman Empire

Ypsilanti, Alexander, unsuccessful revolt led by, in the Danubian Principalities, 16